*Robert J. Illback*
*C. Michael Nelson*
*Editors*

# Emerging School-Based Approaches for Children with Emotional and Behavioral Problems: Research and Practice in Service Integration

*Pre-Publication*
*REVIEWS,*
*COMMENTARIES,*
*EVALUATIONS . . .*

"*E* merging School-Based Approaches for Children with Emotional and Behavioral Problems fills the need for an organized presentation of how the integrated services paradigm can be applied in the context of school settings. The volume can serve as a guide for action to those who endorse and seek to implement the concept of integrated services in order to empower families, eliminate barriers to service, and to capitalize on the strengths of diverse services through the development of an understandable overall organization.

The first section of the book provides an overall picture of national and state trends and the public policy issues that have been raised and addressed by the integrated services paradigm. The clear and concise presentation of a conceptual framework enables the reader to grasp and hang onto the goals. The second section provides the reader with reviews of exemplary programs that have achieved integrated services in a wide variety of ways and which address different local conditions. The programs described are both inspirational and serve as guides for action; they address the full range of issues from organization and structure of services to staff development, program operations, and program evaluation.

*Emerging School-Based Approaches* is a valuable resource for school and public health administrators, mental health personnel, special educators, and community leaders interested in effectively addressing the unmet needs and problems of children with emotional and behavioral problems. The volume is well suited for use as a resource both for community enlightenment, and as training resources in classes for a variety of different disciplines which are concerned about the provisions of services to children, families, and school systems."

**Richard R. Abidin, EdD**
*Director of Clinical Training, Curry Programs in Clinical and School Psychology, University of Virginia*

"This book documents a highly unsatisfactory state of affairs in the country and in its public school system and suggests some new directions that might be taken to correct this. At present, children with emotional and behavioral problems, those called "severely emotionally disturbed" (SED) by educators, fare poorly. They often have a low rate of academic progress and are likely to drop out of school. When they do finish whatever education they attain, these youngsters are more likely than others to be unemployed or even to end up in prison. In their introductory chapter, the editors explain an approach to the problem of SED children known as "service integration," which attempts to deliver mental health services more effectively and to reach out to their families and to the community. Most of the chapters in the book provide particular examples of how such service integration has been employed within a number of different school systems, including descriptions of some individual youngsters, many of whom are the concern not only to the schools but also to many other social agencies such as child welfare or the juvenile court.

The next to the last chapter discusses the challenging problem of evaluating innovative programs within a complex organization such as a school system. Traditional attempts at controlled experiments to evaluate such programs are considered and found wanting. The final chapter paints a vivid portrait of "school culture," contrasting the school as a "tribal center," as "factory," and as "hospital." In it the service integration movement is viewed as a praiseworthy attempt to induce some rather fundamental changes in the way schools operate. All in all, this book is a stimulating and valuable contribution to the topic of how schools should try to help SED youngsters and their families."

**Donald K. Routh, PhD**
*Professor of Psychology, University of Miami, Coral Gables, FL*

# Emerging School-Based Approaches for Children with Emotional and Behavioral Problems: Research and Practice in Service Integration

# Emerging School-Based Approaches for Children with Emotional and Behavioral Problems: Research and Practice in Service Integration

Robert J. Illback
C. Michael Nelson
Editors

Routledge
Taylor & Francis Group
New York London

First published 1996 by The Haworth Press, Inc.

Published 2019 by Routledge
52 Vanderbilt Avenue, New York, NY 10017
2 Park Square, Milton Park, Abingdon, Oxon OX14 4RN

*Routledge is an imprint of the Taylor & Francis Group, an informa business*

*Emerging School-Based Approaches for Children with Emotional and Behavioral Problems: Research and Practice in Service Integration* has also been published as *Special Services in the Schools*, Volume 10, Number 2 1995 and Volume 11, Numbers 1/2 1996.

**Library of Congress Cataloging-in-Publication Data**

Emerging school-based approaches for children with emotional and behavioral problems : research and practice in service integration / Robert J. Illback, C. Michael Nelson, editors.
    p. cm.
    "Has also been published as Special services in the schools. Volume 10, Number 2, 1995 and Volume 11, Numbers 1/2, 1996"–T.p. verso.
    Includes bibliographical references.
    ISBN 1-56024-819-X (alk. paper)
    1. Mentally ill children–Education–United States. 2. Mentally ill children–Services for–United States. I. Illback, Robert J. II. Nelson, C. Michael (Charles Michael), 1941-  .
LC4181.E44 1995
371.92'0973–dc20                           96-4210
                                            CIP

ISBN 13: 978-1-56024-819-4 (hbk)

# INDEXING & ABSTRACTING

Contributions to this publication are selectively indexed or abstracted in print, electronic, online, or CD-ROM version(s) of the reference tools and information services listed below. This list is current as of the copyright date of this publication. See the end of this section for additional notes.

- *Cabell's Directory of Publishing Opportunities in Education (comprehensive & descriptive bibliographic listing with editorial criteria and publication production data for selected education and education-related journals)*, Cabell Publishing Company, Box 5428, Tobe Hahn Station, Beaumont, TX 77726-5428

- *Child Development Abstracts & Bibliography*, University of Kansas, 2 Bailey Hall, Lawrence, KS 66045

- *CNPIEC Reference Guide: Chinese National Directory of Foreign Periodicals*, P.O. Box 88, Beijing, People's Republic of China

- *Contents Pages in Education*, Carfax Information Systems, P.O. Box 25, Abingdon, Oxfordshire OX14 3UE, United Kingdom

- *Education Digest*, Prakken Publications, Inc., 416 Longshore Drive/P.O. Box 8623, Ann Arbor, MI 48107

- *Educational Administration Abstracts (EAA)*, Sage Publications, Inc., 2455 Teller Road, Newbury Park, CA 91320

- *ERIC Clearinghouse on Counseling and Student Services (ERIC/CASS)*, University of North Carolina-Greensboro, 101 Park Building, Greensboro, NC 27412-5001

- *ERIC Clearinghouse on Rural Education & Small Schools*, Appalachia Educational Laboratory, 1031 Quarrier Street, P.O. Box 1348, Charleston, WV 25325

- *Exceptional Child Education Resources (ECER), (online through DIALOG and hard copy)*, The Council for Exceptional Children, 1920 Association Drive, Reston, VA 22091

(continued)

- *International Bulletin of Bibliography on Education*, Proyecto B.I.B.E./Apartado 52, San Lorenzo del Escorial, Madrid, Spain

- *INTERNET ACCESS (& additional networks) Bulletin Board for Libraries ("BUBL"), coverage of information resources on INTERNET, JANET, and other networks.*
  - JANET X.29: UK.AC.BATH.BUBL or 00006012101300
  - TELNET: BUBL.BATH.AC.UK or 138.38.32.45 login 'bubl'
  - Gopher: BUBL.BATH.AC.UK (138.32.32.45). Port 7070
  - World Wide Web: http: // www.bubl.bath.ac.uk./BUBL/ home.html
  - NISSWAIS: telnetniss.ac.uk (for the NISS gateway)
  The Andersonian Library, Curran Building, 101 St. James Road, Glasgow G4 ONS, Scotland

- *Inventory of Marriage and Family Literature (online and CD/ROM)*, Peters Technology Transfer, 306 East Baltimore Pike, 2nd Floor, Media, PA 19063

- *Mental Health Abstracts (online through DIALOG)*, IFI/Plenum Data Company, 3202 Kirkwood Highway, Wilmington, DE 19808

- *National Clearinghouse for Bilingual Education*, George Washington University, 1118 22nd Street NW, Washington, DC 20037

- *OT BibSys*, American Occupational Therapy Foundation, P.O. Box 31220, Rockville, MD 20824-1220

- *Social Work Abstracts*, National Association of Social Workers, 750 First Street NW, 8th Floor, Washington, DC 20002

- *Sociology of Education Abstracts*, Carfax Publishing Company, P.O. Box 25, Abingdon, Oxfordshire OX14 3UE, United Kingdom

- *Special Educational Needs Abstracts*, Carfax Information Systems, P.O. Box 25, Abingdon, Oxfordshire OX14 3UE, United Kingdom

- *Urban Affairs Abstracts*, National League of Cities, 1301 Pennsylvania Avenue NW, Washington, DC 20004

(continued)

# SPECIAL BIBLIOGRAPHIC NOTES

*related to special journal issues (separates)*
*and indexing/abstracting*

☐ indexing/abstracting services in this list will also cover material in any "separate" that is co-published simultaneously with Haworth's special thematic journal issue or DocuSerial. Indexing/abstracting usually covers material at the article/chapter level.

☐ monographic co-editions are intended for either non-subscribers or libraries which intend to purchase a second copy for their circulating collections.

☐ monographic co-editions are reported to all jobbers/wholesalers/approval plans. The source journal is listed as the "series" to assist the prevention of duplicate purchasing in the same manner utilized for books-in-series.

☐ to facilitate user/access services all indexing/abstracting services are encouraged to utilize the co-indexing entry note indicated at the bottom of the first page of each article/chapter/contribution.

☐ this is intended to assist a library user of any reference tool (whether print, electronic, online, or CD-ROM) to locate the monographic version if the library has purchased this version but not a subscription to the source journal.

☐ individual articles/chapters in any Haworth publication are also available through the Haworth Document Delivery Services (HDDS).

# ABOUT THE EDITORS

**Robert J. Illback, PsyD,** is Executive Director of R.E.A.C.H. of Louisville, Inc., and Professor of Psychology at Spalding University in Louisville, Kentucky. He holds a PsyD from the Graduate School of Applied and Professional Psychology at Rutgers University and has worked in various school and community agency settings. His professional and research interests include "systems of care" in child mental health, school-linked integrated service programs, community-based intervention, program evaluation, and planned organizational change. An APA Fellow and member of Divisions 16, 33, and 37, Dr. Illback is licensed in Kentucky and Indiana and is a member of the Kentucky Board of Psychology.

**C. Michael Nelson, EdD,** a well-known and respected educator, researcher, and leader in the fields of special education and psychology, with special emphasis on behavioral, emotional, and learning disorders, is Professor of Special Education and Rehabilitation Counseling at the University of Kentucky in Lexington. His current research projects are *Emotional and Behavioral Disorders Preparation* and *Improving the Interactive Teaming Skills of Professionals and Family Members Serving Children and Youth with Serious Emotional Disturbance,* both supported by the U.S. Office of Special Education Programs. An active participant in national and international conventions and symposiums, Professor Nelson has presented more than 80 papers and has published numerous books and nearly 70 articles. He occupies several editorial positions for important academic journals, including the *Journal of Special Education Technology,* for which he has been Consulting Editor since 1979, and *Teacher Education and Special Education,* for which he has been Associate Editor since 1984. Professor Nelson is a member of many professional organizations, including the Council for Exceptional Children, the Council for Children with Behavioral Disorders, and the Association for Behavior Analysis.

# Emerging School-Based Approaches for Children with Emotional and Behavioral Problems: Research and Practice in Service Integration

## CONTENTS

## INNOVATIVE SCHOOL-BASED APPROACHES TO SERVICE INTEGRATION

# CONCEPTUAL FOUNDATIONS OF SCHOOL-BASED INTEGRATED SERVICES

# School-Based Integrated Service Programs: Toward More Effective Service Delivery for Children and Youth with Emotional and Behavioral Disorders (EBD)

Robert J. Illback

R.E.A.C.H. of Louisville, Inc.

C. Michael Nelson

University of Kentucky

Educational, social, mental health, and juvenile systems for children and youth with emotional and behavioral disorders (EBD) are struggling

Address correspondence to: Robert J. Illback, R.E.A.C.H. of Louisville, Inc., 101 East Kentucky Street, Louisville, KY 40203.

[Haworth co-indexing entry note]: "School-Based Integrated Service Programs: Toward More Effective Service Delivery for Children and Youth with Emotional and Behavioral Disorders (EBD)." Illback, Robert J., and C. Michael Nelson. Co-published simultaneously in *Special Services in the Schools* (The Haworth Press, Inc.) Vol. 10, No. 2, 1995, pp. 1-6; and: *Emerging School-Based Approaches for Children with Emotional and Behavioral Problems: Research and Practice in Service Integration* (ed: Robert J. Illback, and C. Michael Nelson) The Haworth Press, Inc., 1996, pp. 1-6. Single or multiple copies of this article are available from The Haworth Document Delivery Service [1-800-342-9678, 9:00 a.m. - 5:00 p.m. (EST)].

to provide appropriate and effective services. While there have been numerous positive developments and innovations over the past two decades, such as special education and related services and family support and preservation programs, substantial difficulties remain. Increasingly, it has become clear that these problems are not entirely related to the lack of financial and programmatic resources (e.g., health care). The "patchwork quilt" of education, health, and human services also serves to complicate and impede community efforts to respond to complex child and family needs in a thoughtful, comprehensive, and integrative manner (National Commission on Children, 1991). Current child-serving organizations have thus been described as fragmented, inaccessible, duplicative, and ineffective (Saxe, Cross, & Silverman, 1988; Tuma, 1989).

Recently, local, state, and federal efforts have been initiated to reform the child service system, resulting in considerable progress toward a more integrated system of care for this population (Nelson & Pearson, 1991). CASSP, the Child and Adolescent Service System Program within the National Institute of Mental Health, promotes systems change in mental health services for children with severe emotional disabilities (SED) by encouraging states to provide more comprehensive and coordinated services (Day & Roberts, 1991). Relatedly, numerous regional and statewide service integration initiatives are occurring that emphasize: (1) more broad-based community services, (2) less restrictive child placement, (3) prevention of hospitalization and out-of-home placement, (4) interagency collaboration, (4) flexible and individualized services, and (5) cost containment and efficiency (Stroul, Goldman, Lourie, Katz-Leavy, & Zeigler-Dendy, 1992).

Two parallel developments have been the family support movement (Dunst, Trivette, & Deal, 1988; Kagan & Weissbourd, 1994), which has empowered families of children with EBD to advocate for services, and school-linked social and mental health services, which has encouraged collaborative relationships between the education and mental health disciplines (Dryfoos, 1994). Although parental advocacy has played a major role in educational reform, especially in terms of creating public school programs for students with disabilities, until recently parents have had little voice in directing the mental health services received by their children. Also, partnerships between education and mental health or social service agencies traditionally have been created to support educational programs in residential or day-care facilities. The idea of having mental health staff and programs in the public schools is relatively new.

While schools often are involved in system of care re-structuring through interagency agreements, the literature on the nature and scope of their participation is not well developed. Considerable school-based integrated service delivery is underway across the nation, but these innovative programs and practices have not received as much attention as have approaches that occur within mental health and social service systems. This volume fulfills a growing need for an organized discussion of how the integrated service paradigm can be applied in the context of school settings, with special reference to the issues and problems that are idiosyncratic to schools as institutions.

The fundamental assumption underlying this publication is that the integrated services movement in children's services holds much promise as a means to create more comprehensive and coordinated school-based systems of care for children and families. For purposes of this discussion, integrated services are defined as: (1) accessible without reference to physical, psychological, social, or other barriers; (2) comprehensive and appropriate, in that they address priority needs the family has identified, at a level of service sufficient to their need; (3) formulated and delivered at a high level of quality such that the family perceives them as an organized whole and can participate in a consistent and effective manner; (4) facilitative of psychological competence and self-sufficiency rather than focusing exclusively on dysfunction and pathology; (5) oriented toward the full participation and empowerment of family members, such that they attribute change in part to their own efforts; (6) sensitive to cultural, gender, and racial issues; (7) driven by concern for the needs and desires of the consumers (i.e., children and families) and emphasize explicit outcomes stated in a positive manner; and (8) inclusive of prevention and early intervention activities (Illback, 1994).

The manuscripts contained in this volume feature conceptual, practice, and research issues relevant to school-based integrated service programs for children and youth with emotional and behavioral disorders. In the initial section, David Osher and Thomas Hanley present a thoughtful analysis of the National Agenda for Children and Youth with EBD formulated by the United States Department of Education Office of Special Education and Rehabilitation (OSERS). The National Agenda targets seven major areas that are seen as essential in moving toward a responsive, school-based system of care re-structuring. Following this, Ronda Talley and Rick Short describe the growing movement toward structuring schools to become primary delivery sites for a range of health and social services, an alternative model for school re-structuring in the service of more integrated, family-centered services. Importantly, there is not universal agreement as to how schools should change in order to become more responsive, and a variety of approaches are described herein.

The following section is comprised of descriptions of exemplary programs from across the country that have as their focus the integration of services. Douglas Cheney, Craig Barringer, Dayle Upham, and Barbara Manning depict Project Destiny in New Hampshire, a team-building approach targeted toward middle school students, with especially promising results reported by teachers in terms of skill-building. Given the poor transition to adulthood experiences of adolescents with EBD, an innovative and comprehensive competitive employment and service management program for youth in western Oregon is outlined by Michael Bullis and Kathleen Paris. Then, Carla Cumblad, Michael Epstein, Kimberly Keeney, Talitha Marty, and Jennifer Soderlund describe the Children and Adolescents Network program in DuPage County, IL, which uses an interagency child and family planning team process to conduct strength-based assessments, write unified service plans, coordinate services, and involve families. An illustrative case study and initial service data are also presented.

The evaluation of a school-linked, family support initiative in Maryland called Linkages to Learning is the subject of the paper by Peter Leone, Sean Lane, Nancy Arllen, and Haifa Peter. Findings demonstrate the need to articulate clear understandings between participating organizations in school-linked support programs, and create appropriate infrastructure for program operation. Lucille Eber then portrays Project WRAP, an extraordinary five-year systems change initiative in Illinois designed to improve outcomes for children and youth with EBD. Based on the wraparound approach developed within child mental health, this project has field tested a variety of approaches to assure integrated, appropriate services.

Judy Faris and Gerry Nichol describe a nationally recognized integrated service program in operation since 1969 within the Memphis (TN) City Schools, a comprehensive, school-based delivery system for mental health and substance abuse services. While not exclusively targeted toward children with EBD, this program is remarkable for its breadth and emphasis on community outreach and prevention. In the paper that concludes this section, Ron Nelson and Geoff Colvin describe proactive strategies to improve school environments for all students and staff. They present data showing that straightforward modifications in the school ecology and routine can lead to reductions in disruptive school behavior.

The final section serves to explicate issues facing those who are involved with school re-structuring. In a seminal analysis, Barbara Friesen and Trina Osher review the challenges and opportunities of involving families in change processes in schools. Major foci of integrated service programs are to become more family-centered and to empower families through meaningful involvement; however, the potential contribution of families remains under-appreciated in schools, and many programs are struggling to become more inclusive. The authors' guidelines for family involvement are especially salient. Contemplating the complexity of planning and evaluating integrated service programs in schools, John Kalafat argues that the prevailing positivist research model is too narrow, and should give way to broader, developmental perspectives on hypothesis generation and testing, methodology, and evaluator role. The paradigm shift that is recommended for the way evaluative questions are asked and answered can thus be seen to parallel the shift required to create a more integrated service system. Cindy Carlson reflects on the complexities of change processes in school organizations.

While the educational system alone has a mandate to accommodate all children and youth, historically those identified as having emotional and behavioral difficulties have not been well served . . . Schools are often blamed for poor outcomes experienced by students identified as EBD. However, it is becoming recognized that the multiple and complex problems of these children and families exceed the capacities of any single system, and furthermore, that increasing the number of services or the number of agencies involved in their delivery will not necessarily improve these outcomes. The articles contained in this volume support our contention that not only *should* schools have a key role in the provision of integrated services, they *are*, in fact, proactive in seeking solutions to the complex problems posed by this challenging population.

## REFERENCES

Day, C., & Roberts, M.C. (1991). Activities of the child and adolescent service system program for improving mental health services for children and families. *Journal of Clinical Child Psychology, 20*, 340-350.

Dryfoos, J.G. (1994). *Full service schools: A revolution in health and social services for children, youth, and families.* San Francisco: Jossey-Bass.

Dunst, C.J., Trivette, C.M., & Deal, A.G. (1988). *Enabling and empowering families: Principles and guidelines for practice.* Cambridge, MA: Brookline Books.

Illback, R.J. (1994). Poverty and the crisis in children's services: The need for services integration. *Journal of Clinical Child Psychology, 23*, 413-424.

Kagan, S.L., & Weissbourd, B. (Eds.). (1994). *Putting families first: America's family support movement and the challenge of change.* San Francisco: Jossey-Bass.

National Commission on Children (Final report). (1991). *Beyond rhetoric: A new American agenda for children and families.* Washington, D.C.: U.S. Government Printing Office.

Nelson, C.M., & Pearson, C. (1991). *Integrating services for children and youth with emotional or behavioral disorders.* Reston, VA: The Council for Exceptional Children.

Saxe, L., Cross, T., Silverman, N., Batchelor, W.F., & Dougherty, D. (1987). *Children's mental health: Problems and services.* Durham, NC: Duke University Press.

Stroul, B., Goldman, S., Lourie, I., Katz-Leavy, J., & Zeigler-Dendy, C. (1992). *Profiles of local systems of care for children and adolescents with severe emotional disturbances.* Washington, DC: Georgetown University Child Development Center, CASSP Technical Assistance Center.

Tuma, J. (1989). Mental health services for children: The state of the art. *American Psychologist, 44,* 188-199.

# Implications of the National Agenda to Improve Results for Children and Youth with or at Risk of Serious Emotional Disturbance

David Osher

Chesapeake Institute

Tom V. Hanley

U.S. Department of Education

**SUMMARY.** Fragmented, agency-centered services contribute to poor educational and social outcomes. *The National Agenda to Improve Results for Children and Youth with Serious Emotional Disturbance* targets approaches that are knowledge-based and have a high likelihood of improving outcomes. This article explores the implications of the Agenda's seven targets and the importance of early identification and prevention. *[Article copies available from The Haworth Document Delivery Service: 1-800-342-9678.]*

## OVERVIEW

It is not a recent notion that schools play an important role in the social and emotional development of children and youth. Schools, Progressive

---

Address correspondence to: David Osher, Chesapeake Institute, Suite 400, 1000 Thomas Jefferson Street, NW, Washington, DC 20007.

[Haworth co-indexing entry note]: "Implications of the National Agenda to Improve Results for Children and Youth with or at Risk of Serious Emotional Disturbance." Osher, David, and Tom V. Hanley. Co-published simultaneously in *Special Services in the Schools* (The Haworth Press, Inc.) Vol. 10, No. 2, 1995, pp. 7-36; and: *Emerging School-Based Approaches for Children with Emotional and Behavioral Problems: Research and Practice in Service Integration* (ed: Robert J. Illback, and C. Michael Nelson) The Haworth Press, Inc., 1996, pp. 7-36. Single or multiple copies of this article are available from The Haworth Document Delivery Service [1-800-342-9678, 9:00 a.m. - 5:00 p.m. (EST)].

Era reformer Robert Hunter wrote in a turn-of-the-century study of poverty, must take on "responsibilities which the school, more than any other public agency, is fitted to master" (1904, p. 260). Schools, too, as Barbara Biber wrote half a century later, have a particularly important responsibility, ". . . to give the growing child a solid feeling that the world is more safe than threatening, more giving than denying, more accepting than rejecting" (1955, p. 159). Schools, Minuchin and his colleagues observed a decade and a half later, are ". . . responsible for nurturing individuality, for the experience that contributes to feelings of worth and self-realization, to the capacity for emotional investment, and to the building of a separate identity" (Minuchin, Biber, Shapiro, & Zimiles, 1969, p. 130).

Also recognized for a long time is the inextricable relationship between schools and social problems. The school provides the "critical social context" that generates delinquent behavior. In a seminal study, Delbert Elliott argued that delinquency is "a way to deal with the immediate social and psychological consequences of school failure, degradation, and rejection" (1974, p. 204). Nicholas Hobbs was even more pointed in his important *The Troubled and Troubling Child*, in which he wrote, "School figures more frequently than any other setting, even the family itself, as the place where adjustment difficulties become manifest" (1982, p. 288).

## THE NEED FOR APPROPRIATE, LINKED SERVICES

Although the "mutually reinforcing aspects of education and mental health" (The Joint Commission on Mental Health of Children, 1973, p. 378) and the link between education and social outcomes may seem obvious, the institutional response to those connections is not. Although schools do have some mental health and social service personnel–with, in fact, the number of such personnel increasing over time (Cremin, 1988; Tyack, 1992; Knitzer, Steinberg, & Fleish, 1990; Digest of Educational Statistics, 1994; Dryfoos, 1993)–the impact of such services, with some exceptions, is marginal at best. There are, for example, too few school psychologists working in too many schools to have a sustained and pervasive impact on the climate of schools as a whole (e.g., Fine, 1991); and psychologists who do work in the schools typically spend so much of their time doing assessments that their time available for counseling, therapy, or teacher consultation is extremely limited.

If one looks at this matter from the perspective of young people who could most benefit from school-based counseling services–students with serious emotional disturbance (SED)–the matter looks no different. A 1988 study of 60 school districts in 18 states found that 58 percent of reporting schools simply lacked the capacity to provide counseling of any sort (Moore, Strang, Schwartz, & Braddock, 1988). According to national studies, only 25-40 percent of students with SED are provided personal counseling or therapy by their schools (McInerney, Kane, & Pelavin, 1992; Wagner, Blackorby, Cameto, Hebbeler & Newman, 1993). Moreover, according to the National Longitudinal Transition Study of Special Education Outcomes (NLTS), the average amount of counseling provided annually to students with SED was 22.8 hours, with only 13 percent of these students receiving more than 40 hours of counseling (Valdes, Williamson, & Wagner, 1991).

The lack of coordinated or school-linked services mediates how students with SED leave school, as such students are less likely to receive mandated transition planning than are any other group of students with disabilities; and schools are less likely to contact state Vocational Rehabilitation agencies on behalf of students with SED than they are for any other group of students with disabilities. More significantly, the NLTS researchers reported that no contacts with mental health agencies were made on behalf of youth with SED (Wagner, Blacborby, Cameto, Hebbeler, & Newman, 1993).

Historical analyses and contemporary policy studies document the marginalization of mental health in schools. For example, up until the 1960s, the mental health system assumed primary responsibility for children with emotional and behavioral disorders; and even when social work and mental health personnel were added to schools, those workers were likely to be the first casualties of retrenchment (Paul & Warnock, 1980; Grob, 1994; Tyack, 1992). Jane Knitzer's 1990 *Beyond the School House Door* and the 1992 report of McInerney and his colleagues delineated the continuation of marginalization, of which there are (according to Knitzer) two typical patterns: "Either the child has no access to any mental health services and supports or, in a *sub-rosa* effort to accommodate the child's needs without incurring the fiscal liability, the teacher, or other school personnel, outside of the formal area of the individualized education program (IEP) process, suggest to a family that they seek services from a mental health center" (p. 13). In many cases, the consequences are predictable–only those students whose parents can afford services get them. Moreover, even if appropriate services are provided, those services tend to be isolated–and do not build upon or utilize other services.

Fragmented, agency-oriented services have historically characterized the array of settings and systems that can support (or undermine) the emotional and mental well being of children and youth with or at risk of developing emotional and behavioral problems. Some of those systems include (a) general and special education, (b) health, (c) mental health, (d) rehabilitative services, (e) welfare, (f) recreation and youth work, (g) protective services, and (h) juvenile justice. These systems are fragmented by differences in five critical areas:

- legislative mandates,
- target groups,
- organizational cultures,
- theoretical and research paradigms, and
- approaches and models of service delivery.

As a 1992 Packard Foundation Report suggests, fragmented services ". . . divide the problems of children and families into rigid and distinct categories," and prevent agencies from ". . . responding in a timely, coordinated and comprehensive fashion to the multiple and interconnected needs of children and families" (Packard Foundation, 1992, p. 8; Dryfoos, 1993).

Not only are these services uncoordinated, but they reflect agency and school-centered approaches to planning and service delivery that fail to involve families and students in the design, implementation, and evaluation of supports and services (U.S. Department of Education, 1995). Rather than connectedness and responsiveness, many students with emotional and behavioral problems and their families experience unresponsive and fragmented services. As two groups at a 1991 Teleconference on SED said, "There *are* holes in the safety net and students *do* fall through the cracks" (as quoted in Osher, 1992, p. 2).

The absence of a strong student- and family-centered link between education and other services is particularly troubling, especially since education does play five distinctive service delivery roles. First, general education is a universal (in terms of the United States) entitlement that reaches all students. In other words, schools have direct access to more children than do other community institutions; and schools provide an available mechanism for overcoming such barriers to service delivery as time and transportation (Catron & Weiss, 1994; Tapp & Niarhos, 1994).

Second, schools have an obligation to serve students, and Federal special education law provides students and parents with due-process rights. While other systems may choose to provide due-process rights, and even the right to "treatment," those rights, in fact, are mandated under special education legislation.

Third, schools provide academic skills and credentials that structure the life chances of all young people independent of disabilities. The lack of those skills and credentials–what Basil Berstein (1971) aptly described as social capital–compounds the impact of a disability.

Fourth, schools are "sorting station[s]," wherein children and youth first ". . . come to think of themselves as consistently inadequate or dumb, and especially as bad or troublesome" (Wheeler, Cottrell, Jr., & Romasco, 1966, p. 436). Schools label students, parcel out credentials and access to academic and vocational training, and sustain an environment in which students define themselves (Willis, 1977).

Finally, schools and school-related activities are where many young people spend the single largest portion of their days. Travel to and from school, recess, formal and informal extra-curricula activities, homework (whether done or ignored)–all of these structure the lives of young people; and, because of the five roles schools play, ". . . an educational dimension is crucial to an effective system of care for troubled children" (Stroul & Friedman, pp. 77-8). Unfortunately, reports on model systems of care suggest that (a) education remains on the margins of many systems of care and that (b) in spite of espousing child and family-centered core principles, settings remain agency-directed, as opposed to consumer-centered or consumer-directed (Stroul, Lourie, Goldman, & Katz-Leavy, 1992; Osher & Weisel, 1995).

## THE IMPACT OF FRAGMENTED SCHOOL AND AGENCY-CENTERED SERVICES

Fragmented school and agency-centered services contribute to what Lisbeth Schorr described as nothing less than "rotten outcomes" (1988, p. 259)–outcomes that are particularly bleak for students and youth who are or could be identified as having SED. While positive educational experiences play a prominent role in both the development and the remediation of emotional problems (Hobbs, 1982; Osher & Osher, 1995), educational outcomes for young people with SED are dismal.

Dryfoos (1990, p. 201) defined seven "measures of success in the evaluation or prevention of school failure": poor grades, low achievement, low expectations for achievement, non-promotion, dropping out, truancy, and suspensions and expulsions. In each of these, schools do more poorly with students with SED than they do with many or all other groups of students, particularly if we factor in data on race, ethnicity, and social class. In fact, compared to other students with disabilities, students with SED in regular and special education classes have the lowest grades at each secondary school grade level, fail more courses, are retained at the same grade more frequently, drop out more frequently, miss school more frequently, and graduate less frequently (Wagner, Newman, D'Amico, Jay, Butler-Nalin, Marder, & Cox, 1991).

Teacher expectations for students with SED reinforce the poor performance of schools, and such students are pushed out of school by transfer, suspension, and plain hostility (Walker, Reavis, Rhode, & Jenson, 1984; Rumberger & Larson, 1994; Osher & Osher, 1995). Graduation and dropout statistics for these young people are particularly stunning, with only 42 percent of students with SED graduating from high school, and more than 54 percent of students with SED simply dropping out of school all together (Wagner, Blackorby, & Hebbeler, 1993). Perhaps it is needless to say that the implications of such data are portentous for the future of young people with SED. Instead of remaining in school, succeeding there and gaining skills, socializing with "non-disabled" peers, and participating in extra-curricular activities–actions that contribute to the long-term adjustment of most young people–for students with SED, the opposite occurs. They miss more days of classes, are placed in more restrictive settings, and have less transition planning done for them by their schools than the schools do for any other group of students with disabilities.

Arrest rates for students with SED also speak to a level of systemic failure, with 58 percent of all students with SED arrested within 5 years of leaving school. Among dropouts, the rates are an even more appalling (73 percent) (Wagner, D'Amico, Marder, Newman, & Blackorby, 1992).

## TOWARD A NATIONAL AGENDA

Since 1975, Federal special education law has included students with SED. However, although P.L. 94-142 covered students with SED, many such students have remained unidentified, and still others have received inappropriate services (Walker, Reavis, Rhode, & Jenson, 1984; Knitzer, Steinberg, & Fleisch, 1990). In the Individuals with Disabilities Education Act (IDEA) of 1990, Congress addressed this matter by adding to Part C of IDEA a discretionary program on serious emotional disturbance. "It is generally agreed that children with serious emotional disturbance remain the most undeserved population of students with disabilities," the House Committee on Education and Labor stated in a report that described "the pervasive and deep-seated nature of the problem." Both the House and Senate committees (1990) conceptualized that problem in broad terms– (a) the stigma attached to the SED label, (b) the poor treatment of parents of these children, (c) the differential treatment of African American, Latino, and other minority children of ethnic backgrounds, (d) the need for coordination and collaboration among the multiple agencies, and (e) the need to improve prevention efforts and to reduce the use of out-of-community residential placements.

In addition to establishing an SED research and demonstration program in 1990, Congress mandated a planning process that, when applied to the SED program, would involve individuals with disabilities, parents, professionals, and representatives of state and local educational agencies, private schools, institutions of higher education, and national organizations with interest or experience in the program.

This mandate set the stage for an extensive four-year planning effort that mined and tested the ideas generated by thousands of individuals–family members, former students with SED, special and general education teachers, early childhood and Head Start personnel, school psychologists, mental health and juvenile justice professionals, experts on systems change, behavioral disorders, and mental health, and local, state, and national education and mental health administrators. These culturally and geographically diverse individuals addressed three essential questions:

- *What needs must be targeted to improve outcomes for children and youth with or at risk of developing serious emotional disturbance?*
- *Can these targets be implemented?*
- *Are these targets consistent with validated research and practice?*

The planning process defined a consensus centered around seven strategic targets and three cross-cutting themes that were knowledge-based, had a high likelihood of having a significant impact, and reached well beyond education. This consensus was incorporated into the *National Agenda to Improve Results for Children and Youth with Serious Emotional Disturbance* (U.S. Department of Education, 1994). The agenda identified seven strategic targets that are listed in Figure 1, "Reorientation and Preparedness to Achieve Better Results." In addition, the SED National Agenda identified three "cross-cutting themes" that should infuse linked services and should represent core principles for improving results for children with SED. These three themes emphasize the following principles that must be considered in activities related to all of the targets:

- *Prevention:* For children *with* SED, all efforts must be directed toward arresting the escalation of their mental health, behavioral, and educational problems "replacing problems with solutions and successes. For children *at risk* of SED, efforts must be directed toward reversing that trajectory and providing them with support and guidance that will prevent development of a "serious emotional disturbance."
- *Cultural Sensitivity and Respect:* The continuing resource that enriches the American experience and makes this country singular among nations is its cultural, ethnic, racial, and linguistic diversity.

This resource also is a challenge that daily confronts individuals and institutions–the challenge of communicating and understanding across cultural and linguistic barriers. Cultural differences should never be interpreted as weaknesses, and failures to communicate or understand should never translate into inappropriate identifications of SED or, alternatively, into failures to address and serve emotional and behavioral conditions when they present themselves.

- *Empowerment:* The collaborative "wrap-around" service delivery model must embrace service deliverers *and* receivers. All individuals must feel that their perspectives are respected and that their participation is constructive and influential. Even though the SED National Agenda clearly highlights reaching out to previously underserved and under-represented individuals (e.g., families), all participants and stakeholders need to feel that reform will strengthen their ability to achieve better results for these children. This is, in effect, a "win-win" model. The school psychologist needs the capability to exercise therapeutic, rather than simply diagnostic skills. The classroom teacher needs to know that behavioral and mental health resources, as well as training, are available to him or her. Mental health and juvenile justice professionals need to do their work without barriers, to allow them to interact effectively with the schools. Families and young people need to feel that they are full participants in designing and evaluating wrap-around plans.

The remainder of this article will first describe these seven targets and suggest the relationship to school-linked services.*

## SEVEN TARGETS OF THE NATIONAL AGENDA

### Target 1: Expand Positive Learning Opportunities and Results

*To foster the provision of engaging, useful, and positive learning opportunities. These opportunities should be result-driven and should acknowledge as well as respond to the experiences and needs of children and youth with serious emotional disturbance.*

---

*Those interested in receiving a copy of the *National Agenda for Achieving Better Results for Children and Youth with Serious Emotional Disturbance* should contact David Osher at the Chesapeake Institute, 1000 Thomas Jefferson Street, N.W., Suite 400, Washington, DC 20007 (202) 944-5373 or DOsher@AIR-DC.ORG.

FIGURE 1. Reorientation and Preparedness to Achieve Better Results

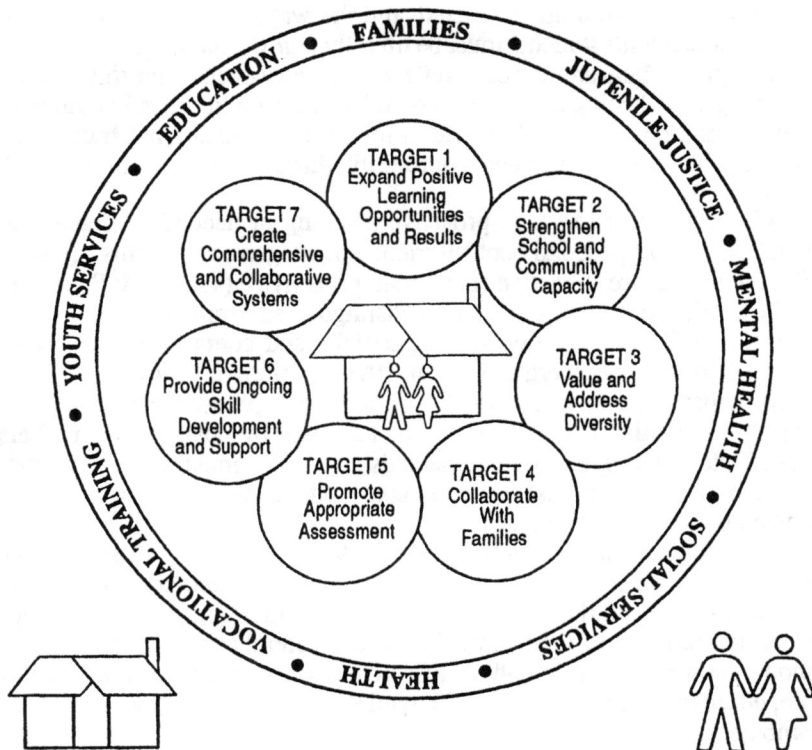

SCHOOL AND COMMUNITY RESULTS
● Community Strength
● Family Preservation
● Fiscal Efficiency
● Teacher Retention
● School Effectiveness

STUDENT RESULTS
● Improved Grades
● Enhanced Learning
● Higher Graduation Rates
● Increased Equity
● Successful Transition to Adult Roles

COLLABORATE ➡ IMPLEMENT TARGETS ➡ ACHIEVE RESULTS

Source: *National Agenda for Achieving Better Results for Children and Youth with Serious Emotional Disturbance (1994)*

School and community factors are reflected in the dismal outcome data cited in this review. In other words, the data reflect ecological factors–not just intrapsychic or biological factors. To change outcomes for young people with emotional or behavioral problems, the environments in which these children learn must be altered–and the ways in which teachers and others interact with students must be literally *transformed*. The first report on the agenda-building process reflected a "consensus" on this matter: "Nothing truly lasting could be accomplished for children and youth with serious emotional disturbance within the current educational framework that largely seeks to achieve conformity through systems of control" (Osher, 1991, p. 4).

This target calls for ". . . proactive teaching of needed academic and social skills as opposed to control-oriented management systems" (Osher, 1992, p. 9) that are "reactive rather than proactive" (Walker & Severson, 1990, p. 1). This approach can be distinguished from a curriculum of control that focuses on ameliorating deficits and containing undesirable actions (Knitzer, Steinberg & Fleisch, 1990; Cambone, 1994).

Some participants in the 1991 teleconference phrased the matter this way: ". . . positive results can only be achieved by positive means. This means altering our traditional methods. . . . We must get away from coercive methods that just serve to make students and teachers aversive" (quoted in Osher, 1992, p. 4).

Like other at-risk students (Levin, 1993; Fine, 1991; Rossi, 1994), students with SED require culturally responsive, student-centered opportunities to learn, marked by high expectations, attention to skill development, and tailored to their individual needs (Steinberg & Knitzer, 1992; Rhode, Jenson, & Reavis, 1993). Effective teaching practices must, therefore, *adapt* instruction to individual requirements and strengths–and use or combine the following:

- Planned, direct instruction and reciprocal teaching that enable students to understand what is expected of them and to receive feedback and support in developing mastery;
- Cooperative learning and peer tutoring, which can enable students to develop academic and social skills; and
- Experiential learning (including the creative use of computers), which engages students and enables them to test and to internalize new skills.

Proactive teaching and creative classroom management require school-based services and supports to enable teachers (and other school staff) to teach and to support in other ways the academic, social, and emotional development of students with and at risk of developing emotional or behavioral problems. The Agenda does not ignore the issue of behavior. Instead, the agenda calls for preventative and timely interventions to stop problems from developing in the first place, and for providing teachers (and others who work with students) with the training and the support required for them to act proactively and to use appropriate behavioral strategies. Hence, the second and sixth targets: strengthening school and community capacity and providing ongoing training and support.

### Target 2: Strengthen School and Community Capacity

> *To foster initiatives that strengthen the capacity of schools and communities to serve students with serious emotional disturbance in the least restrictive environments appropriate.*

Students with emotional and behavioral problems are often removed from mainstream classes, neighborhood schools, and even from their own home communities. Such removal reflects a lack of will or a lack of capacity to support these young people in mainstream settings (Walker, Reavis, Rhode, & Jenson, 1984); and it demonstrates an equivalent inability to support those who work and live with them. The removal of these young people also reflects the confounding of restrictive placement (e.g., a residential school) with intensity of need and service (Knitzer, 1993).

If we are to successfully integrate these students into neighborhood schools and into regular classrooms, schools must do more than they currently do. NLTS data on mainstreamed students suggest the dimensions of the challenge. Of those students with SED who participated in mainstream settings, 41 percent were in schools that expected them to "keep up" without any special help. Of equal importance is the fact that only 38 percent of students with SED were in schools that provided teachers with in-service training, while only 26 percent were in schools that provided classroom aides, and only 11 percent were in schools that reduced class size (Valdes, Williamson, & Wagner, 1991). It is, therefore, not surprising that many families and teachers worry about what they characterize as "dumping."

Changing placement will not work without changing the capacity of people and settings to support young people. For example, teachers may not be able to improve learning outcomes without an allocation of planning time, a lower student/faculty ratio, and the support of school psychologists or mental health personnel. Similarly, a call for reintegration that does not address the commitment of support underestimates what it really takes to effectively serve students with emotional or behavioral problems.

Fortunately, as Jane Knitzer recently observed, ". . . it is possible to create the appropriate level of intensity using natural environments by 'wrapping services around' a child and family in his or her own home, classroom, and community" (1993, p. 10). Similarly, it is possible to wrap supports around teachers and school-based personnel, to enable them to work more effectively with challenging students (Eber, 1994 and infra; Osher & Osher, 1995). The National Association of State Boards of Education (NASBE) stated that including students depends upon a ". . . seamless web of services tailored to the individual needs of students and their families" (NASBE, 1992, p. 35). Improving results cannot, then, be conceptualized as a teacher-by-teacher problem. Rather, the improvement of results must be seen as a *systems problem* that must be addressed by schools and other service agencies generating supportive environments and services that enable families, teachers, students, and others who work with students to function together as a team to achieve better results (Nelson & Pearson, 1991; Koyanagi & Gaines 1993).

The remaining five targets of the agenda focus on issues that must be addressed, if meaningful efforts are to succeed: addressing diversity, collaborating with families, improving assessment, supporting individuals in new professional roles, and generating effective community-based collaborations.

### Target 3: Value and Address Diversity

> *To encourage culturally competent and linguistically appropriate exchanges and collaborations among families, professionals, students, and communities. These collaborations should foster equitable outcomes for all students and result in the identification and provision of services that are responsive to issues of race, culture, gender, and social and economic status.*

Diversity has been a challenge since the 19th Century establishment of the U.S. system of public education (Tyack, 1974; Lazerson, 1971; Fass, 1989); and that endemic challenge of diversity has been particularly pronounced for students with emotional and behavioral problems–for whom rates of identification, placement, services received, and achievement vary across gender, racial, and cultural dimensions (Valdes, Williamson, & Wagner, 1991; Osher & Osher, 1995).

For example, white students are less likely to be identified as SED than are black students. In fact, compared to black students, white students are even more likely to spend time in regular education classes and even less likely to be placed in restrictive settings. White students with SED are more likely to receive school-based counseling, much more likely to receive higher grades, and much more likely to graduate (46 percent to 28 percent) than are their black counterparts (Valdes, Williamson, & Wagner, 1991).

Improving results for children and youth with emotional and behavioral problems requires approaches that improve the capacity of individuals and systems to respond skillfully, respectfully, and effectively to youth, families, teachers, and other providers in ways that recognize, affirm, and value their worth and dignity (Hilliard, 1989; Gordon & Yowell, 1994). This will not be easy, as ethnocentric approaches have played a powerful role in the development of public education, psychology, social work, and juvenile justice in the United States (Kaestle, 1983; Grob, 1994; Lubove, 1969).

Still, it is both necessary and possible to develop culturally competent services that address the needs of all children and youth with serious emotional disturbance (Isaacs & Benjamin, 1991; *Focal Point,* 1994). Cultural competency, however, is not a set of tools to be mastered at some point and applied indiscriminately over and over again. Rather, cultural competency is an *approach* to reflective practice (Schoen, 1983), which recognizes (a) the cultural grounding of service providers' assumptions, knowledge, behaviors, and methods; and (b) a set of skills that must be adapted to each new individual encounter.

Culturally competent approaches attend to the power of language and communicative style; they view family and community as critical parts of a young person's support system; and they demonstrate a willingness and ability to draw on family and community-based values, traditions, customs, and resources. Furthermore, implementing culturally competent approaches requires an understanding of the extent to which school-family and professional-family encounters are often bi-cultural encounters (Cross, Bazron, Dennis, & Isaacs, 1989; Harry, 1992)–an understanding that also requires breaking out of traditional top-down professional-parent relations (issues that target 4 addresses).

### Target 4: Collaborate with Families

> *To foster collaborations that fully include family members on the team of service providers that implements family-focused services to improve educational outcomes. Services should be open, helpful, culturally competent, accessible to families, and school–as well as community-based.*

Families are critical to interventions aimed at improving outcomes for children and youth with emotional and behavioral problems–yet, although families frequently represent a child's most intimate and long-term support system, familial support (or even family participation in education and service systems) has not been, historically, a priority (Tyack, 1992; Friesen & Korloff, 1990; Upshur, 1991). In fact, families often have been blamed for their children's problems–a tendency that has been particularly pronounced for families of children with emotional and behavioral problems (Lipsky, 1989; Lefley, 1989; Wahl, 1989). Moreover, schools and services often have been designed to insulate children from economically poor and socially marginalized families who have been traditionally viewed as the cause of other children's *deviance* (Tyack, 1992; Rothman, 1980; Franklin, 1994).

Although frequently ignored and stigmatized, families of children and youth with emotional and behavioral problems often serve as their children's advocates and case coordinators, negotiating between and among the education, health, mental health, substance abuse, welfare, youth services, and correctional systems. In fact, strategies for linking services and for improving results for children and youth with emotional and behavioral problems cannot work unless families are seen as central to the solution, and strategies build upon family strengths. This requires expanding our definition of family to include birth, extended, adoptive, and foster families; and reconceputalizing the role of families in a manner that will transform the relationship between schools and professionals, on the one hand, and family members, on the other.

One aspect of reconceptualization involves thinking about family support services as central to interventions for students with emotional and behavioral problems, in general, and to such students' individualized educational programs (IEPs), in particular. There often is a reciprocal relationship between home-based support and the success of least restrictive placements "since the success of interventions often depends upon the families' ability to obtain the educational, mental health, and other support services required to maintain their child in their home.

In addition, if families are to meet the needs of their children *and* be full-partners in planning and evaluation activities, they may require support (e.g., transportation or respite). Necessary services, then, should be designed to accommodate family strengths and requirements, and be provided in an easily accessible manner–including counseling services, training, support groups, and immediate crisis intervention.

Services, as important as they are, are not enough. A second aspect of reconceptualization involves both *voice* and *power*. If we are to support children and youth, we must work with family members as partners who have knowledge to contribute to planning, evaluation, and service delivery. Instead of the top-down model of professionalized help, in which professional voices dominate and professionals are viewed as the source of all solutions (Goffman, 1959; Biklen, 1988), this target calls for collaborations marked by (a) full family participation, (b) respect as well as compassion for family members, (c) an appreciation of the knowledge as well as the commitment that family members bring, and (d) a willingness to reconfigure meetings to enable families to participate fully.

Working together requires an understanding of the fact that many family members have often had painful experiences with school and social service agencies, either as students or consumers themselves or as individuals seeking services for their children (e.g., Schrag & Divorky, 1975). Collaboration, then, requires (a) the ability to accommodate different styles of social interaction and to use straightforward language, (b) the demonstration of respect for a family's culture and experience, and (c) a willingness to provide families with crucial information and viable options at a time and in a manner that will support full participation.

Finally, to collaborate with families requires analyzing the barriers to family participation—whether they be scheduling, transportation, language, an "awe" of schools and professionals (Valdivieso & Nicolas, 1994, p. 104), or previous experiences with schools and professionals—and addressing them in a straightforward manner.

### Target 5: Promote Appropriate Assessment

> *To promote practices ensuring that assessment is integral to the identification, design, and delivery of services for children and youth with SED. These practices should be culturally appropriate, ethical, and functional.*

Assessment frequently is a key to effective special education and human service interventions; and appropriate, ongoing, cost-effective, and practical assessment is essential to improving outcomes for troubling youth. If done in a manner that controls for biases of class, race, and culture, screening, monitoring, and assessment can identify children at risk and can support preventive interventions that may reduce more costly and stigmatizing interventions at a later time. Effective assessment can augment planning and can monitor the implementation of comprehensive services. Unfortunately, this often is not the case. Although many young people with emotional and behavioral disorders can be identified early, few are, in fact, so identified. When students are identified, assessment practices often are overly subjective, use inappropriate tools, ignore the impact of culture and language, and fail to effectively involve students and family members (Epstein & Cullinan, 1992). In addition, assessments that are done in one setting or service area are rarely used in other settings or areas. This lack of articulation wastes resources and burdens consumers and families, who have to participate in duplicative assessment procedures. More importantly, such practice does not support consistency between and across settings.

Culturally competent, linguistically appropriate, multi-disciplinary assessments that involve families can help providers build on the strengths of young people and their families, and they can help to address the changing developmental needs of troubling youth. Ongoing assessments that focus on the youth's environment (including the school) can target service provisions (Greenwood, Carta, & Atwater, 1991; Arreaga-Mayer, Carta, & Tapia, 1994) and can prevent emotional problems from intensifying, thus avoiding the need for more protracted and more expensive future interventions.

Current assessments practices frequently fail to identify the support and modifications necessary for the successful integration or reintegration of students with SED into regular education settings. This target supports practical and timely assessments that enable teachers and schools to identify appropriate strategies and to assure that interventions are producing desired results.

More generally, the target supports early screening and identification of children with emotional or behavioral problems by a multidisciplinary team of professionals and parents, in order that these children's problems are addressed before a cycle of failure, truancy, dropping out, and delinquency is established. The procedures themselves must be accurate, linguistically appropriate, and culturally fair, and should provide necessary information to enable educators and other service providers to use appropriate educational experiences and services for young people with emotional and behavioral disorders.

### Target 6: Provide Ongoing Skill Development and Support

> *To foster the enhancement of knowledge, understanding, and sensitivity among all who work with children and youth with and at risk of developing serious emotional disturbance. Support and development should be ongoing and aim at strengthening the capacity of families, teachers, service providers, and other stakeholders to collaborate, persevere, and improve outcomes for children and youth with SED.*

Research on school-based change suggests that ongoing staff development is central to making change work (Fullan & Miles, 1992; Gersten & Woodward, 1992). This is particularly important in the case of culturally competent family and child centered cross-disciplinary collaborations aimed at improving results for children and youth with emotional and behavioral problems. The need for new approaches and behaviors, coupled with the complex nature of serious emotional disturbance requires staff capacity building.

These new demands create a gap between what is learned in professional school and what teachers and service providers face in environments that link services in a child-centered and accessible manner. Professionals and others who work with young people require ongoing skill development and training that enables them to teach and to effectively address the needs of students with emotional and behavioral problems, to value and address diversity, to work with families in a respectful manner, to engage in effective assessment practices, and to collaborate effectively.

"One-shot" workshops that lack follow-up and are not integrated into day-to-day work will not address the above matter. Those who work with young people with SED require ongoing support and professional development in order to (a) increase their capacity to teach and work effectively, (b) reduce their sense of isolation, and (c) enhance their commitment to meeting the needs of troubling youth and their families. Parent and family training should be offered so that all those working with troubling youth can develop new skills, acquire knowledge of promising intervention techniques, and become aware of new and successful innovations and practices. Effective approaches include mentoring, coaching, collaborative action research across participants, the employment of change-facilitators, and the designing of ongoing, field-based workshops that enable families, teachers, aides, administrators, and mental health professionals, and others (e.g., school bus drivers and cafeteria workers) to share information and experiences regarding the diversity, the complexity of needs, and the potential of children and youth with emotional and behavioral problems.

## *Target 7: Create Comprehensive and Collaborative Systems*

> *To promote systems change resulting in the development of coherent services built around the individual needs of children and youth with and at risk of developing serious emotional disturbance. These services should be family-centered, community-based, and appropriately funded.*

As many troubling youth and their families attempt to maneuver through a fragmented, confusing, and overlapping aggregation of services in education, mental health, health, substance abuse, welfare, youth services, correctional, and vocational agencies, they encounter and must endure competing definitions, regulations, and jurisdictions in a delivery system marked by formalism, categorical funding, and regulatory road blocks. To effectively plan, administer, finance, and deliver the necessary educational, mental health, social, and other support services to students and their families, coordination among the numerous agencies involved must increase and improve.

Systemic change is needed to enhance regional and community capacity to the point where those involved can meet all of the needs of troubling youth. Simultaneously, systems must be developed that can bring services into the child's environment, whether it be the home, the school, or the community. Furthermore, to achieve desired outcomes, public and private funding streams must be coordinated.

This strategic target supports initiatives to help generate comprehensive and seamless systems of appropriate, culturally competent, child and family-centered services and supports that are mutually reinforcing; and this target envisions systems that are more than linkages of agencies. Instead, this target aims at developing new systems, built around the needs of students, families, and communities–systems that coordinate services, articulate responsibility, implement student and family-centered approaches to planning and evaluation, and provide system-wide and agency-level accountability.

Local systems should remain school- and community-based, to provide desired responses to local needs and to reflect the cultures of the communities served. Systems should be outcome oriented, employ uniform definitions, provide individualized and family-centered services, and respond promptly, flexibly, and effectively during any crisis. Within a coordinated, collaborative system, services should reflect the best approaches to wraparound services. Family members and students should play a key role in defining and evaluating services and supports that are customized to address their needs and strengths. Services should follow needs, and funds should follow children and their families. Young people and their families should be able to enter the entire system from any point at which specific services are first offered.

Finally, while the new systems should be community-based, policy must be coordinated at the state and national levels, for such coordination will eliminate bureaucratic road blocks, establish and reinforce commitment among agencies, and extend initiatives that coordinate previously non- or unaligned services, blending funding streams, both public and private.

## PREVENTION

The pervasive importance of the principles of prevention, cultural respect and sensitivity, and empowerment across the seven targets is readily apparent. Each of the principles should influence (1) opportunities for learning, (2) systems capacity, (3) approaches to diversity, (4) family involvement, (5) assessment, (6) training, and (7) collaboration. However, of the three themes, one stands out as an area in which appropriate approaches are generally considered less self-evident and, especially related to the responsibilities of the schools, controversial and troubling—the area of prevention. The article will conclude with a discussion of prevention.

### Prevention Under IDEA

The sources of perplexity around the areas of *prevention* include the following:

- In general, funding under IDEA is legislatively restricted to children with classified disabilities and not intended for use to "prevent" the development of a disability;
- The current Federal definition of "serious emotional disturbance" (34 CFR, Chapter III, Sect. 300.7, (b)(9)) explicitly excludes ". . . children who are socially maladjusted, unless it is determined that they have a serious emotional disturbance" (7-1-93 Edition, p. 14). This "social maladjustment exclusion clause" is used by many schools to deny special education services to many students with antisocial behavior and conduct disorders (Walker, 1993); and
- Schools and the public at large have a tendency to blame students for their behaviors. With this blame there is a reluctance to identify students with emotional or behavioral disorders for fear that identification requiring special education services would limit the schools' ability to apply to these children what are regarded as "normal disciplinary procedures" (i.e., suspension and expulsion) (McLaughlin, Leone, Hopfengardner Warren, Schofield, & Pasco, 1994).

The problem also may reflect two general assumptions:

- That services from special education staff can only be provided to students who are classified with a specific disability and provided with an IEP; and
- That students who are not "in" special education do not need special accommodations or approaches in the regular education classroom.

Both of these assumptions are, of course, false.

In fact, many of the concerns and premises that make it difficult for some schools to engage in prevention activities rest on misinterpretations of Federal laws, regulations, and policies. It is true that Federal Part B funding, the principal formula (state and local) grants, can be expended only for instructional and related services to children with disabilities, or for evaluative and diagnostic services for children who have or are suspected of having a disability. Nevertheless, the second component–evaluative and diagnostic services–includes "child find" services (34 CFR Sect. 300.128 and 300.220) and, in numerous states, allows for a great variety of what are known as "prereferral strategies." These strategies permit schools and their special and general education staff, working collaboratively, to examine the effects of curricular modifications and other accommodations, prior to a determination of eligibility for special education services. Understandably, the purpose of these prereferral strategies is to improve the accuracy and fairness of the assessment process–to assure that students with disabilities are appropriately identified and that students without disabilities are not identified. However, in that process, the strategies can provide some useful prevention-related activities.

More directly, it is important to note that although Part B funds are generally restricted to services for children with disabilities, Federal policy does not interfere with state and local rights to assign staff and services *where they are needed.* On average, Part B funds cover only 8.3 percent of expenditures, per child, for students in special education (U.S. Department of Education, 1994); and many States and localities use proportionately more of their Part B allotments for related services personnel than to directly support teachers. Consequently, a significant portion of the salary of most special education teachers is provided from local funds and, at least from the Federal perspective, the allocation of such staff time is under state or local discretion.

This issue was treated in 1991 by Judy Schrag, Director of the Office of Special Education Programs (OSEP), in response to questions related to Part B funding issues regarding *inclusion practices* (placement of students with disabilities in regular classrooms). The import of her response can be generalized to other areas, including prevention activities for students with emotional and behavioral problems.

> In general, the Department's position is that personnel may be split-funded across more than one program (e.g., Part B, Chapter I Migrant, Chapter I LEA, regular education, etc.), so that a teacher or other staff member may actually provide services to children with similar needs who are eligible for more than one program. Split-funding of personnel does, however, require time-and-effort documentation so that funding from various programs may be tracked. (Schrag, 1991)

Following this statement of policy, the Department also issued new guidelines (U.S. Department of Education, 1992) that provided more flexibility and more certainty in meeting Federal requirements related to split-funding:

> Teachers belong in class, not in court. The new guidelines will help recipients better understand how to meet the requirements, thus avoiding disputes and increasing flexibility for your teachers and administrators. The guidelines will also encourage the creative use of resources from different Federal, State, and local programs in the same classroom setting . . . Please note that you have the option of developing a simplified, substitute system if it meets certain requirements. . . . (Alexander, 1992)

In addition, there is one notable exception in IDEA itself related to prevention activities, and it is found in the 1990 authorization of the SED Program. When Congress authorized discretionary grants ". . . for the purpose of improving special education and related services to children and youth with serious emotional disturbance," it also stipulated that such projects may include:

> . . . developing and demonstrating innovative approaches to assist and prevent children with emotional and behavioral problems from developing serious emotional disturbances that require the provision of special education and related services. (20 U.S.C. 1426)

This language is especially significant, as it is the only instance of a funding authorization in IDEA related to elementary and secondary school children that explicitly recognizes and authorizes prevention activity under the Act. The language also explains why the SED National Agenda, with its development funded under the most recent (1990) reauthorization, has been able to address the needs of both students with SED and students at risk of SED.

### Why Prevention Is Important

In addition to the litany of poor outcomes mentioned earlier in this article, the short-term and long-term costs of services are extremely high, particularly as children with SED are placed in restrictive environments. During the 1991-92 school year, 19.4 percent of children with SED were placed in settings (separate school, residential facility, homebound–hospital) outside their regular school, compared to an average outside placement rate of 5.3 percent for all children with disabilities (U.S. Department of Education, 1994).

According to the National Institute of Medicine (1989), the cost in 1985 of providing direct mental health services to children under 14 was over $1.5 billion. About $1 billion annually is spent for their residential treatment and hospitalization (Yelton, 1991); and a survey of 37 states (Epstein, Nelson, Polsgrove, Coutinho, Cumblad, & Quinn, 1993) found an average cost of $50,000 per year for services to SED children placed outside their homes. These costs do not even begin to approach the costs to society and to families from untreated emotional and behavioral disorders.

Alternatively, an evolving research base is documenting the effectiveness of some approaches in arresting the escalation of emotional and behavioral disorders, both for children with severe disorders (e.g., Rivera & Kutash, 1994) and for students at risk of SED (e.g., Walker, Colvin, & Ramsey, 1995). These authors and others, however, recognize the complexity of the issues and the limited documentation of past programs intended to effectively address the needs of these children and their families.

### Developmental Contextualism

A recent article by Pellagrini and Horvat (1995) extends the construct of "developmental contextualism" (Gottlieb, 1983; Hinde, 1980; Lerner, 1989) to children with Attention Deficit Hyperactivity Disorder (ADHD). Faced with the variability of symptoms present in children with ADHD, across different settings, and the concomitant difficulties in assessing and addressing that disorder, Pellagrini and Horvat propose a ". . . transitional, not unidirectional, relation between individual organisms and their environment . . . [C]hildren and their environments influence each other."

This model has implications that reach far beyond children with ADHD, and may be extended to many disabilities and conditions in general–and to children with emotional and behavioral problems in particular. In essence, the model encapsulates two very important ideas:

- The behavior and performance of a child, at any point along a time continuum, is a function of the interaction between the child (organicity and development) and the environment (e.g., specific stimuli sets: home, school, playground); and
- The development of a child, over time, as well as the state of any condition present in the child (e.g., ADHD, SED) is a product of the specific (and often continuing) interactions between the child and particular environments, in which the child develops "in context."

It is the second of these positions that is most innovative and critical to the discussion of prevention. Not only does the environment (setting) influence current events, but a history of settings sets a pattern of behaviors and responses that, in some situations, become conditions, disorders, and disabilities. A child with behavioral problems becomes a healthy youth or a disturbed youth in response to a history of interactive patterns within her or his environment.

## *Prevention Is Everybody's Business*

Between the ages of 5 (or increasingly younger) and 18, children spend a great deal of their time in school and in classrooms. From all reports, many children in even the earliest grades have "behavioral problems." Many are ignored, tracked, or subjected to "cold, foreboding" (Montgomery & Rossi, 1994, p. 9) environments that are unresponsive to their cultural and developmental needs. In other words, these students are placed at risk both when they are ignored and when they are placed in insensitive or overly restrictive settings–which can be a strong and potentially disastrous "signal" to a child's self-esteem and sense of belonging (Gordon & Yowell, 1994; Rumberger & Larson, 1994; Franklin, 1994).

By some standards, relatively few of these students are identified or served in special education under the SED classification. This is both a function of the generally narrow interpretation that schools draw for the category (in comparison to mental health agencies that estimate a 5 to 10 percent incidence rate) and the reluctance of some parents and educators to apply the term "seriously emotionally disturbed" to a young child. In addition, the developmental possibilities that the future holds may auger against the premature application of a disability label or what sociologists describe as the "medicalization of deviance" (Zola, 1972; Conrad, 1992). These concerns, however, do not justify a failure to act preventively. Rather, developmental contextualism as well as the fact that so few children in primary grades are classified SED and served by special education reinforce the importance of prevention, and, consequently, the significance of the regular education classroom experience for children with emotional and behavioral problems. (Children with SED have the oldest initial classification age of any children with disabilities.)

The collaborative focus in the SED Agenda (cross-cutting theme and Target 7) often is interpreted as the need to increase inter-agency relations and communications between schools, mental health, juvenile justice, welfare, and other community agencies, which are all important and crucial linkages. However, for those who have been working in SED areas in the schools, the most immediately critical linkage is between special and regular education. The middle and junior high school students who will be classified SED in the future are the very children sitting (or running about) in regular education elementary classrooms today. In this age of overall school reform, innovative and creative approaches to collaboration between regular educators and all of the professionals committed to the mental health of children are essential. True collaboration and, with it, a reorientation of our commitment to *all* children, represent our best hope for an improved future for these too-long neglected children and youth.

## REFERENCES

Alexander, L. (Secretary of U.S. Department of Education) (1992). *Letter accompanying the Department of Education's revised guidelines for split-time expenditures of Federal funds.* Washington, DC: Department of Education.

Arreaga-Mayer, Carta, J., & Tapia, Y. (1994). Ecobehavioral assessment: A new methodology for evaluating instruction for exceptional culturally and linguistically diverse students. In S. B. Garcia (Ed.), *Addressing cultural and linguistic diversity in special education* (pp. 10-29). Reston, VA: The Council for Exceptional Children.

Biber, B. (1955). Schooling as an influence in developing healthy personality. In R. Kotinsky & H. L. Witmer, (Eds.), *Community programs for mental health* (pp. 158-224). Cambridge, MA: Harvard University Press.

Bernstein, B. (1971). *Class, codes, and controls: Theoretical studies towards a sociology of language.* London: Routledge and Kegen Paul.

Biklen, D. (1988). The myth of clinical judgement. *Journal of Social Issues, 44:1,* 127-140.

Brofenbrenner, U. (1979). *The ecology of human development: Experiments by nature and design.* Cambridge, MA: Harvard University Press.

Cambone, J. (1994). *Teaching troubled children: A case study in effective classroom practice.* New York: Teachers College Press.

Catron, T. & Weiss, B. (1994). The Vanderbilt school-based counseling program: An interagency, primary-care model of mental health services. *Journal of Emotional and Behavioral Disorders, 2,* 247-253.

Cremin, L. (1988). *American Education: The Metropolitan Experience, 1876-1980.* New York: Harper & Row.

Cross, T., Bazron, B., Dennis, K., & Isaacs, M. (1989). *Towards a culturally competent system of care.* Washington, DC: CAASP Technical Assistance Center, Georgetown University Child Development Center.

Conrad, P. (1992). Medicalization and social control. *Annual Review of Sociology,* 18, 209-32.

Caplan, P. J. & Hall-McCorquodale, I. (1985). Mother-blaming in major clinical journals. *American Journal of Orthopsychiatry, 55,* 345-353.

Dryfoos, J. G. (1990). *Adolescents at risk: Prevalence and prevention.* New York: Oxford University Press.

Dryfoos, J. G. (1993). *Full-Service schools.* San Francisco: Josey Bass.

Eber, L. (Fall, 1994). The wraparound approach: Toward effective school inclusion. *Claiming Children,* 1, 4-9.

Elliott, D. S. (1974). *Delinquency and dropout.* Lexington, MA: Lexington Books.

Epstein, M. H. & Cullinan, D. (1992). Assessment practices used in programs for adolescents with behavior disorders. Preventing School Failure, *36: 3* (Spring, 1992), 20-25.

Epstein, M.H., Nelson, M., Polsgrove, L., Coutinho, M., Cumblad, C., & Quinn, K. (1993). A comprehensive community-based approach to serving students with emotional and behavioral disorders. *Journal of Emotional and Behavioral Disorders*, 1, 127-133.

Fass, P. S. (1989). *Outside in: Minorities and the transformation of American education.* New York: Oxford University Press.

Fine, M. (1991). *Framing dropouts.* New York: Teachers College Press.

Friesen, B. J. & Koroloff, N. M. (1990). Family-centered services: Implications for mental health administration and research. *The Journal of Mental Health Administration, 17*, 13-25.

*Focal Point* (1994). Special issue on developing culturally competent organizations, Focal Point, 8(2).

Franklin, B. M. (1994). *From "backwardness" to "at-risk": Childhood Learning difficulties and the contradictions of school reform.* Albany: State University of New York Press.

Fullan, M., & Miles, M. (1992). Getting reform right: What works and what doesn't. *Phi Delta Kappan, 73*, 744-752.

Gersten, R. M. & Woodward, J. (1992). The quest to translate research into classroom practice: Strategies for assisting classroom teachers' work with at-risk students and students with disabilities. In D. Carnine, & E. Kameenui, (Eds.), *Higher cognitive functioning for all students* (pp. 201-218). Austin, TX: Pro-Ed.

Goffman, E. (1959). *Asylums.* Garden City, NY: Anchor Books.

Gottlieb, G. (1983). The psychobiological approach to developmental issues. In M. Haith & J. Campos, (Eds.), *Handbook of child psychology: Vol. 2* (pp. 1-26). New York: Wiley.

Greenwood, C. R., Carta, J. J., & Atwater, J. (1991). Ecobehavioral analysis in the classroom. *Journal of Behavioral Education, 1*, 59-77.

Gordon, E. W. & Yowell, C. (1994). Cultural dissonance as a risk factor in the development of students. In R. J. Rossi, (Ed.), *Schools and students at risk: Context and framework for positive change* (pp. 51-69). New York: Teachers College Press.

Grob, G. N. (1994). *The Mad Among Us: A history of the care of America's mentally ill.* New York: Free Press.

Harry, B. (1992). *Cultural diversity, families, and the special education system: Communication and empowerment.* New York: Teachers College Press.

Hinde, R. (1980). *Ethology.* London: Fontana.

Hobbs, N. (1982). *The troubled and troubling child.* San Francisco: Josey-Bass.

Hilliard, A. G. III (1989). Teachers and cultural styles in a pluralistic society. *National Education Association, 7*, 65-69.

Hunter, R. (1904). *Poverty.* New York: Macmillan.

Isaacs, M. R. & Benjamin, M. P. (1991). *Towards a culturally competent system of care,* II. Washington, DC: CAASP Technical Assistance Center.

Joint Commission on Mental Health of Children (1973). *Mental health: From infancy through adolescence: Report of the Joint Commission on Mental Health of Children.* New York: Harper & Row.

Kastle, P. (1983). *Pillars of the republic: Common schools and American society.* New York: Hill and Wang.

Katz, M. (1992). Chicago school reform as history. *Teachers College Record, 94,* 56-72.

Knitzer, J. (1993). Children's mental health policy: Challenging the future. *Journal of Emotional and Behavioral Disorders,* 1, 8-16.

Knitzer, J., Steinberg, Z., & Fleisch, B. (1990). *At the schoolhouse door: An examination of programs and policies for children with behavioral and emotional problems.* New York: Bank Street College of Education.

Koyanagi, C. & Gaines, S. (1993). *All systems failure: An examination of the results of neglecting the needs of children with serious emotional disturbance.* Alexandria, VA: National Mental Health Association.

Lazerson, M. (1971). *Origins of the urban school.* Cambridge, MA: Harvard University Press.

Lefley, H. P. (1989). Family burden and family stigma in major mental illness. *American Psychologist, 44,* 556-560.

Lerner, R. (1989). Developmental contextualism and the life-span view of person-context interaction. In M. Bornstein & J. Bruner (Eds.), *Interaction in human development* (pp. 217-239). Hillsdale, NJ: Erlbaum.

Levin, H. M. (1993). Learning from accelerated schools. In J. H. Block, S. T. Everson, and T. R. Guskey, (Eds.), *Selecting and integrating school improvement programs.* New York: Scholastic Books.

Levine, A. & Levine, M. (1992). *Helping children: A social history.* New York: Oxford University Press.

Lipksy, D. K. (1989). The role of parents. In D. K. Lipsky & A. Gartner, (Eds.), *Beyond Separate Education: Quality Education for All* (pp.159-179). Baltimore. Paul H. Brooks.

Lubove, R. (1969). *The professional altruist: The emergence of social work as a career, 1880-1930.* New York: Atheneum.

McLaughlin, M.J., Leone, P.E., Hopfengardner-Warren, S., Schofield, P.F., & Pasco, S. (1994). *Issues and options for creating comprehensive school-linked services for children and youth with emotional and behavioral disorders.* College Park, MD: Center for Policy Options in Special Education.

McInerney, M., Kane, M., & Pelavin, S. (1992). *Services to children with serious emotional disturbance.* Washington, DC: Pelavin Associates.

McIntyre, T. (1992). The culturally sensitive disciplinarian. *Severe Behavior Disorders Monograph.* 107-115.

Meier, T. & Brown, C. R. (1994). The color of inclusion. *Journal of Emotional and Behavioral Problems, 3*(3), 15-19.

Minuchin, P., Biber, B., Shapiro, E., & Zimles, H. (1969). *The psychological impact of school experience.* New York: Basic Books.

Montgomery, A. F. & Rossi, R. J. (1994). Becoming at risk of failure in America's Schools. In R. J. Rossi, (Ed.), *Schools and students at risk: Context and framework for positive change* (pp. 3 - 22). New York: Teachers College Press.

Moore, M., Strang, E., Schwartz, M., & Braddock, M. (1988). *Patterns in special education service delivery and cost.* Washington, DC: Decision Resource Corp.

National Association of State Boards of Education (NASBE) (1992). *Winners all.* Alexandria, VA: Author.

National Institute of Medicine (1989). *Research on children and adolescents with mental, behavioral, and developmental disorders: Mobilizing a national initiative.* Washington, DC: National Academy Press.

Nelson, C. M. & Pearson, C. A. (1991). *Integrating services for children and youth with emotional and behavioral disorders.* Reston, VA: The Council for Exceptional Children.

Osher, D. (1992). *An analysis of the responses to the SED national town meeting.* Technical Report Prepared for the Office of Special Education Programs, U.S. Department of Education. Washington, DC: Chesapeake Institute.

Osher, D. M. & Osher, T. W. (1995). Comprehensive and collaborative systems that work: A national agenda. In C. M. Nelson, R. Rutherford, & B. I. Wolford, (Eds.), *Developing comprehensive systems that work for troubled youth.* Richmond, KY: National Coalition for Juvenile Justice Services.

Osher, D. & Weisel, L. (1995). Riding shotgun or riding herd: A close look at key factors in delivering basic skill and literacy services to persons with learning disabilities. In *Proceedings of the National Association for Adults with Special Learning Needs.* Bryn Mawr, PA: National Association for Adults with Special Learning Needs.

Osher, T. (1991). Using a focus group to assess in establishing a national agenda for children and youth with serious emotional disturbance: Formulating a national policy for the education system. Paper Presented at the Conduct Disorders Conference, May 8, 1991, Alexandria, VA.

Page, R. N. (1991). *Lower track classrooms.* New York: Teachers College Press.

Paul, J. & Warnock, N. (1980). Special education: A changing field. *The Exceptional Child, 27,* 3-28.

Pellagrini, A.D., & Horvat, M. (1995). A developmental contextualist critique of Attention Deficit Hyperactivity Disorder. *Educational Researcher, 24,* 13-19.

Richardson, V. & Colfer, P. Being at-risk in school. In J. I. Goodlad, & P. Keathing, (Eds.), *Access to knowledge: An agenda for our nation's schools* (pp. 107-124). New York: The College Board.

Rothman, D. J. (1980). *Conscience and convenience: The asylum and its alternatives in Progressive America.* Boston: Little-Brown.

Rothman, D. J. (1971). *The discovery of the asylum: Social order and disorder in the new republic.* Boston: Little Brown.

Rossi, R. J. (1994). *Schools and students at risk: Context and framework for positive change.* New York: Teachers College Press.

Rumberger, R. W. & Larson, K. W. (1994). Keeping high-risk Chicano students in school: Lessons from a Los Angeles Middle School Dropout Prevention Program. In Rossi, R. J. (Ed.), *Schools and students at risk: Context and framework for positive change.* New York: Teachers College Press (pp. 141-162).

Schoen, D. (1983). *The reflective practitioner.* San Francisco: Jossey-Bass.

Schorr, L. (1988). *Within our reach: Breaking the cycle of disadvantage.* Garden City, NY: Doubleday.

Schrag, J.A. (1991). *Letter to Jeffrey V. Osowski.* Washington, DC: U.S. Department of Education, Sept. 20.

Schrag, P. & Divorky, D. (1975). *The myth of the hyperactive child.* New York: Pantheon.

Smey-Richman, B. (1991). *School climate and restructuring for low-achieving students.* Philadelphia: Research for Better Schools.

SRI (1991). *Dropouts with disabilities: What do we know? What can we do?: A Report from the National Longitudinal Transition Study of Special Education Students,* Menlo Park, CA, Author.

Steinberg, Z., & Knitzer, J. (1992). Classrooms for emotionally and behavioral disturbed students: Facing the challenge. *Behavioral Disorders, 17,* 145-156.

Stroul, B. A. & Friedman, R. M. (1986). *A system of care for children and youth with severe emotional disturbances,* (revised edition). Washington, DC: CAASP Technical Assistance Center.

Stroul, B. A., Lourie, I. S., Goldman, S. K., & Katz-Leavy, J. W. (1992). *Profiles of local systems of care for children and adolescents with severe emotional disturbance.* Washington, DC: CAASP Technical Assistance Center.

Taylor, S. J. & Bogdan, R. (1992). Defending illusions: The institution's struggle for survival. In P. M. Ferguson, D. L. Ferguson, & S. J. Taylor, S. J., (Eds.), *Interpreting disability: A qualitative reader.* New York: Teachers College Press.

Tyack, D. (1992). Health and social services in public schools: historical perspectives. In *The future of children: School-Linked services.* Los Altos, CA: Center for the Future of Children, David and Lucile Packard Foundation, (Spring 1992), 19-31.

Tyack, D. (1974). *The one best system: A history of American urban education.* Cambridge, MA: Harvard University Press.

Tuma, J. M. (1989). Mental health services for children: The state of the art. *American Psychologist,* 188-199.

U.S. Department of Education. (1992). *Guidelines for support of salaries and related costs under programs of the U.S. Department of Education for entities governed by OMB Circular A-87.* Washington, DC: Author.

34 CFR: U.S. Department of Education. (1993). *Code of Federal Regulations: Education: 34: Parts 300-399.* Washington, DC: Office of the Federal Register, National Archives and Records Administration, July 1.

U.S. Department of Education. (1994). *Sixteenth annual report to Congress on the implementation of the Individuals with Disabilities Act.* Washington, DC: Author.

U.S. Department of Education (1994). *Digest of Educational Statistics.* Washington, DC: Author.

U.S. Department of Education, Office of Educational Research and Improvement (1993). *Educational reforms and students at-risk: A review of the current state-of-the-art.* Washington, D.C.: Author.

U.S. Department of Education (1994). *National agenda for achieving better results for children and youth with serious emotional disturbance.* Washington, DC: Office of Special Education Programs, September 1, 1994.

U.S. Department of Education, Office of Civil Rights (1993, July). Revised Data circulated to individuals who attended The Forum on Disproportionate Participation of Students from Ethnic and Cultural Minorities in Special Education, convened by Project FORUM at NASDSE as revised. Alexandria, VA.

U.S. House of Representatives (1990). *Report of the House Committee on Education and Labor on the Education of the Handicapped Act Amendments of 1990,* 101st Cong., 2nd. Sess.

U.S. Senate (1990). *Report of the Senate Committee on Labor and Human Resources on the Education of Individuals With Disabilities Act of 1989,* 101st Cong., 1st Sess.

Upshur, C. C. (1991). Families and the community service maze. In Seligman, M. (Ed.), *The family with a handicapped child,* 2nd. ed., Boston: Allyn and Bacon (pp. 91-118).

Valdes, K., Williamson, J. & Wagner, M. (1991). *Student statistical almanacs: Vol 3: Youth categorized as emotionally disturbed.* Menlo Park, CA: SRI.

Valdivieso, R. & Nicolau, S. (1994). "Look me in the eye": A Hispanic cultural perspective on school reform. In R. J. Rossi, (Ed.), *Schools and students at risk: Context and framework for positive change* (pp. 90-115). New York: Teachers College Press.

Wagner, M. (1993). *The secondary school programs of students with disabilities.* Menlo Park, CA: SRI International.

Wagner, M., D'Amico, R., Marder, C., Newman, L., and Blackorby, J. (1992). *What happens next? Trends in postschool outcomes of youth with disabilities. The second comprehensive report from the national longitudinal transition study of special education students.* Menlo Park, CA: SRI International.

Wagner, M., Newman, L., D'Amico, R., Jay, E.D., Butler-Nalin, P., Marder, C., & Cox, R. (1991). *Youth with disabilities: How are they doing. The first comprehensive report from the national longitudinal transition study of special education students.* Menlo Park, CA: SRI International.

Wagner, M., Blacborby, J., Cameto, R., Hebbeler, K., and Newman, L. (1993). *The transition experiences of young people with disabilities.* Menlo Park, CA: SRI International.

Walker, H.M. (1993). Anti-social behavior in schools. *Journal of Emotional and Behavioral Problems, 4,* 20-24.

Walker, H. M., Colvin, G., & Ramsey, E. (1995). *Antisocial behavior in schools: Strategies and best practices.* Pacific Grove: CA: Brooks/Cole.

Walker, H. M., Reavis, H. K., Rhode, G., & Jenson, W. R. (1984). A conceptual model for delivery of behavioral services to behavior disordered children in educational settings. In P. H. Bornstein, & A. E. Kazdin, (Eds.), *Handbook of clinical behavior therapy with children* (pp. 700-741).

Wahl, O. F. (1989). Schizophrenogenic parenting in abnormal psychology textbooks. *Teaching of Psychology, 16* (1989), 31-33.

Wheeler, S., Cottrrell, Jr., L. S., & Romasco, A. Juvenile delinquency–Its prevention and control. In P. Lerman, (Ed.), *Delinquency & social policy* (pp. 428-442). New York: Praeger.

Willis, P. (1977). *Learning to labor: How working class kids get working class jobs.* New York: Columbia University Press.

Yelton, S.W. (1991). Family preservation from a mental health perspective. *The Child, Youth, and Family Services Quarterly, 14*, 6-8.

Zola, I. (1972). Medicine as an institution of social control. *The Sociological Review,* 20, 487-504.

# Schools as Health Service Delivery Sites: Current Status and Future Directions

Ronda C. Talley
Rick Jay Short

The American Psychological Association

**SUMMARY.** The health of our nation is inextricably linked with the health of our children. While families and professionals alike have recognized this truth for decades, current social reform movements in education and health services have provided an unprecedented opportunity for schools to become equal partners in addressing the needs of children, families, and communities in a wholistic, boundary-free, and collaborative manner. Since schools are the one social institution with which every child has contact, they offer a natural environment for assessment, services, and follow-up to promote the convergent education and health agendas articulated in *Goals 2000* and *Healthy People 2000*. This article examines the components of education and health care reform with particular attention to a reconceptualization of health care services in schools. Within this framework, special services professionals are highlighted as leaders in service coordination and delivery for students, staff, and the community at large. *[Article copies available from The Haworth Document Delivery Service: 1-800-342-9678.]*

In American society today, there is a massive convergence of social issues that affect the schools (Talley & Short, 1995; Short & Talley, in

Address correspondence to: Ronda C. Talley, Education Directorate, The American Psychological Association, 750 First Street, NE, Washington, DC 20002-4242.

[Haworth co-indexing entry note]: "Schools as Health Service Delivery Sites: Current Status and Future Directions." Talley, Ronda C., and Rick Jay Short. Co-published simultaneously in *Special Services in the Schools* (The Haworth Press, Inc.) Vol. 10, No. 2, 1995, pp. 37-55; and: *Emerging School-Based Approaches for Children with Emotional and Behavioral Problems: Research and Practice in Service Integration* (ed: Robert J. Illback, and C. Michael Nelson) The Haworth Press, Inc., 1996, pp. 37-55. Single or multiple copies of this article are available from The Haworth Document Delivery Service [1-800-342-9678, 9:00 a.m. - 5:00 p.m. (EST)].

press). The most well known of these for educators is, of course, the education reform movement with its eight national education goals. However, a parallel and sometimes overlapping reform movement may be found in the health care arena. With many schools throughout the nation adding school health centers to their list of basic services (Peak & Hauser, 1994; Shearer & Holschneider, 1995), it is clear that health care services essential for child growth and development are increasingly recognized as prerequisites to student learning (Comer, 1992; Maddux et al., 1986a; McElhaney, Roth & Constantine, 1995; Russell, & Barton, 1993).

Both education legislation and health care reform initiatives have acknowledged the critical importance of schools and school-community partnerships for quality services to American citizens (American Academy of Pediatrics, 1993; Tyack, 1992). As a common setting for America's children and their families, schools may constitute an optimal system and mechanism for comprehensive human service delivery. Throughout America's history, schools have served as a mirror of broad social change. As the one institutionalized social program that has touched the lives of every American, schools reflect the merging of cultures, values, and priorities of a diverse mix of citizens in the surrounding communities and society at large. Schools and educational agencies are primary settings for the delivery of services with this orientation, and student services personnel are uniquely prepared to provide comprehensive preventive services in schools and communities. Therefore, as social reform movements gain periodic prominence throughout the nation, concurrent reforms are reflected in the structure, function, and language of schools (Short & Talley, in press) (see Table 1).

Whereas American education traditionally has occurred within the confines of the school building (Carlson, Paavola, & Talley, in press; Dryfoos, 1994), the social change of education reform is occurring in tandem with health care concerns (American Psychological Association, 1994; Chervin & Northrop, 1994; Gurkin, in press; Talley, 1995). Neither can be achieved without a coordinated, integrated, and interdisciplinary effort that also includes parents, social and health agencies, and communities (Matarazzo, 1982; Smrekar, 1994; Stone, 1993). In fact, service delivery within education reform and health care reform initiatives may share many mechanisms and objectives. These two reform movements, sometimes overlapping and sometimes in parallel, may provide special services providers within the schools with an unprecedented opportunity to redefine school service delivery for the 21st century (Talley & Short, 1994a).

TABLE 1. Comparison of Education Reform and Health Care Reform Language

| Education Reform | Health Care Reform |
| --- | --- |
| Support school readiness | Provide prevention & early intervention services, including health care services, nutrition, & physical education |
| Reduce school drop-outs | Decrease health problems (i.e., teen pregnancy) |
| Increase achievement in basic subjects & citizenship | Improve health status |
| Provide staff development on new teaching/assessment strategies | Provide staff development for personnel to work as school-based, school-linked & community-based integrated service teams |
| Offer safe, disciplined schools | Prevent violence |
| Assure drug-free students & school environment | Reduce substance abuse |
| Involve communities and parents | Link communities & schools |
| Apply opportunity to learn standards | Increase access/equity for all |

*Note.* Adapted from "How School Health Components Are Implemented at the State Level," by L. Zedosky, 1995. Paper presented at the conference on Creating a Blueprint: Comprehensive School Health Program Working Group Meeting, Washington, DC.

## EDUCATION REFORM AND HEALTH

America is witnessing a clear change in direction in education and health care policy (Short, 1993). President Clinton signed into law the foundation for school reform, *Goals 2000: The Educate America Act,* on March 31, 1994 (National Education Goals Panel, 1994; Payzant, in press; U.S. Department of Education, 1994). During this same time frame, the U.S. Congress struggled to develop and pass some form of health care reform for the American people. The President's health care reform initiative, the *Health Security Act of 1994* (HSA), formally addressed schools as health service delivery sites and as public health mechanisms (Talley & Short, 1994b). Of the numerous pieces of health care reform legislation introduced in the U.S. Congress during 1994, only the HSA contained a specific section devoted to schools. In Title III, Subtitle G of the *Act,* two dimensions of school health care were addressed: comprehensive school health education and school-related health services. Health, prevention, and education rather than disease, intervention, and mental health were emphasized.

Although Congress failed to enact national health care reform legislation, many states, with support from federal agencies and other interested groups, have begun to pursue school health initiatives as promising avenues for improving health services to American citizens (Copeland, 1995; Kolbe, Collins, & Cortese, in press; "States Lead the Way," 1995; Zedosky, 1995). For example, Peak and Hauser (1994) report that the number of school-based health centers identified by the Center for Population Options increased significantly from 31 in 1984 to 327 in 1991. By late 1992, 415 school-based and 95 school-linked health centers had been identified, operating in 42 states, the District of Columbia, Puerto Rico, and Guam. Of these, 79 of the school-based centers served elementary school students, 53 served junior or middle school students, 214 served high school students, and 69 centers served a combination of kindergarten through high school students. While most centers (60%) operated in urban school districts, 31% and 9%, respectively, were found in rural and suburban areas.

In addition, a number of coalitions of agencies, professional associations, and advocates have generated a number of initiatives on school health and have provided a framework for school health programs (Allensworth & Kolbe, 1987). All of these groups have concluded that school health programs are essential to achieve the national education goals, the national health objectives, education reform, and health care reform. The eight components of comprehensive school health programs found in Table 2 are currently undergoing revision by work groups convened by CDC (Kolbe, 1995).

Although health and education reform initiatives address different service domains and may seem disparate in their focus, their school-related components share several innovative characteristics (Short & Talley, 1994). First, both enterprises have been multifaceted and inter-related, addressing comprehensive health, welfare, mental health, and education services for children and families. Second, both agendas emphasize the school as an integral component of a larger network of service delivery. And third, both assume an intimate and reciprocal link among education, social issues, and health, often addressing the same problems (e.g., violence, substance abuse) in the same settings (schools and communities).

The education reform movement as embodied by *Goals 2000* (1994) and the health promotion goals contained in *Healthy People 2000* (1990) constitute broad guidelines for comprehensive services for children, adults, and school systems. To lend these guidelines greater support, U.S. Secretary of Education Richard W. Riley and U.S. Secretary of Health and Human Services Donna E. Shalala issued a joint statement on the impor-

## TABLE 2. Components of a Comprehensive School Health Program

| | |
|---|---|
| Health education | planned sequential K-12 curriculum that addresses the physical, mental, emotional, and social dimensions of health; |
| Physical education | planned, sequential K-12 curriculum that provides cognitive content and learning experiences in a variety of activity areas; |
| Health services | services provided for students to appraise, protect, and promote health; |
| Nutrition services | nutrition to promote the health and education of students by providing access to nutritious meals; |
| Health promotion for staff | programs for school staff that provide health assessments, health education, and health-related fitness activities; |
| Counseling, psychological and social services | services provided that include broad-based individual and group assessments, interventions and referrals for the mental, social and emotional needs of students; |
| Healthy school environment | environment that addresses the physical and aesthetic surroundings and the psycho-social climate and culture of the school to maximize the health of students and staff; |
| Parent/community involvement | integrated school, parent, and community approach which establishes a dynamic partnership to enhance the health and well-being of students. |

*Note.* From "The Comprehensive School Health Program: Exploring an Expanded Concept," by D. D. Allensworth and L. J. Kolbe, *Journal of School Health, 57*(10) December 1987, pp. 411-412. Reprinted with Permission. American School Health Association, Kent, Ohio.

tance of school health (1992). Their joint statement emphasizes that "America's children face many compelling education, health, and developmental challenges that affect their lives and futures; to help children meet these challenges, education and health must be linked in partnership; school health programs support the education process, integrate services for disadvantaged and disabled children, and improve children's health prospects; reforms in health care and in education offer opportunities to forge the partnerships needs for our children in the 1990's; and that *Goals 2000* and *Healthy People 2000* provide complementary visions that, together, can support our joint efforts in pursuit of a healthier, better educated Nation for the next century."

We believe that to fully address the charges articulated in the Joint Statement, a services integration model that links schools and communities in a multitude of patterns with health, social needs, mental health, and developmental issues as well as education is needed (McGinnis & De-Graw, 1991). Whereas American education traditionally has occurred within the confines of the school building, given the expanded scope of current social reform movements, success cannot be achieved without a coordinated, integrated, and interdisciplinary effort that also includes parents, extended family members, social service, health, welfare and juvenile justice agencies, businesses, and communities (American Academy of Pediatrics, 1995; Blank & Hoffman, 1994; Morrill, 1992; Paavola, Cobb, Illback, Joseph, Torruella, & Talley, 1995).

## HEALTH SERVICES IN SCHOOLS

The federal, state, agency, and coalition initiatives are diverse in their origin, focus, and content. However, Talley and Short (1994b) have noted that all of the current initiatives have several common characteristics, each of which have considerable implications for health services in schools. These common characteristics include emphases on health rather than mental health or mental health services, prevention and education rather than treatment, social and public health problems rather than educational or psychological problems, and integrated communities rather than schools-in-isolation.

### Health vs. Mental Health and Mental Health Services

Most health care initiatives provide enumerations or descriptions of the problems they address, as well as the types of services that fall within their sphere. Problems typically include primary health problems, such as minor injuries, and health risk behaviors–behaviors that increase the likelihood of negative health outcomes (Council of Chief State School Officers, 1991). Health risk behaviors include such areas as violence, substance abuse, and sexual risk behaviors (American Psychological Association, 1993; Epstein & Collinan, 1986). Although these primary health problems and health risk behaviors certainly relate to mental illness and mental health, mental health problems as such receive relatively little attention in most school health initiatives. For example, the school health section of the HSA mentioned mental health services in two passages: representation on community-level advisory councils for comprehensive school health education, and as a referral component in school health service sites. The components of comprehensive school health programs listed in Table 2 include counseling, psychological, and social services.

### Prevention and Education vs. Treatment

As noted above, schools constitute an important service delivery site for community-based public health services, as well as for some community primary health services. The nature, mission, and structure of schools make them key agents for integrating health care and education into a comprehensive, community-based prevention medium. Most school health initiatives acknowledge the schools' primary promise as health education and preventive agencies (Simeonsson & Covington, 1994; Zins et al., 1988). Although schools probably are conceptualized best as important components of comprehensive public health programs (American Public Health Association, 1975), they sometimes also must collaborate with other community health agencies for treatment of existing health conditions (American School Health Association, 1993). It is important to note, though, that schools and school-communities are seen in school health policy initiatives primarily as *public* health mechanisms, rather than as *primary* health care sites.

### Social and Public Health vs. Educational and Psychological Problem Conceptualizations

Although this point may seem to be one of common sense given the context of school health initiatives, it may reflect a considerable shift in the way that problems occurring in schools and communities are framed and addressed. An example of such a reframe is aggressive behavior. Psychologists have a long history of studying and treating aggression, as do educators within the framework of school discipline and special education. However, psychologists and educators typically have formulated aggressive behavior as an individual behavior problem with implications for social and educational performance. Interventions often have included diagnosis and treatment of the problem in individual students. Within a social or public health framework, aggressive behavior might be seen in aggregate as a social problem (violence) with negative health implications (death and injury) that must be prevented (Short & Brokaw, 1994). Public health interventions might include assessment of the prevalence and incidence of the problem in the community, assessment of risk factors, and development of coordinated school and community prevention programs (Dunkle, 1994; Gottlieb, 1983; Kean, 1989; Thoresen & Eagleston, 1985).

### Integrated Communities vs. Schools as Autonomous Units

As mentioned previously, the traditional mission of American schools has been the education of our children (Fagan, 1992; Paavola, Carey, Cobb, Illback, Joseph, Routh, & Torruella, in press). Accordingly, schools often have considered social issues other than education to be outside of their area of responsibility. However, current policy acknowledges the complex nature of social phenomena, including learning, so that the reciprocal effects of health, education, and social and economic status are emphasized throughout policy and legislation. Because learning depends on the multitude of characteristics brought by the learner to the learning environment, the mission of schools must expand to address them as they relate to education (Bagnato, 1994; Darling-Hammond, 1994; Elkind, 1989).

The dimensions of school reform are multifaceted, therefore, the contributions of student services staff must be correspondingly complex. Some of the key roles that school service providers play in conceptualizing and implementing fundamental change in each component of school health are addressed in the next section. Although the list obviously is not exhaustive in regard to the myriad ways by which student services personnel may address the school health issues, it uses the eight school health components identified by the U.S. Public Health Service, Centers for Disease Control and Prevention, Division of Adolescent and School Health, as a framework to highlight the contributions we can make and the emerging roles we can play in reformed schools.

## Component 1: Health Education

*Priorities.* Health education is defined as a planned, sequential, K-12 curriculum that addresses the physical, mental, emotional, and social dimensions of health. The curriculum is designed to be comprehensive and address such issues as personal, family, community, consumer, environmental, and mental/emotional health; sexuality education; injury prevention and safety; and prevention and control of disease. Health education has been traditionally provided by qualified teachers trained in this area.

*Potential Roles.* Special services professionals are skilled in assessment of individual needs and abilities. As essential members of the school team, they can offer knowledge on learner characteristics, teaching strategies, developmental sequencing of curricula, and task analysis which can be applied to all the content areas mentioned above. Given their expertise in assessment of students and systems, school services staff can assist in the process of matching curricular needs to student readiness, thus helping produce increased understanding of the subject matter and its application to real world situations.

## Component 2: Physical Education

*Priorities.* Physical education is also defined as a planned, sequential K-12 curriculum; this one provides cognitive content and learning experiences in activity areas such as basic movement skills, physical fitness, rhythms and dance, games, sports, and gymnastics. Like health education, physical education is taught by qualified, trained teachers.

*Potential Roles.* Special services providers in schools have an opportunity to work in concert with physical educators emphasizing the unique perspectives of their disciplines. For example, physical and occupational therapists may assist the physical education process by working with teachers to teach students about how the body works during physical activity and how to work and play in ways to avoid injury. Similarly, recreation specialists can provide information on the variety and types of physical activities to which many children may have limited exposure, thus introducing children and youth to positive activities for life-long fitness and enjoyment.

## Component 3: Health Services

*Priorities.* Health services form the basic core of health care delivery. These services are designed to assess, protect, and promote health, and historically have been provided by medical personnel, such as physicians, nurses, dentists, and other allied health personnel. Health services are designed to insure access to primary health care services, prevent and control communicable diseases, provide emergency care for illness or injury, and provide educational and counseling opportunities for the promotion and maintenance of individual, family, and community health.

*Potential Roles.* While health services have been primarily defined as a medical domain, now physicians and nurses are working collaboratively with special service providers to meet a challenging range of student needs (Talley, 1995). For example, triage teams combining medical and traditional "mental health" services providers, such as psychologists, counselors, and social workers, are now functioning in some schools to address a comprehensive range of student problems. This is an important reconceptualization of the health services component since it increases the person resources available to address an increasingly complex set of student and environment characteristics. In order for this movement to gain additional support, it will be important for national professional associations in pupil services to articulate their desire for the more integrated services model that this reconceptualization represents.

## Component 4: Nutrition Services

*Priorities.* School nutrition services reflect the U.S. Dietary Guidelines for Americans; they are structured to promote the health and education of students by providing access to a variety of nutritious and appealing meals. In addition, school nutrition programs offer an opportunity for students to experience good nutrition and learn these precepts. Services are provided by qualified child nutrition professionals.

*Potential Roles.* The special services personnel team has much to offer to traditional food services. These staff can assist food services professionals by providing research on issues that often may be seen only by food service experts–conditions like eating disorders, such as bulimia and anorexia nervosa, and other behaviorally based problems with food consumption. In addition, given the vital link of good nutrition to appropriate cognitive development (D'Augelli, 1981), special service professionals have a vested interest in assisting students to access these essential services.

### Component 5: Health Promotion for Staff

*Priorities.* Health promotion programs are designed to provide school staff with health assessment, education, and health-related fitness activities so that they may display a greater commitment to the health of students and offer positive role modeling. While designed to improve productivity, decrease absenteeism, and reduce health insurance costs, staff health promotion is offered to ensure a greater personal commitment by staff to the school's overall comprehensive health program.

*Potential Roles.* Health promotion for staff offer an opportunity for expanded service and practice opportunities for special services providers in schools. Since the roles of special services personnel have often been restricted to a subcategory of the student population, primarily those identified as needing special education or other adapted instruction, expanding our roles to address the health concerns of school staff offers an exciting opportunity to reframe special services in the schools. Professionals in student services in many cases have the requisite skills to address content issues represented by staff health promotion opportunities, however, in some cases, may wish to acquire additional training and guided practice in addressing the needs of an adult population.

### Component 6: Counseling, Psychological, and Social Services

*Priorities.* Traditionally provided by psychologists, school counselors, and social workers, the school health component of counseling, psychological, and social services is conceptualized as discrete from the school health services component mentioned earlier. The services include broad-based individual and group assessment, intervention, and referrals that address mental, emotional, and social health issues for students. In addition, organizational assessment and consultation that contributes to the overall health of students and the health environment of the school are considered part of this health component.

*Potential Roles.* Providing counseling, psychological, and social services has been a traditional strength of special services providers (Graham, 1985). As mentioned earlier, psychologists, counselors, and social workers, as well as others, receive university training to provide these necessary functions, only to find limited practice opportunities upon graduation (Fagan & Wise, 1994). Emphasis of this health component in graduate curricula, in school-based internship experiences, and in local school district priorities would provide the necessary preparation and organizational sanctions for such services to be delivered. Given the essential connection between behavior, emotion, and learning (National Health/Education Consortium, 1990a, 1990b), schools of the future will find it highly desirable to have these teams of personnel to help students be prepared to receive good instruction and to help teachers be prepared to deliver it.

### Component 7: Healthy School Environment

*Priorities.* A healthy school environment addresses the physical and aesthetic surrounding of the school, including the psycho-social climate and culture of the school. It also includes the psychological environment, which is defined as the interrelated physical, emotional, and social conditions that affect the well-being and productivity of students and staff. These may include issues of physical and psychological safety, positive interpersonal relationships, recognition of the needs and successes of the individual, and support for building self-esteem in students and staff.

*Potential Roles.* Much attention has been paid in recent literature about the importance of offering a school environment conducive to learning (Stokols, 1992). However, many schools are seeking ways to achieve this goal. With safe schools being a recognized feature of both health and education reform, monies from several legislative sources are available to support efforts in this area. Special service providers in schools are critically positioned to advise schools on how to make their buildings and surrounding environment safe, disciplined, drug-free, and conducive to learning.

### Component 8: Parent/Community Involvement

*Priorities.* This school health component seeks to support the concept of an integrated school, one which brings the community and families into a dynamic partnership designed to enhance the health and well-being of students. Schools are encouraged to actively solicit parent involvement and engage community resources to respond in a services integration model to the health-related needs of students.

*Potential Roles.* In order to be successful, education and health reform must involve communities, families, and businesses as integral members of the planning, implementation, and evaluation team (Davies, 1991; Delgado & Lutzker, 1988; Jason, 1982; Lehman, 1995). Under these reform initiatives, special services professionals have the opportunity to solicit community involvement in school plans, recruit businesses and other entities to support health services in schools, and work with researchers to determine that the services that are being provided are on-target and effective in addressing the established goals. Traditionally, school-based special services personnel have worked with students as members of the larger family and community units. In reformed schools, these initiatives increasingly will be supported and expanded to draw upon the wealth of resources, including support and information, that children need for learning and development.

## CONFLUENCE OF INFLUENCE: IMPLICATIONS OF HEALTH AND EDUCATION REFORM FOR SPECIAL SERVICES IN SCHOOLS

Combined with education reform, health care reform may create a sufficient mass of changes in the system for education to respond in new and innovative ways. These include emphasizing health rather than mental health, prevention rather than treatment, social problems rather than educational or psychological problems, and integrated communities rather than solely schools. These new areas of emphasis can guide us in positioning special services personnel to be a responsive leader in schools of the future.

Comparing the two present perspectives above, several important concepts become apparent in relation to health services in schools.

### Intraprofessional Practice

With the convergence of the major social issues of health care reform, education reform, and services integration, special service providers in the schools may find an opportunity to consider new ways of viewing their profession and how it relates, both directly and indirectly, to health care issues as they are increasingly addressed within school settings. For example, special service professionals within a discipline, such as psychology, may wish to call upon expertise from a variety of its specialties to contribute to each of the eight school health components. Sports psychologists may contribute to the school health component for physical education; educational psychologists may advise on the development of curricula for health and physical education and on learner-centered principles of instruction; behavioral psychologists may assist in applying principles of reinforcement to encourage students to eat healthy meals; and school, counseling, and clinical psychologists may work as part of the health services team, addressing issues facing students, faculty, families, and communities. In the future, many special service disciplines may be challenged to reexamine what constitutes "school" practice and consider issues of matching expertise within the discipline to service needs within school. Rather than viewing the entry of discipline-specific, but traditionally non-school-based personnel into the schools as a challenge to well entrenched service delivery models, school-based special services personnel, as the most knowledgeable staff regarding student, faculty, and community needs, must be poised to serve as *leaders* in reformed schools, assessing the total system needs and orchestrating comprehensive, coordinated, and community-sensitive service delivery to the system as a whole.

## *Interprofessional Practice*

While traditional service delivery paradigms for health care allowed each discipline to work in relative isolation, heath reform mandates coordinated collaborative services to address whole-child, whole-school, whole-system, and whole-community issues. In order to accomplish the delivery of health care services within a services integration model, school service providers increasingly will find themselves working in teams of professionals across a variety of disciplines with services occurring both on and off school grounds. Additional numbers of school staff may choose to acquire additional training in order to meet the emerging health care roles. Both education reform and health care reform, which have many overlapping features, will call for new and creative ways for special services staff to work with teachers, administrators, parents, agencies, and the community.

## *Organization and Funding of Services*

Health care reform initiatives are designed to address the complexity of children's problems and consider service delivery from a holistic perspective. Addressing the whole child requires expanding the service delivery field to encompass all settings in which the child develops and operates—with the school as a possible coordinating and service delivery hub. Special services personnel providing such services must be able to negotiate and cross boundaries adroitly. In order to do this, new organizational and funding arrangement will be required. For example, coordinated service delivery would be enhanced if all special services personnel within a school district reported through a single management line. The person directing the program would also be responsible for coordinating all services provided by "adjunct" student services personnel, those hired through arrangements other than the typical employer-employee relationship, thus assuring maximum efficacy for school-based as well as school-linked staff. Funding from several sources could be merged and expended based on established district/school priorities as established by the responsible system entity (e.g., site-based decision-making team, school principal, superintendent, community advisory committee, etc.).

### Training for Service Provision

In the area of training, student services professionals will need greater breadth and flexibility, with opportunities for training as team members with other health service professionals. School professionals will be asked to assume leadership roles within integrated services programs, providing program administration and supervision, building collaborative teams, and facilitating planned change in the direction of more integrated services. Practitioners will be able to exercise greater flexibility in the range of activities with which they engage, and not be restrained in regard to funding source and eligibility considerations. And finally, special services professionals will be trained to conduct research on the efficacy of integrated service delivery approaches for children and families, thus providing a unique opportunity to demonstrate the impact of these emerging special services in the schools.

## HEALTHY STUDENTS, HEALTH SCHOOLS: AMERICA'S FUTURE

Because public schools are a fundamental, universal social structure in the United States, we have argued for their importance in providing comprehensive health services to America's children and their families. However, we also have made the case for an *integrated* approach to advocating for schools in social reform. As we have written elsewhere, social problems affecting children, their families, and the schools are multifaceted and require multidimensional solutions. Accordingly, we have conceptualized health care reform and education reform as simultaneous and complementary initiatives.

In addition to the traditional charge to American schools to educate the nation's youth, schools may play a large role in public and primary health care in the future. The importance of schools to public health was recognized by inclusion of a specific section on schools as health education and health service delivery sites in the *Health Security Act of 1994*. The *HSA*, along with other federal and state initiatives, acknowledged that many health risk factors and health problems are school-related, either by age group or by setting. These factors include intentional and unintentional injury, alcohol and substance abuse, AIDS and other sexually-transmitted diseases, and adolescent pregnancy. It gave credence to the importance of the school setting as a focal point of public health initiatives. And finally, school health care systems acknowledge the inter-relatedness of children's health and education: children's health problems interfere with their learning and school performance.

Special services providers in the schools have not always been alert to emerging societal, political and legislative trends which affect both practice and training. However, the confluence of education reform and health care reform, combined with emerging reforms in human services, offers special services personnel in the schools an opportunity to assume leadership in redefining service delivery models to provide a wider array of services for children, youth, and families. The initial systems changes mandated through education reform have broken ground in this area and the considerable changes proposed through health care reform may serve as the catalyst for major breakthroughs in service delivery. Dramatic changes in the substance and process of providing education and health care services are on the horizon. Special services professionals who choose to practice in schools as well as trainers of those personnel would do well to recognize the changing landscape and readjust the direction in which they are moving in order to capture emerging opportunities to redefine services of the future.

## REFERENCES

Allensworth, D. D., & Kolbe, L. J. (1987). The comprehensive school health program: Exploring an expanded concept. *Journal of School Health, 57*(10), 409-412.

American Academy of Pediatrics. (1993). *School health: Policy and practice.* Elk Grove Village, IL: Author.

American Academy of Pediatrics. (1994). *Integrating education, health, and human services for children, youth, and families: Systems that are community-based and school-linked.* Final Report of the National Consensus Building Conference on School-Linked Integrated Service Systems. Washington, DC: Author.

American Psychological Association. (1994). *Schools as health service delivery* sites: *Historical, current, and future roles for psychology (draft report).* Washington, DC: Author.

American Psychological Association. (1993). *Violence and youth: Psychology's response.* Washington, DC: Author.

American Public Health Association. (1975). Resolutions and position papers: Education for health in the community setting. *American Journal of Public Health, 65*(2), 201.

American School Health Association. (1993). School health services: School-based primary health care. *American School Health Association Compendium of Resolutions,* 52-53.

Bagnato, S. J. (1994). *The child health resource partnership: Collaborative health interventions for learners with disabilities.* Pittsburgh, PA: University of Pittsburgh Medical School.

Blank, M. J., & Hoffman, E. (1994). *Services integration in the United States: An emerging agenda.* Washington, DC: Institute for Educational Leadership.

Carlson, C. I., Paavola, J. C., & Talley, R. C. (in press). Historical, current, and future models of schools as health care delivery settings. *School Psychology Quarterly.*

Chervin, D. D., & Northrop, D. (1994). *Education and health: Partners in school reform.* Boston, MA: Education Development Corporation.

Comer, J. P. (1992). Organize schools around child development. *Social Policy, 22*(3), 28-30.

Copeland, T. L. (1995). *Putting children first: State-level collaboration between education and health.* Washington, DC: National Health and Education Consortium.

Council of Chief State School Officers. (1991). *Beyond the health room.* Washington, DC: Author.

Darling-Hammond. L. (1994). Performance based assessment and educational equity. *Harvard Educational Review, 64*(1), 5-30.

D'Augelli, A. R. (1981). Healthy eating: A human development intervention perspective. *Journal of Nutrition Education, 13*(1), 554-558.

Davies, D. (1991, August). Implementing a national strategy for school reform through family-community partnerships: The league of schools reaching out. Paper presented at the Annual Meeting of the American Psychological Association, San Francisco, CA.

Delgado, L. E., & Lutzker, J. R. (1988). Training young parents to identify and report their children's illnesses. *Journal of Applied Behavior Analysis, 21*(3), 311-319.

Dryfoos, J. G. (1994). *Full-service schools: A revolution in health and social services for children, youth, and families.* San Francisco: Jossey-Bass.

Dunkle, M. (1994). *Linking Schools with health and social services: Perspectives from Thomas Payzant on San Diego's New Beginnings.* Washington, DC: Institute for Educational Leadership.

Elkind, D. (1989). Developmentally appropriate practice: Philosophical and practical implications. *Phi Delta Kappan, 71*(2), 113-117.

Epstein, M. H., & Cullinan, D. (1986). Depression in children. *Journal of School Health, 56*(1), 10-12.

Fagan, T. K. (1992). Compulsory schooling, child study, clinical psychology, and special education: Origins of school psychology. *American Psychologist, 47*(2), 236-243.

Fagan, T. K., & Wise, P. S. (1994). *School psychology: Past, present, and future.* New York: Longwood.

Gottlieb, B. H. (1983). Social support as a focus for integrative research in psychology. *American Psychologist, 38*(3), 278-287.

Graham, P. (1985). Psychology and the health of children. *Journal of Child Psychology and Psychiatry and Allied Disciplines, 26*(3), 333-347.

Gutkin, T. B. (in press). School psychology and health care: Moving our field into the twenty-first century. *School Psychology Quarterly.*

*Healthy people 2000: National health promotion and disease prevention objectives.* (1990). (DHHS Publication No. (PHS) 91-50212). Washington, DC: U.S. Government Printing Office.

Jason, L. A. (1982). Community based approaches in preventing adolescent problems. *School Psychology Review, 11*(4), 417-424.

Kean, T. H. (1989). The life you save may be your own: New Jersey addresses prevention of adolescent problems. *American Psychologist, 44*(5), 828-830.

Kolbe, L. J. (1995, April). *Building the capacity of schools to improve the health of the nation: A call for assistance from school health professionals.* Paper presented at the conference on Creating a Blueprint: Comprehensive School Health Program School Health Program, Washington, DC.

Kolbe, L. J., Collins, J., & Cortese, P. (in press). Building the capacity of schools to improve the health of the nation: A call for assistance from psychologists. *American Psychologist.*

Lehman, C. (1995, Spring). Preparing professionals to work in community integrated service delivery systems. *Service Bridges, 1*(1), 1-2.

Maddux, J. E., & Others. (1986a). Developmental issues in child health psychology. *American Psychologist, 41*(1), 25-34.

Maddux, J. E., & Others. (1986b). Health psychology for children: A step child/stepping stone. *Journal of Clinical Psychology, 42*(2), 383-386.

Matarazzo, J. D. (1982). Behavioral health's challenge to academic, scientific, and professional psychology. *American Psychologist, 37*(1), 1-14.

McElhaney, S. J., Russell, M., & Barton, H. A. (1993, May). *Children's mental health and their ability to learn.* Washington, DC: National Health/Education Consortium.

McGinnis, J. M., & DeGraw, C. (1991). Healthy schools 2000: Creating partnerships for the decade. *Journal of School Health, 61*(7), 292-297.

Morrill, W. A. (1992). Overview of service delivery to children. *The Future of Children: School Linked Services, 2*(1), 32-43.

National Education Goals Panel. *National education goals report: Building a nation of learners.* (1994). Washington, DC: U.S. Government Printing Office.

National Health/Education Consortium. (1990a). *Creating sound minds and bodies: Health and education working together.* Washington, DC: Author.

National Health/Education Consortium. (1990b). *Crossing the boundaries between health and education.* Washington, DC: Author.

Paavola, J. C., Carey, K., Cobb, C., Illback, R. J., Joseph, H. M., Jr., Routh, D., Torruella, A. (in press). Interdisciplinary school practice: Implications of the service integration movement for psychologists. *Professional Psychology: Research and Practice.*

Paavola, J. C., Cobb, C., Illback, R. J., Joseph, Jr., H. M., Torreulla, A., & Talley, R. C. (1995). *Comprehensive and coordinated psychological services for children: A call for service integration.* Washington, DC: American Psychological Association.

Payzant, T. W. (in press). Education reform in the United States: National policy and legislation. *American Psychologist.*

Peak, G., & Hauser, D. (1994). *School based health centers*: Update. Washington, DC: Center for Population Options.

Phillips, V., & Boysen, T. C. (in press). Psychology's role in state wide education reform: Kentucky as an example. *American Psychologist.*

Riley, R. W., & Shalala, D. E. (1992). Joint statement on school health. *Journal of School Health, 64*(4), 135.

Roth, R., & Constantine, L. M. (1995, February). Heath-care access easier through education reform. *The APA Monitor,* p. 44.

Seffrin, J. R. (1994). America's interest in comprehensive school health education. *Journal of School Health, 64*(10), 397-399.

Shearer, C. A., & Holschneider, S. O. M. (1995). *Starting young: School-based health centers at the elementary level.* Washington, DC: National Health and Education Consortium.

Short, R. J. (1993, December). *The role psychology can play in improving America's schools.* (Available from the American Psychological Association, 750 First Street, NE, Washington, DC 20002-4242.)

Short, R. J., & Brokaw, R. (1994). Externalizing behavior disorders. In R. J. Simeonsson (Ed.), *Risk, resilience, and prevention: Promoting the well-being of all children* (pp. 203-217). Baltimore, MD: Brookes Publishing.

Short, R. J., & Talley, R. C. (1994). Half full/half empty: Health care and education advocacy. *The School Psychologist, 48*(4), pp. 1, 9.

Short, R. J., & Talley, R.C. (in press). Rethinking psychology and the schools: Implications of recent national social reform policy. *American Psychologist.*

Simeonsson, R. J., & Covington, M. (1994). Policy and practice: Implications of a primary prevention agenda. In R. J. Simeonsson (Ed.), *Risk, resilience, and prevention: Promoting the well-being of all children* (pp. 299-320). Baltimore: Brookes Publishing.

Smrekar, C. (1994). The missing link in school-linked social service programs. *Educational Evaluation and Policy Analysis, 16*(4), 422-433.

States lead the way for school-based health centers. (1995, Winter). *Access to Comprehensive School-Based health Services for Children and Youth,* 1-2.

Stokols, D. (1992). Establishing and maintaining healthy environments: Toward a social ecology of health promotion. *American Psychologist, 47*(1), 6-22.

Stone, E. J. (1993). Cycles of change and challenges for health professions involved in multidisciplinary approaches to prevention. *Journal of Health Education, 24*(6), 347-355.

Talley, R.C. (1995). Best practices in APA policy and advocacy for school psychology practice. In A. Thomas & J. Grimes (Eds.), *Best practices in school psychology–III*, Washington, DC: National Association of School Psychologists.

Talley, R. C., & Short, R. J. (1994a). Health care reform and school psychology: A wake up call to school psychologists from school psychologists. *The School Psychologist, 48*(3), pp. 1, 3, 15.

Talley, R. C., & Short, R. J. (1994b). Health care reform and the schools: Just the facts. *The School Psychologist, 48*(2), pp. 1, 7, 11.

Talley, R. C., & Short, R. J. (1995). *Reforming America's schools: Psychology's role: A report to the nation's educators.* Washington, DC: American Psychological Association.

Thoresen, C. E., & Eagleston, J. R. (1985). Counseling for health. *Counseling Psychologist, 13*(1), 15-108.

Tyack, D. (1992). Health and social services in public schools: Historical perspectives. *The Future of Children: School Linked Services, 2*(1), 19-31.

U.S. Department of Education. (1994). *Goals 2000: A world-class education for every child.* Washington, DC: Author.

U.S. Department of Health and Human Services. (1993). *School-based health centers and managed care: Examples of coordination.* Washington, DC: Authors.

Zedosky, L. (1995, April). How school health components are implemented at the state level. Paper presented at the conference on Creating a Blueprint: Comprehensive School Health Program School Health Program, Washington, DC.

Zins, J. E, & Others. (1988). Primary prevention: Expanding the impact of psychological services in schools. *School Psychology Review, 17*(4), 542-549.

# INNOVATIVE SCHOOL-BASED APPROACHES TO SERVICE INTEGRATION

## Project Destiny: A Model for Developing Educational Support Teams Through Interagency Networks for Youth with Emotional or Behavioral Disorders

Douglas Cheney
Craig Barringer
Dayle Upham
Barbara Manning

Keene State College

**SUMMARY.** Students with emotional and behavioral disorders present significant challenges to educators and community profes-

Address correspondence to: Douglas Cheney, Director, Project Destiny, Institute on Emotional Disabilities, Keene State College, Keene, NH 03435-2903.

Preparation of this manuscript was funded in part with the support of Grant No. H237D30012 from the U.S. Office of Special Education Programs.

[Haworth co-indexing entry note]: "Project Destiny: A Model for Developing Educational Support Teams Through Interagency Networks for Youth with Emotional or Behavioral Disorders." Cheney, Douglas et al. Co-published simultaneously in *Special Services in the Schools* (The Haworth Press, Inc.) Vol. 10, No. 2, 1995, pp. 57-76; and: *Emerging School-Based Approaches for Children with Emotional and Behavioral Problems: Research and Practice in Service Integration* (ed: Robert J. Illback, and C. Michael Nelson) The Haworth Press, Inc., 1996, pp. 57-76. Single or multiple copies of this article are available from The Haworth Document Delivery Service [1-800-342-9678, 9:00 a.m. - 5:00 p.m. (EST)].

sionals in contemporary practice. At the same time, parents of middle school students experience parenting as a difficult time period that is laden with a variety of feelings. A central strategy for assisting both parents and professionals during this developmental period is to work collaboratively with one another. This sharing of ideas and strategies is helpful in attaining goals for students that are usually not met in the absence of cooperative team work. Furthermore, the recommended direction for service provision for these youth is to work through a coordinated, interagency approach across the community.

This paper presents the first year's methods and initial findings from Project Destiny, a three year study that is attempting to enhance the knowledge and strategies of professionals, parents and community teams for working with middle school students having emotional or behavioral disorders (EBD). Initial results from the project's work in three communities suggest that teachers at the middle schools have been interested and able in acquiring new knowledge and skills for working with the youth. These gains were evident in self-evaluations completed by the teachers. Additionally, 60% of parents of youth with EBD were recruited and participate regularly in parent support and advocacy groups. Efforts to integrate the project with local interagency teams have been somewhat less successful due to the current political and economic climate that has eliminated essential resource personnel on local teams. The Project Destiny model has merit for further replication and further analysis of student performance and will be completed in the final year of the project. *[Article copies available from The Haworth Document Delivery Service: 1-800-342-9678.]*

Much progress has been made over the past two decades in delivering specialized educational services to children and youth in our public schools. Much ground is yet to be covered, however, before public education agencies have the capacity to implement effective educational services for children and youth with emotional or behavioral disorders. A litany of findings have concluded that educational programs are ineffective at meeting the social, academic or mental health needs of students with emotional or behavioral disorders (Knitzer, Steinberg, & Fleisch, 1990; Kortering & Blackorby, 1992; Marder, 1992; Neel, Meadows, Edgar & Levine, 1988; US Department of Education, 1994). One frequent recommendation from such studies is that practitioners require a sophisticated knowledge and skill base to work successfully with these students. Additionally, coordinated services need to be provided across agencies with parents aligned in the service delivery for both support and advocacy (Coe & Pole, 1994; Knitzer, 1993; Nelson & Pearson, 1991). Under the best of circumstances, communities would have highly skilled practitioners working in a coordinated system of care with frequent parental input to design and deliver services for children and youth with emotional or behavioral disorders (EBD).

The U.S. Department of Education, recognizing the need for improving services to students with EBD, implemented an initiative to address these shortcomings for youth with EBD in Public Law 101-476. Within the law, known as the Individuals with Disabilities in Education Act, the U.S. Office of Special Education and Rehabilitative Services (OSERS) has identified several goals that include: (a) maintaining an adequate number of qualified personnel; (b) enhancing the capacity of school and community systems to meet the needs of diverse populations; (c) expanding the inclusion of students with disabilities in general education programs; and (d) improving educational results of students with disabilities (US Department of Education, 1994). In the area of emotional or behavioral disorders, OSERS has stressed the need to expand the capacity of schools and communities for working with students having EBD, the importance of collaboration between agencies and families, and the necessity of improving the knowledge and skills of professionals and parents working with these students.

## TEACHERS' KNOWLEDGE AND SKILLS FOR WORKING WITH STUDENT'S HAVING EBD

Within school programs, teachers of students with EBD are inadequately prepared and in high demand (US Department of Education, 1994). In 1994, The Department of Education reported that 4,724 teachers of students with certification in the area of EBD were needed nationally. This was a high area of need, approximated only by low incident disabilities such as traumatic brain injury and deaf-blind. An additional reported shortage of 1,154 psychologists, 745 school social workers and 5,448 instructional assistants indicates related service providers for students with EBD are also in demand. Given that students with EBD are considered to be an underidentified population (Kauffman, 1989), there is perhaps an even greater demand for trained professionals than indicated in the US-DOE report.

Data from our state of New Hampshire also reveal an increasing number of students identified as having serious emotional disturbance (the state's administrative label for emotional or behavioral disorders). In January of 1988, there were 1,468 students with this disability, and by October of 1994, this population increased to 1,963 (Davis, 1995). This trend is consistent with other states and creates the need for qualified teachers to work with the students. Yet, from 1990 to 1994, teachers of students with serious emotional disturbance continued to represent the highest categorical area of need, with a range of 40-60 additional teachers required each year during the time period (Davis, 1995). This trend will continue to undermine the goal of providing broad-based services to students and parents until it is remedied.

Practicing teachers also report they require improved skills to deal with the increasing numbers of students with EBD. In a 1992 needs analysis of training desired by special education teachers in New Hampshire, a number of areas related to services for children with EBD surfaced (NH Department of Education, 1992). Based on responses of 1,350 educators and administrators, the top training needs were:

a. increased knowledge of children's diagnostic syndromes (87% of respondents);
b. knowledge and strategies for using alternative instructional approaches (85% of respondents); and
c. skills to structure classrooms for effective instruction (85% of respondents), use behavior management techniques (83% of respondents), and increase coordination between regular and special educators (80% of respondents).

An array of inservice training and classroom supports are therefore indicated for teachers if educational, social, and affective outcomes are expected to improve for students with EBD.

## COLLABORATION FROM AN EDUCATIONAL PERSPECTIVE

The central strategy for improving the educational services for all children has been the use of collaboration between professionals. Collaboration in this context was defined by Bruner (1991) as a process that leads to the attainment of goals that cannot efficiently be reached by any one single agent. At the school level, collaborative efforts have effectively impacted on problems related to students' behavior, attendance, and achievement (Kretovics, Farmer & Armaline, 1991). Small cluster teams of teachers working across content areas have improved their instructional strategies; problem-solved structural issues; and utilized broad research findings to improve the academic performance, attendance, and motivation factors of their students.

Collaboration from a special education perspective has most frequently been used to bring teachers together in teams (e.g., teacher assistance teams, mainstream assistance teams, prereferral teams) to formally or informally discuss student performance problems and determine appropriate interventions (Fuchs, Fuchs & Bahr, 1990; Graden, 1989; Pugach & Johnson, 1988). The collaborative approach focuses on processes that affect educators' attitudes, skills, and knowledge. This process has a commensurate relationship with student's schoolwide performance. Much of this work has focused on short-term interventions for student's learning or behavioral problems. While this approach has been helpful for students with learning disabilities, there has been limited reporting about the effectiveness of collaborative schoolwide teams in meeting the educational needs of students with more serious emotional or behavioral disorders.

## COORDINATING SERVICE SUPPORTS WITH FAMILIES

There is considerable agreement that parents of students with emotional or behavioral disorders must be more involved in the educational programs of their children (Allen, Brown & Finlay, 1992; Jones, 1992; Knitzer, 1993). Boyer (1991) suggested that we have failed to provide necessary supports to families in our country, and that family, not schools, may be our country's most imperiled institution. Many students enter school with biologic, economic, and familial risk factors that have been present from the prenatal period (Allen et al., 1992; Boyer, 1991). Additional supports to parents could provide them an improved understanding of special education procedures, opportunities to learn techniques for effective parenting, and a forum for developing positive relationships with other parents and school personnel. Just as most schools have not yet figured out how to facilitate strong parent involvement, neither have they adjusted to new family realities (Edwards & Young, 1992). A critical bridge between the family and school is needed to build these positive partnerships.

Mobilizing and aligning families to advocate for appropriate services for their children is not easy (Knitzer, 1993). This appears more related to service providers' biases than it is to families' willingness or ability to participate. Historically, families were perceived to be the "cause" of children's emotional or behavioral problems and were dismissed from involvement with their child. Children were removed from homes and placed in a specialized treatment setting. Recently, however, an interest in creating comprehensive systems of care for children has led communities to involve and preserve families to the greatest extent possible (Cole & Poe, 1993; Knitzer & Cole, 1989). Most families of children who receive specialized services at school also ask for assistance in dealing with their children's problems at home (Knitzer & Cole, 1989). When problems are observed in school and home, an opportunity exists for developing an alliance between the family, school and other agencies to benefit the growth of the family and child.

## COMMUNITY COORDINATION OF CARE

The direction of service provision for children with emotional or behavioral disorders has been to establish interagency networks (Nelson & Pearson, 1991; Stroul & Friedman, 1986). The recommended participants include educators, specialists, mental health workers, child welfare workers and families. The Peacock Hill Working Group (1991) proposed several suggestions for improving collaborative efforts. These included: (a) developing cross-agency collaboration for case management and service provisions; (b) changing the social expectation that school programs alone can address the complex nature of student's emotional or behavioral disorders; (c) developing integrated collaborative programs that involve an array of social service programs for supporting students and their families; (d) integrating researchers across disciplines to share information on a wider scale with educators; and (e) expanding inservice training of educators to emphasize classroom practices, multidisciplinary collaboration, and family/community interventions.

Agencies that provide services to students with emotional or behavioral disorders and their families have typically lacked the history or mechanisms to work in a coordinated fashion (Knitzer, 1993). While it is not uncommon for families to be involved with multiple agencies for service delivery, there has been little common planning or direction for the service delivery. Complicating this is the high cost when services overlap or are duplicated. As a result of this uncoordinated service delivery, an inevitable outcome has been irrational expenditures in excessively restrictive environments (Cole & Poe, 1993).

Since 1990, the Mental Health Services Program for Youth (MHSPY) has attempted to rectify this systems problem by funding demonstrations projects in states. The focus of the MHSPY has been to create systems of care for the population of families having children/youth with SED. The programs were started in eight states and emphasize community-based care in normative settings, use of effective clinical practices, integration of financial and clinical decision-making across agencies and families, and accountability for outcomes (Cole & Poe, 1993). Initial findings from these and other projects show promising results and merit further replication.

## THE SCHOOL AS SITE FOR COLLABORATIVE ENTERPRISE

Across communities, collaborative efforts of juvenile justice, mental health, child welfare, and the school system have identified the school as the primary point of contact to provide health, welfare and family services to families (Payzant, 1992; Dryfoos, 1994). This system of care has assisted teachers to identify a singular referral spot for students experiencing academic, behavioral, attendance, or health problems. Teachers, families, and social service providers are reported to benefit from more frequent contact and access to vital service needs for students.

School-based services open access to students and families for an array of health and social services. In their most fully developed form they include before- and after-school programs, family resource centers, dental and medical services, and mental health clinics. Dryfoos (1994) and Comer (1988) give several examples of the significant impact these integrated services have on the health of individuals and neighborhoods. One school in Comer's project, for example, moved from a district's last rank (out of 33 schools) to third in the district on achievement and social measures during a ten-year period. Mental health teams were constructed to apply interventions to assist students and their families. The school became a natural part of the community, and commitment to education became a priority for staff and families. A community was created that allowed for inclusion of all stakeholders in the management of the school.

Further implementation of similar models of school, family, and community cooperation are needed to build upon our successes in developing community systems of care for individuals with EBD. These additional projects could lead to the paradigm shift Knitzer (1993) has called for so that interagency collaboration becomes a reality in the service provisions for youth with emotional or behavioral disorders.

## PROJECT DESTINY MODEL AND APPROACH

In the Fall of 1993, the Institute on Emotional Disabilities at Keene State College, Keene, New Hampshire, received a grant from the Office of Special Education Projects at the U.S. Department of Education to conduct a three year research project to enhance the knowledge, skills and strategies of practicing professionals in the area of emotional or behavioral disorders. The project's title, **Designing Educational Support Teams through Interagency Networks for Youth (DESTINY)** with emotional or behavioral disorders describes the overarching goal of our research. We are working at three middle school sites that are attempting to include students with EBD in their general education programs to the greatest extent possible. Project Destiny provides essential supports to the middle schools to: (a) enhance and expand teacher's knowledge, skills, and strategies for working with students; (b) improve collaborative efforts of school teams of 4-8 members for working with students in grades 6-8; (c) provide education and support to parents of students with EBD; and (d) coordinate service provisions for students that may center in the school but spread across other agencies and persons in the community.

The middle school years for this study were chosen because they are a particularly sensitive developmental period. Children with emotional and behavioral problems are at great risk for rejection from their peers during this time (Ladd, Price, & Hart, 1990), may experience poor relations with their teachers (Conduct Problems Prevention Research, 1992), and have increased tension and conflict with their parents (Patterson, Reid & Dishion, 1992). School leaders in participating schools were particularly cognizant of these issues and recommended that Project Destiny be implemented at their middle schools to counteract these negative influences on students. The purpose of this paper is to discuss the multidimensional interventions used in Project Destiny that seek to:

a. enhance the knowledge and skills of teachers working with students having EBD;
b. support and coalesce parent groups so that they become active members with one another and with school teams to improve services for youth with EBD; and
c. integrate service improvements at the school with interagency teams in the community.

## *ENHANCING AND EXPANDING TEACHER'S KNOWLEDGE, SKILLS, AND STRATEGIES FOR WORKING WITH STUDENTS*

Project Destiny's first step in expanding the knowledge, skills, and strategies of practitioners was to hire a staff that reflected a broad base of knowledge and skills. To this end, our project staff includes a child clinical psychologist, a special educator, and a family services coordinator who is the parent of a son with a disability. This multidisciplinary team brought over fifty years of multidisciplinary experience to the project. The project team has the initial responsibility for developing and implementing two levels of training at the middle school.

The first level of training is to impart a broad base of knowledge to the school faculty involved. Schools that agreed to participate in the study did so on the basis of a full school faculty vote. Faculty at the schools were given an overview of the project by the project director and informed that all staff would be involved in knowledge-based training, case studies of individual students, and intervention work in their classrooms. Types of training that would occur and the desired outcomes of the training were discussed in the overview. Faculty voted in the project with a greater than 90% approval in all schools.

Each school's entire faculty received eight training units during the 1994-95 school year. These units were developed to meet the objectives of the project and were derived from empirical findings at the schools regarding teachers knowledge and skill base and student functioning in social, affective and academic areas (Cheney & Barringer, in press). The training units were presented to full school faculty on a monthly basis and took approximately 90 minutes to cover the knowledge objectives of the units. They are viewed as presenting requisite knowledge and giving a general awareness for effectively working with students with EBD and their parents. The training units are outlined in Table 1.

## INITIAL RESULTS OF THE TRAINING

Assessment of school staff's knowledge and skills for working with students having EBD was done by using the Emotional or Behavioral Disorders Teacher Competency Survey (Braaten, 1993). The Teacher Competency Survey is a self-rating form that includes all of the core competencies recommended by the Council for Exceptional Children for working with students with disabilities (Swan & Sirvis, 1992). Additionally, items from the five categories cover all the competencies suggested by Bullock, Ellis and Wilson (1994) for working with students having EBD. The EBD Teacher Competency Survey has excellent content and face validity due to its consistency with the competencies from CEC and Bullock et al. (1994). While the original survey includes over 200 items, we selected 48 representative items of the knowledge and skills that were being discussed in our units. Teachers completed self-ratings of their competence on these items on a 3-point scale, with 1 being little or no competence, 1.5 being some competence, 2 being moderate competence, 2.5 being strong competence, and 3 indicating mastery.

TABLE 1. Staff Development Topics for Project Destiny, 1994-95 School Year

| Topic | Topic Description |
|---|---|
| 1. Team assessment and program planning for students with emotional or behavioral disabilities. | 1. This session focuses on how team members can contribute to understanding students through observations, personal judgments, and archival data. Through the use of the data, team members develop and monitor intervention plans for students. |
| 2. Understanding individual differences of students. | 2. Project staff prepare descriptions of students from a variety of diagnostic categories. Participants learn defining characteristics of students with different diagnoses and discuss suitable intervention strategies. Distinctions between externalizing and internalizing behaviors are emphasized. |
| 3. Implementing a social skills curriculum. | 3. School faculty review existing social skill approaches. Project staff make suggestions for instructional strategies to teach the skills. School faculty or teams identify social skills to teach, modify curriculum as necessary, design an implementation plan and teach sets of desirable behaviors in their classroom. Project staff assist the team in monitoring the use of skills by faculty and staff. |
| 4. Crisis prevention and intervention. | 4. Methods for thwarting behavioral problems through the development of positive learning environments are discussed. Participants practice the methods to enhance interpersonal interactions and relationships. In addition, participants develop plans for crisis intervention and identify critical features of a school wide plan. |
| 5. Life space interviews. | 5. Life space interviews are one of many problem-solving approaches for students in crisis. It involves six steps; (a) identifying incidents, (b) getting youth to talk, (c) identifying central issues and goals, (d) choosing youth valued solutions, (e) successful plans to use the solutions, and (f) preparing to resume classroom activities. |
| 6. Behavioral contracting. | 6. Contracting allows the youth and adult to identify specific behaviors of concern and make agreements on performance of acceptable behaviors. Performance of the desired behavior leads to a mutually agreed upon reinforcer. The contract delineates expectations of youth and adults, timelines and is signed by all involved. |
| 7. Collaborative teaming across the disciplines. | 7. Skills regarding communication, sharing of feelings, problem-solving, reaching shared decisions, and monitoring shared goals are discussed. Teams then use the skills to develop interventions for youth. |

| Topic | Topic Description |
|-------|------------------|
| 8. Engaging families as positive partners. | 8. The family coordinator presents issues that parents confront raising their children as well as issues they have dealing with community professionals. The goal is to reach a better understanding of the complexities of parenting youth with emotional or behavioral disabilities. |

To date, analysis of 43 teacher's self-ratings across a one-year period have shown promising results regarding the effects of the project on teacher's self-perceptions of their knowledge and skills for working with youth having EBD. Most of these teachers were practicing in general education classrooms ($n = 36$), while seven were teaching in special education or chapter one programs.

Table 2 displays results on selected items from pre- and post-testing on the EBD Teacher Competency Survey. Only a subset of the items were selected for presentation in this paper that related directly to the training units covered in the school year. A full report on the changes across all items is available from the senior author. A review of the items presented in Table 2 suggests that the teachers perceived positive and rather significant gains across the year of this staff development. When the two testing periods were compared using a T-test, positive changes in the desired direction were found. These results suggest that the teachers were able to assimilate new knowledge regarding characteristics and strategies for working effectively with students having EBD. This is a particularly important finding since this was a somewhat experienced group of teachers (average years experience = 12 years, range = 1 to 33 years). The teachers were therefore able to self-report their own increase in knowledge and skills across the first year of the project. Further assessment of the relationship between these gains and student performance will be completed at the end of the second year of the study.

## COLLABORATIVE TEAMING SKILLS FOR TEACHERS IN GRADES 6-8

The second step in Project Destiny's approach has been to apply the knowledge acquired in the training sessions in a case review format. Educational support teams have been formed at the grade levels in each school for this purpose. These teams are composed of four general education content teachers, specialists from music or physical education, and special education or guidance support staff. When possible, parents are

TABLE 2. Teacher Means and Comparisons from Competency Survey for Emotional or Behavioral Disorders

*(n* = 43 teachers)

| Area/Item | Year 1 | | Year 2 | | P-value |
|---|---|---|---|---|---|
| | M | SD | M | SD | |
| **General Knowledge** | | | | | |
| 1. Definitions of Emotional Disturbance or Behavior Disorder. | 1.81 | .45 | 2.24 | .35 | .0001 |
| 2. Characteristics of students with EBD. | 1.84 | .43 | 2.24 | .37 | .0001 |
| 3. Definitions and Classifications from DSM-IIIR. | 1.40 | .49 | 1.8 | .45 | .0001 |
| **Assessment & Evaluation** | | | | | |
| 1. Techniques for screening student's emotional/behavioral disorders. | 1.40 | .49 | 2.34 | .38 | .0001 |
| 2. Evaluating effectiveness of intervention plans. | 1.40 | .54 | 1.86 | .58 | .0001 |
| 3. The role of educators and other professionals in assessing specific emotional or behavioral disorders. | 1.43 | .50 | 2.02 | .48 | .0001 |
| 4. Assessing and evaluating emotional patterns of students. | 1.68 | .65 | 2.10 | .44 | .002 |
| **Skills & Strategies with Students** | | | | | |
| 1. Procedures for helping students to solve social/interpersonal problems. | 1.93 | .51 | 2.25 | .43 | .003 |
| 2. Methods for enhancing individual's social skills. | 1.81 | .55 | 2.17 | .42 | .001 |
| 3. Strategies for observing and recording behavior. | 1.66 | .62 | 2.13 | .47 | .001 |
| 4. Developing crisis intervention plans for your school. | 1.48 | .50 | 1.90 | .48 | .0001 |
| 5. Establishing positive, interpersonal rapport with students having EBD. | 1.9 | .62 | 2.28 | .47 | .0001 |

| Area/Item | Year 1 | | Year 2 | | |
|---|---|---|---|---|---|
| | **M** | **SD** | **M** | **SD** | **P-value** |
| 6. Strategies to diffuse the emotional intensity of students in crises. | 1.83 | .58 | 2.22 | .43 | .0001 |
| 7. Teaching students to monitor their own behavior. | 1.68 | .52 | 2.10 | .44 | .0001 |
| 8. Implementing schoolwide approaches that promote positive social and emotional behavior. | 1.56 | .59 | 1.95 | .47 | .001 |
| **Skills & Strategies with Parents** | | | | | |
| 1. Strategies to improve family-school relationships. | 1.50 | .51 | 1.87 | .53 | .003 |
| 2. Planning and conducting parent conferences on students with EBD. | 1.60 | .59 | 1.88 | .49 | .04 |
| **Skills & Strategies with Colleagues** | | | | | |
| 1. Collaborating with colleagues on instructional planning and team teaching. | 1.79 | .47 | 2.14 | .50 | .001 |
| 2. Identifying group dynamics that create barriers or support successes. | 1.68 | .57 | 2.06 | .52 | .002 |
| 3. Methods for effective team building. | 1.74 | .54 | 2.01 | .37 | .005 |

invited to team meetings, and when appropriate, professionals from other community agencies participate.

A case study format is used to apply skills and strategies during these team meetings. Students whose parents have given informed consent to participate are scheduled for review and information concerning their school and community performance, is organized on a case study worksheet developed by project staff. The case study worksheet assesses the student's strengths and weaknesses in five areas: social/interpersonal, affective, academic, familial, and organic/biological. Since these are the five major influences on behavior, all are reviewed with the grade level team. Following review of the student's strengths and weaknesses, teams are asked to generate priority interventions based on the five areas. Project staff assist the teams in using knowledge about strategies from staff development units into the intervention approaches. In general, teams have been developing social, affective, and academic interventions for use during the school program, but occasionally new strategies are generated for ways to communicate with parents and to discuss medical issues with doctors.

Our final approach to assisting teachers with new skills and strategies is to have our educational coordinator spend time in classrooms. The purpose of this involvement is to have the educational coordinator observe use of new skills by faculty and to coach them in the use of the skills. Several studies suggest that coaching is a key variable in actual use of efficacious procedures by teachers (Gersten & Woodward, 1990). The coaching phase in Project Destiny began in the Winter of 1995 and has been very well received by teachers. In particular, teachers have been receptive to observation of their use of new skills in their classrooms and for suggestions on how to use new strategies in their daily work.

## PROVIDING SUPPORT AND EDUCATION TO PARENTS OF STUDENTS WITH EBD

The Family Services Coordinator meets with all parents/guardians of special education identified students with EBD in each middle school and invites them to participate in the project. Participation has included a commitment to attend twice monthly meetings in the local community and to provide all requested assessment data on youth and parent functioning. Across the three schools, 60% (18 of 30) of the parents of students with EBD have agreed to and consistently participate in the group meetings. This participation ranges from a low of 6 of 12 parents in one community to a high of 6 of 8 parents in another town.

Groups across the 1994-95 school year have focused on three major goals. The first has been to understand the nature of emotional and behavioral disorders and to discuss the impact this disability had on each family. Within discussions on this topic, parents have been able to share their personal experiences, reveal the impact of the disability on family members, and understand the relationship between this impact and the grieving process. Most parents were able to discuss how their lives had changed over the period of parenting their son or daughter, and the group has focused on ways to empower each other to support personal growth and self-esteem building. An additional topic in this goal area has been assisting group members with issues related to depression and, in some cases abuse. Coping strategies and mutual support have been emphasized to help group members.

The second goal of the group has been to help members improve on their own communication skills. Within the context of group meetings, members have explored their own cultural differences, personal values, and expectations for their children and themselves. Activities used to meet this goal have focused directly on the development of skills to coalesce the group. This movement toward group cohesion has provided members the much needed support to develop a functional parent support network.

Our final goal for parents has been to assist them in understanding community resources and developing personal skills to help them with their children's school and community functioning. To meet this goal, groups have spent time discussing their children's individualized education plans, and planning ways to participate more effectively in I.E.P. meetings. Parents simulate these meetings and discuss ways to collaborate with educators around I.E.P. objectives. They also have an opportunity to discuss teachers' roles and responsibilities in the daily implementation of an I.E.P. Finally, when parents feel prepared and have the time, they are invited to join case study teams at the schools. To date, 4 of our 18 parents have been able to join the team meetings. During the 1995-96 school year, we plan to increase this number by exploring optional meeting times and places for the case studies. We are also working with four of the parents to prepare as presenters at a week-long summer institute regarding best practices for students with EBD, that our institute staff will sponsor.

A variety of resources have been used in preparing content of support group meetings. Materials have been coordinated with activities in each goal area and used to understand specific concepts. For example, the grieving cycle (Kübler-Ross, 1969) has been helpful for the impact of disability unit, while the parent's support and advocacy book (Federation for Children with Special Needs Parents, 1991) and Clarke's (1981) book on self-esteem have been helpful for most members in the other topics. Parents relate concepts from these materials to their own experiences and discuss them in the safe and caring atmosphere of the group. Trust breeds growth, and the family service coordinator assists group member to feel equal, protected, and valued. Ground rules are set so that each member can participate and become responsible for his/her own actions and opinions. Everyone gets a chance to speak and group members have concluded that it is by listening closely to others that changes can be made that have meaningful impact on their own and other's lives.

Families have been very positive about these sessions. Their attendance rate at sessions has exceeded 75% for all participants during the 1994-95 school year. They have begun to report improvements in their children's behavior. All of the parents have been surprised to find out how much their own understanding of the disability has helped them. When asked about specific changes they have experienced during this year some of their responses include:

"Because of my constant awareness, I'm now more able to help my child before his behavior gets out of control."

"It's nice to have support from others who share aspects of my life that most people just don't understand."

"I never thought much about what it was like to have my son in the class as far as how the teacher feels."

"This is the first time I've begun to understand what I can be doing to help my child within our community."

"It's great to just be able to cry and share my joys and sorrows."

"It's nice to know that having a child with emotional disturbance is difficult for all the other families and that I'm not a bad parent."

"Finally, I can meet with the teachers and feel like I know how to relate to them."

The parents continue to use the group process to solidify their relationships and have become verbally and emotionally more open with each other and with the facilitator. They seem eager to talk and have ongoing questions about emotional disabilities. Recently, there has been increased rapport as evidenced by the parents exchanging phone numbers, and scheduling social engagements. Additional changes in parental behavior and attitudes will be analyzed in the summer of 1995 and 1996.

## COORDINATING SERVICE PROVISIONS FOR STUDENTS ACROSS THE SCHOOL AND COMMUNITY

Coordinating the school and family segments of Project Destiny with community interagency teams began in the summer of 1994, and has been met with varied success across the past year. The two essential factors that have influenced the coordination of these efforts have been: (a) the availability of a key person from the interagency team who could attend school team meetings, and (b) the intensity of individual student needs in the community.

At earlier meetings with the interagency teams, formal mechanisms to involve team members in case studies at school were discussed. Since most interagency teams members were administrators with limited time, the most promising method to accomplish this was to involve intensive case managers (ICM) in a preventative approach at the case study meetings at schools. The ICMs were newly funded positions at the community level that were intended to bridge the service need between the interagency team and the community. Unfortunately, funding for these positions was cut in a mid-year recision of funding from the New Hampshire Department of Developmental Disabilities and Mental Health. At present, it is doubtful that these funds will be restored in the future, as New Hampshire is presently facing a 100 million dollar deficit.

Intensity of student needs has opened the gatekeeper function for a few students. These are the most complex students and have required community level staffings. In these cases, school team members were able to share information with the community team to coordinate some services. The level of need had to reach crisis proportion, however, before this team coordination was successful.

Efforts in this project have been less than successful at creating a more full service school by bringing community services into the school. As Melaville and Blank (1991) noted, there are at least five critical variables in shaping interagency work in communities. The first is to have the social and political climate that makes the change possible; the fourth is overcoming technical difficulties of governing policies; and the last is having available resources to make the changes possible. These three variables all play a major role in maintaining barriers for the interagency teams to effectively reach professionals, parents, and youth at the school level. These barriers need to be overcome because people at the school level have demonstrated their vision and willingness to make the partnership work through an ongoing problem-solving and continuing education format (the other two key variables). In the coming year, the project will continue to engage community team members in its efforts at the school level.

## CONCLUSION

During its first year, Project Destiny has made some critical first steps in broadening the knowledge base of full school faculties to address the social, emotional, and academic challenges of youth with emotional or behavioral disorders. This first and very important step has been complemented by the development of grade level resource teams for all teaching staff. The grade level teams have been able to meet consistently at least two times per month to apply their new knowledge in case studies of individual students. Overall, both the ability to consistently implement a monthly regimen of staff training and to follow-up the training with the case study meetings is no small accomplishment. The most precious element in a teacher's day is time, and the willingness to devote almost weekly meetings to the project is a sign of strong commitment in these schools.

The additional commitment of parents in the project activities is also a notable accomplishment. Stories are often heard in schools about the lack of cooperation that is felt between staff and parents of youth with EBD. In our experience at these middle schools, most of the parents are highly interested in their children's educational programs and are very willing to commit to the work of the parent groups. The attendance and comments of parents who are participating is testimony to the cooperative venture that can occur in trusting and supportive groups. We anticipate that the parents in the project will demonstrate their commitment by further involvement in school meetings, community activities, and project activities as we enter the last year of the project.

There are, of course, some remaining objectives that are yet to be realized. As stated previously, it has been difficult to coordinate the project's in-school work with the communities interagency teams. Additionally, we have yet to analyze student performance in relation to perceived gains of teachers and parents. This analysis will occur through evaluation of both quantitative and qualitative data in the summer of 1995. This data analysis will serve a critical role in justifying the comprehensive work of the project. In the end, empirical findings that support the efforts of full service models will be essential in firmly establishing these programs at the community level.

## REFERENCES

Allen, M., Brown, P., & Finlay (1992). *Helping children by strengthening families: A look at family support programs.* Washington, D.C.: Children's Defense Fund.

Billingsley, B. S. & Cross, L. H. (1992). Predictors of commitment, job satisfaction, and intent to stay in teaching: A comparison of general and special education. *Journal of Special Education, 25* (4), 453-471.

Boyer, E. L. (1991). *Ready to Learn.* Princeton, NJ: Carnegie Foundation for the Advancement of Learning.

Braaten, S. (1993) *Emotional or behavioral disorders Teacher Competency Survey.* Minneapolis: Institute for Adolescents with Behavior Disorders.

Bruner, C. (1991). *Thinking collaboratively: Ten questions and answers to help policy makers improve children's services.* Washington, D.C.: The Education and Human Services Consortium.

Bullock, L. M., Ellis, L. L., & Wilson, M. J. (1994). Knowledge/Skills needed by teachers who work with students with severe emotional/behavioral disorders: A revisitation. *Behavioral Disorders, 19* (2), 108-125.

Cheney, D. & Barringer, C. (in press). Teacher Competence, Student Diversity, and Staff Training for the Inclusion of Middle School Students with Emotional and Behavioral Disorders, *Journal of Emotional and Behavioral Disorders.*

Cole, R. F. & Poe, S. L. (1993). *Partnerships for Care: Systems of care for children with serious emotional disturbances and their families.* Washington, D.C.: Washington Business Group on Health.

Comer, J. (1988). Is 'parenting' essential to good teaching? *NEA Today*, 6(6), 34-40.

Conduct Problems Prevention Research Group. (1992). A developmental and clinical model for the prevention of conduct disorder: The FAST Track Program. *Development and Psychopathology, 4*, 509-528.

Clarke, J. I. (1981). *Self Esteem: A Family Affair.* San Francisco: Harper & Row.

Davis, C. (1995). *Special education personnel census data summary and report.* Concord NH: Comprehensive System of Personnel Development, New Hampshire Department of Education.

Dryfoos, J. G. (1994). *Full-service schools: A revolution in health and social services for children, youth and families.* San Francisco: Jossey Bass.

Edwards, P.A. & Young, L. S. (1992). Beyond Parents: Family, Community, and School Involvement, *Phi Delta Kappan, 74*(1), 72-81.

Federation for Children with Special Needs (September, 1991). *The parents manual: A guide to parent's and children's rights under federal and state special education law.* (Available from the Federation for Children with Special Needs, 95 Berkeley St., Suite 104, Boston, MA 02116.)

Fuchs, D., Fuchs, L., & Bahr, M. (1990). Mainstream assistance teams: A scientific basis for the art of consultation. *Exceptional Children, 57*(2), 128-139.

Graden, J. (1989). Redefining "prereferral" intervention as intervention assistance: Collaboration between general and special education. *Exceptional Children, 56*(3), 227-231.

Gersten, R. & Woodward, J. (1990). Rethinking the regular education initiative: Focus on the classroom teacher. *Remedial and Special Education, 11*(3), 7-16.

Jones, V. (1992). Integrating behavioral and insight-oriented treatment in school based programs for seriously emotionally disturbed students. *Behavioral Disorders, 17*(3), 225-236.

Kauffman, J. M. (1989). *Characteristics of behavior disorders of children and youth (4th Edition).* Columbus, OH: Merrill Publishing.

Knitzer, J. (1993). Children's mental health policy: Challenging the future. *Journal of Emotional and Behavioral Disorders, 1*(1), 8-16.

Knitzer, J. & Cole, E. (1989). Family preservation services: The policy challenge to state child welfare and mental health system. New York: Bank Street College of Education.

Knitzer, J., Steinberg, Z. & Fleisch, B. (1990). *At the school house door: An examination of programs and policies for children with behavioral and emotional problems.* New York: Bank Street College of Education.

Kortering, L. J. & Blackorby, J. (1992). High school dropout and students identified with behavioral disorders. *Behavioral Disorders, 18*(1), 24-32.

Kretovics, J., Farber, K., & Armaline, W. (1991). Reform from the bottom up: Empowering teachers to transform schools. *Phi Delta Kappan, 73*(4), 295-299.

Kübler-Ross, E. (1969). *On death and dying.* New York: Collier Books.

Ladd, G. W., Price, J. M., & Hart, C. H. (1990). Preschoolers' behavioral orientations and patterns of peer contact: Predictive of peer status? In S. R. Asher & J.

E. Coie (Eds.). *Peer rejection in childhood* (pp. 90-115). New York: Cambridge University Press.

Marder, C. (1992). *Secondary school students classified as seriously emotionally disturbed: How are they being served?* Palo Alto: SRI International.

Melaville, A. I. & Blank, M. J. (1991). *What it takes: Structuring interagency partnerships to connect children and families with comprehensive services.* Washington, D.C.: Education and Human Services Consortium.

Neel, R. S., Meadows, N., Levine, P., & Edgar, E. B. (1988). What happens after special education: A statewide follow-up student of secondary students who have behavioral disorders. *Behavioral Disorders, 13.* 209-216.

Nelson, C. M. & Pearson, C A. (1991). *Integrating services for children and youth with emotional or behavioral disorders.* Reston, VA: The Council for Exceptional Children.

New Hampshire State Department of Education. (1992). *Summary report on the survey of continuing education needs related to special education.* Concord, NH: NH State Department of Education.

Payzant, T. (1992). New beginnings in San Diego: Developing a strategy for interagency collaboration. *Phi Delta Kappan, 74*(2), 139-146.

Patterson, G.R., Reid, J.B., & Dishion, T.J. (1992). *Antisocial boys: Vol. 4. A social interactional approach.* Eugene, OR: Castalia.

Peacock Hill Working Group. (1991). Problems and promises in special education and related services for children and youth with emotional or behavioral disorders. *Behavioral Disorders, 16*(4), 299-313.

Pugach, M. C., & Johnson, L. J. (1988). Rethinking the relationship between consultation and collaborative problem-solving. *Focus on Exceptional Children, 21*(4).

Swan, W., & Sirvis, B. (1992). The CEC common core of knowledge and skills essential for all beginning special education teachers. *Teaching Exceptional Children, 25* (1), 16-20.

Stroul, B. A. & Friedman, R. M. (1986). *A system of care for severely emotionally disturbed children & youth.* Washington, D.C.: CASSP Technical Assistance Center at Georgetown University.

U.S. Department of Education, OSEP (Office of Special Education Programs). (1994). *Fifteenth annual report to Congress on the implementation of the Individuals with Disabilities Fifteenth annual report to Congress on the implementation of the Individuals with Disabilities Education Act.* Washington, DC: Author.

# Competitive Employment and Service Management for Adolescents and Young Adults with Emotional and Behavioral Disorders

Michael Bullis
Kathleen Paris

Western Oregon State College

**SUMMARY.** Adolescents with emotional and behavioral disorders (EBD) pose difficult service delivery problems as they display the types of behaviors that are least tolerated in school, work, and community settings. This population has (a) the highest drop-out rate (over 50%) and (b) the highest unemployment rate (52%) four years after leaving high school of all disability groups served by special education. Further, there are few transition programs and interventions with documented long-term benefit for this population and age group. Given the variety and severity of the complex problems associated with EBD (e.g., poverty, substance abuse, family planning, counseling, criminal activities, etc.), and the poor transition experiences of this population, it is imperative that a coordinated sys-

---

Address correspondence to: Dr. Michael Bullis, Secondary Special Education and Transition, 275 College of Education, University of Oregon, Eugene, OR 97403.

Preparation of this document was supported through grants from the Federal Rehabilitation Services Administration. However, no endorsement of the views presented herein by those agencies should be inferred.

[Haworth co-indexing entry note]: "Competitive Employment and Service Management for Adolescents and Young Adults with Emotional and Behavioral Disorders." Bullis, Michael, and Kathleen Paris. Co-published simultaneously in *Special Services in the Schools* (The Haworth Press, Inc.) Vol. 10, No. 2, 1995, pp. 77-96; and: *Emerging School-Based Approaches for Children with Emotional and Behavioral Problems: Research and Practice in Service Integration* (ed: Robert J. Illback, and C. Michael Nelson) The Haworth Press, Inc., 1996, pp. 77-96. Single or multiple copies of this article are available from The Haworth Document Delivery Service [1-800-342-9678, 9:00 a.m. - 5:00 p.m. (EST)].

tem of vocational training and social support be afforded adolescents and young adults with EBD to have maximum effect. This article describes such a service model and summarizes preliminary data on the effect of the program. *[Article copies available from The Haworth Document Delivery Service: 1-800-342-9678.]*

Adolescents and young adults with emotional and behavioral disorders (EBD) pose difficult service delivery problems, as their disability is extremely durable and resistant to intervention efforts (Kazdin, 1987a, 1987b; Patterson, Reid, & Dishion, 1992; Wolf, Braukmann, & Ramp, 1987). A sizeable portion (39% to 55%, depending upon the study) of students with EBD drop out of public school before graduation (Blackorby, Edgar, & Kortering, 1991; Valdes, Williamson, & Wagner, 1990), and the few (15% in one national study; Valdes et al., 1990) who enroll in postsecondary training, usually go to community college or short-term training (Neel, Meadows, Levine, & Edgar, 1988). Finally, the post-high school employment experiences of this population are dismal. In the National Longitudinal Transition study (D'Amico & Marder, 1991), a nationally representative sample of persons with emotional disorders presented an unemployment rate of 52% four years after leaving high school. This was the highest unemployment rate of any disability group included in that study. Coupled with unemployment is the issue of meaningful employment. Persons with EBD who do work tend to secure menial and lower paying jobs (Valdes et al., 1990) with reduced opportunity for advancement through the adult years (e.g., Wolfgang, Thornberry, & Figlio, 1987).

Given these results, programs at the secondary grades that emphasize instruction and experiences to foster successful adjustment in adult life should be provided to adolescents and young adults with EBD (Edgar, 1987, 1988). Adolescence may be an efficacious developmental period to intervene (Hobbs & Robinson, 1982), as entry to adulthood may initiate a desire to learn that was not present in earlier grades. A central component of such programs should be vocational training (Bullis & Gaylord-Ross, 1991; Weber, 1987; Will, 1984) as such interventions can have a positive effect on school completion (Thornton & Zigmond, 1987; Thornton & Zigmond, 1988; Weber, 1987), post-school work success (Hasazi, Gordon, & Roe, 1985), and personal adjustment in community settings (Garrett, 1985; Kazdin, 1987a, 1987b; Massimo & Shore, 1963; Shore, Massimo, & Mack, 1965). Unfortunately, not all persons with EBD are provided vocational training while in school, and the quality of much of this instruction is questionable (Bullis & Gaylord-Ross, 1991). Data from the National Longitudinal Transition Study indicated that 69% of the subjects received some type of vocational education in their last year of school, for an average of six hours per week (Valdes et al., 1990). Halpern (1992), in a study of high school programs in Oregon, found that adolescents with EBD were identified by parents as those most in need of school-based programs of vocational training, yet they were the least likely of all special education students to receive such interventions.

Even though this evidence suggests that vocational training can have a positive impact on the transition experiences of adolescents and young adults with EBD, it must be recognized that these persons pose difficult service delivery problems due to the multi-faceted nature of their behavioral characteristics (e.g., delinquency, drug involvement, unstable living situation, poverty, etc.). Assistance from agencies outside the school that offer vocational services is infrequent and/or inconsistent. For example, Kortering and Edgar (1988) found that only 5% of their sample of adolescents and young adults with EBD in transition had received services from vocational rehabilitation. Marder, Wechsler, and Valdes (1993), in an analysis of a subgroup of 140 adolescents and young adults with emotional disorders from the National Longitudinal Transition Study, found that only 5.7% of this group reported receiving vocational assistance from vocational rehabilitation agencies.

As the majority of persons with EBD do not go on to postsecondary education or receive services from other agencies, interventions offered in the secondary grades are likely to be the last concentrated service delivery effort for these persons. Accordingly, it is essential that these interventions be as powerful and pragmatic as possible. Secondary programs should include both vocational training and the establishment of a system of support services from multiple, specialized agencies from outside the schools (e.g., mental health, substance abuse treatment programs, welfare, criminal justice) (Walker & Bullis, in press).

In an earlier publication (Bullis, Fredericks, Lehman, Paris, Corbitt, & Johnson, 1994), we described a model service delivery program—Job Designs—that emphasized competitive vocational placements. While we were able to secure competitive work placements for the majority of these persons, only half of the placements were judged as positive (did not end from termination or by the worker quitting inappropriately). As we examined and discussed these experiences, it became clear that we had not (a) involved the participants themselves fully in the planning and placement efforts and (b) placed sufficient emphasis on developing a system of support involving multiple social service agencies in the immediate locale. In a subsequent proposal (Bullis, 1992), we re-structured the project to include vocational placement, as well as emphasizing the central role of the participant in planning his or her program and emphasizing service management to develop an integrated system of services for each participant. This article describes (a) this revised service delivery model, (b) preliminary data from the first two years of this second project, and (c) a case study of one participant. Where appropriate, we compare the results from the first Job Designs project with data from years 1 and 2 of the present project.

## *METHOD*

### *Setting and Participants*

*Setting.* Job Designs is located in western Oregon, just outside a town of approximately 40,000, in which a major university is located. Unemployment for this locale is low (over the course of the project the unemployment rate for this county ran from 3% to 4%, as compared to a national unemployment rate of 7% to 9% during the same period. The major employers in the area were the university, the local school system, a large computer manufacturer, and various agricultural and timber businesses.

Project offices were located at a residential facility for adolescents and young adults. The residents were 12 to 18 years of age with EBD who had been removed from their natural homes as a consequence of order by the juvenile or child welfare authorities. A census of around 80 is usual with a 4:1 male to female ratio of residents and an average length of stay is approximately 11 months. Residential services are provided through cottages of 10 to 15 residents who are grouped by gender and age. Individual and group counseling is offered to all residents and, if appropriate, their families by facility staff or through contractual arrangements with private providers. Educational services are provided through an on-campus high school. As residents progress in the on-campus school, they may be transferred to one of two community high schools. At the time Job Designs began, there was no coordinated vocational program that emphasized competitive employment. Other referrals to Job Designs came from the local schools or community agencies (e.g., vocational rehabilitation, mental health, probation and parole).

*Participants.* At this point, the end of the second project year, 60 persons have been formally referred to Job Designs. Age and grade were distributed in a bimodal manner at referral by Job Designs participants: 16 and 17 years of age and tenth and eleventh grades. There were 44 males (73%) and 16 females (27%), and 9 (15%) were of a cultural minority. At referral 28 (47%) were certified for special education and 43 (72%) carried a psychiatric diagnosis (American Psychiatric Association, 1987, 1994). A total of 27 (47%) previously had received treatment for alcohol or drug abuse, 30 (50%) had been adjudicated, 20 (33%) had attempted suicide at least once, 10 (17%) had been placed in an institutional living arrangement, 16 (27%) had a history of running away from natural or foster living placements, and 54 (93%) had a history of some type of competitive work. As compared to the first three years of Job Designs, this present sample is roughly equivalent, but differs in two important ways. First, in the sample from the first three years, 79% presented a profile of antisocial behavior as evidenced by being adjudicated at least once ($n$ = 46) and 67% ($n$ = 39) had a history of alcohol or substance abuse and treatment. Second, that first sample presented a lower incidence of psychiatric diagnoses (53%, $n$ = 31) and none had been institutionalized for mental or emotional disorders.

### Project Structure

Two Service Coordination Specialists (SCSs) are responsible for service delivery. Generally, SCSs maintain a caseload of 10 to 15 participants, with 5 or 6 of these actively working. Their primary duties include intake, job development and support, and service coordination. A half-time project coordinator monitors the day-to-day administration of the project, consults on difficult cases, maintains regular contact with key educational and social service agency staff, and monitors data collection. A senior staff person assumes primary administrative responsibility, analyzes project data, and represents the project to the region and the state. All project staff meet regularly (weekly or biweekly) in a 1 to 2 hour meeting to review the progress and experiences of each participant.

Through previous projects, a comprehensive data collection system has been developed that profiles vocational (e.g., job status, hours worked, average hourly wage), educational (e.g., classes missed, graduation, drop-out status, grades), and social (e.g., arrest status, emotional problems, runaway incidents, outbursts in living situations) experiences on a monthly basis. These data are coded by each participant's SCS, with the project coordinator coding similar forms on a sampling of participants for the purpose of establishing inter-judge reliability. As participants exit the program they are interviewed regarding their impression of the program by a naive interviewer and employers who hire from Job Designs are surveyed yearly about their impressions of the project.

### Philosophy

Both the Individuals with Disabilities Education Act (P.L. 94-142) and the 1992 Amendments to the Rehabilitation Act emphasize the importance of *self determination* in the provision of services to persons with disabilities. Self determination relates to the ability to plan and direct one's own direction and life course in different settings, including those settings comprising transition (i.e., vocational, postsecondary education, independent living, recreation). Further, this ability may be the most important aspect of human functioning, and it is a key element of success in transition endeavors and adult life (Bandura, 1977; Halpern, 1992; Nosek & Fuhrer, 1992; Syzmanski, 1994). In line with this emphasis, we elected to focus on the individual's capabilities and interests to affect strong rapport between the participants and the program in order to lead to more positive, goal-directed services (Burns, 1994). In line with this orientation, each participant is centrally involved in planning his or her service program by (a) identifying his or her own strengths, interests, and needs; (b) being responsible to the maximum extent possible for securing vocational placements and social services; and (c) making decisions regarding his or her goals and desires after leaving Job Designs.

## Service Delivery Procedures

The primary services offered through Job Designs are (a) compilation of a comprehensive and accurate file on each participant's background and interests, (b) service coordination with community-based agencies, (c) job development, and (d) training and on-the-job support.

*Intake.* We believe that intake is crucial to the entire service delivery effort, as accurate and comprehensive information on the individual, his or her emotional and behavioral characteristics, vocational and life goals and interests, and available supports must be considered in service delivery. Intake takes no more than one week and is orchestrated by each participant's SCS. The process is designed to gather the information necessary to identify (a) appropriate worksites for job development and (b) appropriate and necessary support services. For example, questions are asked about the adolescent's daily schedule, so that time is not wasted on investigating possible work sites that would pose schedule conflicts. Hobbies and interests can be a great source of ideas for types of professions to target when job development begins. For example, a person with an interest in reading might do well placed at a library or book store, and an individual with an interest in animals may be placed in an animal shelter. Often adolescents and young adults have very specific ideas about where they would like to work and–equally as important–firm notions about where they would *not* like to work. We have developed a structured interview protocol which asks the individual to rate their level of interest in a variety of career areas on a Likert-type scale (1–high to 4–low). Careers rated as a "1" are targeted first for job development.

Sometimes interviewing a family member is helpful in preliminary job and service development efforts. Family members can be insightful, not only about the work habits and strengths of their son or daughter, but also about deficits which will require additional support and attention. An additional benefit of involving a family member in the service planning is to establish the personal connection with the SCS. Enlisting the family's support for the program provides interest and monitoring for program involvement from both program staff and the family, which–in our experience–can be helpful should problems arise with the participants.

Contact with the referral source (e.g., schools, social service agency) generally describes the emotional and behavioral characteristics of the individual, information with critical implications for job placement and service delivery. For example, if an individual has a recent history of theft, then finding a work setting where there is little or no temptation to steal is important. Likewise, a sex offender should not be placed where victimization could occur. While this type of information is, at times, difficult to obtain, it is essential to service delivery. As a rule, we will work with an individual *only* if a complete and detailed history has been obtained and we can be confident in the placement and service options we can provide. Obviously, safety for the participant, co-workers, and others in the community is paramount and must be considered carefully. Clearly it is critical for participants and environments to be matched as closely as possible to foster success.

*Service coordination.* We believe that effective service coordination with community-based agencies–including vocational, postsecondary, recreational, medical, mental health, and housing agencies–is the key to successful vocational placements and transition for adolescents and young adults with EBD. Appendix A provides a summary of the agencies with which we have worked. Once the services necessary to support successful community integration for an individual are identified, it becomes that person's and his or her SCS's responsibility to locate and contact the appropriate agencies. Maximum responsibility is placed on the individual to take a lead role in this effort; however, in some cases, it may be necessary for the SCS to assist or even take the lead with the participant assisting in the effort. In all instances, the dual goal of service coordination is to (a) secure the necessary services and (b) offer a context in which the participant can learn to interact effectively with other adults and service providers.

Although there are advantages to establishing formal inter-agency agreements at an administrative level to affect service coordination, it has been our experience that informal networks through the SCSs are efficient and effective. The SCS often coordinates these multiple services, while at the same time affording the individual as much responsibility and independence as possible and appropriate.

The SCS's personal relationship with the *individuals* in the agencies is critical. A phone call from an SCS who has taken the time to talk with a staff person is more likely to get results than a call from an anonymous voice on the phone asking for services on behalf of a participant. When a positive relationship has been established it is easier to generate creative solutions that will meet a particular individual's needs. Accordingly, it is important for the SCS to contact local agencies, to meet regularly with key staff, and to determine their referral criteria, the appropriate contacts, the expectations of the persons they serve (e.g., are persons automatically dropped if they miss appointments or don't comply with treatment plans), and unique terminology. While it may not always be possible for agency staff to grant all of the individual's requests, it is usually possible to work together with the SCS to generate service alternatives and to identify other sources of support.

Multiple meetings with all of the agencies involved with an individual are very time consuming. Just scheduling this type of meeting is difficult because of the numerous commitments and meetings required of other social service agencies. It has been our experience that the amount of delay caused by multiple agency meetings can in some cases override the potential benefit of such meetings to the individual. When these types of meetings are unavoidable, the SCS should contact agency representatives ahead of time to inform them of the purpose of the meeting and their particular role in order to arrive at the meeting prepared to answer specific questions and achieve rapid service provision.

*Job development.* Most jobs are located through an individual's personal contacts or through those of family members or friends (Azrin & Besalel, 1980), what many term the self/family/friend network (Edgar & Levine, 1987). As many of the Job Designs participants do not reside with their families, in a very real sense the program and the SCSs fulfill this role. It is important that participants and SCSs work together to develop and secure employment consistent with the participant's career goals and interests. Because these interests may change as varied vocational and academic experiences accrue, it is not unusual for our participants to be placed in multiple jobs.

Job development is time consuming and should be approached in an organized and informed manner to limit the time and resources spent in the effort and to maximize placement successes. Review of our records indicates that, of 10 phone calls to employers, two or three will respond positively and be willing to talk with a staff person about the project. If a personal interview can be secured, roughly 50% of these employers have hired one of our workers. Job development in smaller businesses has proven most successful, as in larger companies it is more difficult to access a person with the authority to hire or create a position for a person with EBD. As employment opportunities often are outside of the regular class hours and in the community away from the school building, it is essential for the SCS to be flexible, pleasant, and have the ability to work independently. The process of job development is really sales, with the goal being for an employer to "buy into" the program as much as hiring a particular individual. The following is the step-by-step process for successful job development.

- *Identify potential work-sites.* The SCSs must use personal contacts, check bulletin boards around local businesses, read the yellow pages, look for new businesses in town which are hiring, speak to local professional organizations to "drum up" possible placements, and regularly review the want advertisement section of the paper. Just because an employer isn't advertising does not mean that they don't have openings or aren't willing to create a position. This information gathering should be organized into a comprehensive and detailed filing system in order to quickly locate employers, previous contacts, notes for future contacts, placements successes, etc.
- *Place an individual or develop a placement site.* There are no firm rules about how to place an individual. Roughly half the time the SCSs will seek a placement for a specific individual; while in the other cases, contacts are made with employers to inform them of the program and to develop a personal relationship with the program.
- *Call the work-site.* The first point of contact is usually a phone call to the business. The SCS asks to speak to the manager or owner. It is important to refrain from stating the purpose of the call to a receptionist who could "shield" the individual with the authority to hire. Once the SCS is connected with the appropriate person, the SCS gives a brief description of the program, provides an overview of the population that is served, and–if possible–gives a *general* description of the specific person seeking employment (e.g., "This is an individual who has experienced some difficult times and who is working hard to turn him/herself around. We believe s/he is a good candidate for a job in a business such as yours"). This conversation should be brief, as time is money for business people. The initial

meeting concludes by asking to schedule a short meeting to discuss the specifics of the program, the types of supports which are provided, and the individual under consideration.

- *Take materials about the program to the meeting.* A brochure describing Job Designs has been developed to introduce the program. The brochure is brief (4 pages), printed on a fine quality paper, professionally structured, and includes statements of praise from local employers, service organizations, and local citizens. If an individual is eligible for the Targeted Jobs Tax Credit (TJTC) (employers who hire individuals with documented disabilities or from low income families are eligible for a federal tax credit), information about that program is taken to the meeting in an organized folder. Finally, if a specific person is being placed, the SCS presents a current, polished resume, which has been developed with that participant.
- *Be positive and honest.* The SCS tells the employer about other jobs held by program participants, emphasizes successes in similar job placements, and uses the names of current or previous employers (after first securing their permission). They mention and discuss appropriate on-site support to be offered to both the worker and the employer to promote initial placement success. An issue that arises invariably relates to the characteristics and background of the individual who is to be placed with the employer. How much information to share with employers on worker's backgrounds is a sensitive issue. Sharing too much information with employers may influence them not to hire and may infringe on the individual's rights to keep his/her history confidential. As a policy, in Job Designs, we share only that information that is directly related to the job duties. Many employers have hired our participants due to a sense of altruism and express that they wish they could have more knowledge of the individual's background in order to be of greater assistance.
- *Close constructively.* If the employer indicates an interest to hire, the SCS schedules an interview for the individual. If the employer is not interested, the SCS asks if he/she might be interested at a later date, and finds out when might be a good time to call again. Regardless of whether the employer shows an interest in the program, it is important to be courteous and professional in closing to leave a positive impression.

*Training and on-the-job support.* Pre-employment training is provided to each participant on an individual basis by the SCS and–if possible–by coordinating with ongoing educational classes. As a rule, all persons who are to be placed in a job are scheduled for an actual job interview with the prospective employer. The interview affords the employer the opportunity to review and approve of the individual before hiring, shifting the responsibility for the decision from the SCS, and offers the individual the experience of interviewing for a position. Most adolescents and young adults will change jobs and career aspirations numerous times, thus these skills have generalized applications and importance for future jobs. Consequently, a fair portion of the pre-employment training involves job search skills, resume writing, and interview techniques and practice. Once a job is secured, the emphasis of the training offered participants shifts to job-related social skill training through discussion of specific problems and role playing of problematic situations between the SCS and the participant. The length of time spent on pre-employment training depends upon the amount of previous training and/or job experience, but typically includes several one-hour meetings per week. Ongoing monitoring by the SCS results in continuing support, training, and intervention as needed by each individual.

Varying levels of support are provided after an individual is hired. The SCS initially is present at all work shifts for the first one to four weeks, depending upon the level of training required. Some employers prefer to do all of the training themselves. If the employer wishes to do all of the training, or when the individual is stable on the job, the SCS observes at the work-site for only 5 to 15 minutes daily and regular contact is maintained by telephone. Subsequent informal contacts then are made outside of working hours (e.g., the SCS takes the participant out for lunch or coffee).

At this stage, the SCS's role becomes that of a mentor, and in most cases time spent with the participant decreases. Work-site check-ins are reduced to once a week and eventually to once every two weeks. Contact with the employer is made every two weeks. Both the participant and the employer know that–if for any reason either party has a concern about the job–the SCS will help to solve the problem. A consistent finding in these projects has been the cyclical nature of the job skills, satisfaction, and attendance of adolescents and young adults with EBD. It is all too common for an individual to be performing well on the job, express satisfaction, appear happy and then to express diametrically opposite views seemingly overnight and for no apparent reason. In these situations, the SCS must be able to talk to the individual, identify the problem, assist in developing a strategy to resolve the issue, and–in some cases–contact the employer regarding the placement. In these instances, the SCS can either save the placement for the worker or save the placement for another participant.

## RESULTS

As we are in the final year of this three year funding cycle, we have not completed the evaluation of the project. Consequently, only preliminary, descriptive results from the first two years of the project are presented, followed by an illustrative case study of a young woman with whom our staff have worked extensively through both Job Designs projects.

### Vocational Experiences

Table 1 presents a summary of vocational data. The last full year of the first Job Designs project, 1991, is used as a baseline for comparison. There has been an overall decrease in the average number of workers in competitive positions on a monthly basis and in average hourly wage, but the average number of hours worked per week has remained fairly constant. In the first Job Designs project, 22% of the workers were fired from at least one position. In contrast, in the first two years of this second project, only 13% of the workers have been fired.

### Interagency Services

Table 2 presents the number and percentage of project participants referred to and/or served by other service agencies from the first Job Designs project contrasted with those from the present project. There has been a considerable increase in the number of participants in the present project who have been referred to other service agencies and/or support systems. In fact, the modal number of agencies with whom the participants have had contact with and/or receive services from is four to five.

TABLE 1. Employment Experiences

|  | 1991 | 1992 | 1993 | 1994 (to May) |
|---|---|---|---|---|
| Average No. of Workers Placed Competitively/Mo. | 10.25 | 6.97 | 8.75 | 5.20 |
| Average No. of Hours Worked/Week | 19.12 | 21.68 | 23.74 | 18.66 |
| Average Hourly Wage | $5.07 | $4.99 | $4.96 | $4.82 |

TABLE 2. Agency Contacts

| Agency | Job Designs 1 (n = 58) | Job Designs 2 (n = 60) |
|---|---|---|
| Vocational Rehabilitation | 17 (29%) | 32 (53%) |
| Mental Health | 7 (12%) | 14 (23%) |
| Public Welfare | 4 (7%) | 5 (8%) |
| Employment Division | 11 (19%) | 10 (17%) |
| Social Security | 9 (16%) | 15 (25%) |
| Alcohol/Drug Treatment | — (0%) | 4 (7%) |
| Probation/Parole | 4 (7%) | 6 (10%) |
| Private Counseling | 11 (19%) | 11 (18%) |
| Alternative Education Programs | 4 (7%) | 12 (20%) |
| Foster Family | 7 (12%) | 12 (20%) |
| Natural Family | 14 (24%) | 28 (47%) |
| Children's Services Division | 11 (19%) | 23 (38%) |
| Job Training Partnership Program | 11 (19%) | 22 (37%) |

## Employer Perceptions

On a yearly basis we survey the employers who hire one of our participants to gain their perspective on the program and ways in which it may be improved. Over the past two years we have received surveys from 26 employers. These respondents gave the following answers to the five questions comprising this form: What was the reason you hired a worker from Job Designs? (three top answers)–had an opening to fill (35%, *n* = 9), wanted to help one of these adolescents and young adults (19%, *n* = 5), and impressed with program (15%, *n* = 4); Are you interested in hiring another worker from Job Designs, 80% answered "yes" (*n* = 20); Impression of the Job Designs staff with whom you worked (1 = high to 4 = low) − mean = 1.15; Impression of the Job Designs program (1 = high to 4 = low) − mean = 1.31; and Impression of the Worker you Employed (1 = high to 4 = low) − mean = 1.84.

## Case Study

Sarah was referred to the first Job Designs program at the age of 17 from two sources: the learning resource center of the local high school and the school district's work experience program. She was on an Individualized Education Plan with work experience identified as an appropriate educational goal. The district's work experience coordinator stated that she did not believe their program had the staffing to place Sarah in competitive employment in a community setting.

At referral Sarah was certified as having an emotional disorder. Her most recent psychological evaluation indicated a full scale I.Q. of 80, verbal I.Q. of 69, and a performance I.Q. of 93. Voluminous medical, social, and psychological information also indicated a neurological deficit and a seizure disorder which was controlled through prescriptions of depakote, and tegritol; however, there was suspicion that she pretended to have seizures at different times to gain attention. Her other behaviors included self-abuse such as picking at her skin or pulling off scabs.

Social Security was one of the first agencies that Job Designs contacted. The SCS assisted Sarah and her parent with the application process, and she was approved for eligibility for Supplemental Security Income and Medicaid resources which addressed growing medical bills. For the two years prior to referral to Job Designs, Sarah had been living in a group home for adolescents and young adults with learning and/or emotional disorders. She had been successful and happy in the group home and had experienced a variety of vocational placements, including a fabric store, a restaurant, and a day care facility. Information from that program's vocational trainer indicated that Sarah was a slow worker, and occasionally "played dumb" to avoid doing a job that she didn't like.

Sarah expressed a strong desire to work in a restaurant, so the SCS helped her to obtain a Food Handlers Permit from the local health department. The officials at the health department allowed the SCS to read and explain the questions to Sarah so that she could answer the questions in a valid manner.

Sarah was then placed at a pizza parlor for 10 to 12 hours per week as a bus person, food handler, and salad maker. Initially she required daily supervision for the duration of each shift. It became apparent that her hygiene needed improvement and that she needed rules about what was appropriate to discuss with co-workers. Her clothing often was wrinkled and dirty, she smelled and discussed personal topics, such as her menstrual cramps. She would bring up the subject loudly and in front of customers. The SCS assisted Sarah's supervisors in confronting her about these inappropriate outbursts and helped them learn to reinforce her when she discussed appropriate topics. To deal with her hygiene, the SCS purchased toiletries and discussed with her the use of each of these items and the need for daily bathing. A check list was developed by the SCS that Sarah was to use each day prior to dressing. Every day that Sarah demonstrated appropriate hygiene on the job, she was allowed a soft drink from her employer.

Sarah maintained this job without incident for two years until she graduated from high school at the age of 20. Upon graduation she seemed to have trouble finding activities to fill her time. Sarah began pretending to have seizures, fought with her family members, and missed numerous mental health appointments. As problems escalated, the SCS approached other agencies such as mental health, vocational rehabilitation, and senior and disabled services to provide supports for Sarah. Eventually, she began to make suicide threats and attempted suicide on at least one occasion. In the winter, she was admitted to the local hospital for psychiatric evaluation.

After this evaluation, she was sent to a residential training program for persons with chronic mental illnesses. Unfortunately, the other residents in the foster home were all elderly and she did not adjust well, making suicide attempts and threatening another resident. By the fall Sarah was placed in a hospital for psychiatric patients. The SCS worked closely with her family, the State and local mental health agencies, and Senior and Disabled Services to find an alternative placement for her. Through a process of local meetings, and pressure exerted at the state level, an appropriate group home was found for Sarah, but at a distance of four hours away from her family and home. At her current residence she participates in leisure activities, has two part-time paid jobs, and is making friends. Job Designs has begun working with the father to explore possibilities for establishing a similar program in the local community so that Sarah could remain in the immediate locale and still receive necessary treatment and services to live and work in the least restrictive yet appropriately supportive arrangement possible.

## *CONCLUSION*

We believe that the revised model of services offered through the current Job Designs project is logical and that it addresses the very real needs and characteristics of the population of adolescents and young adults with EBD. The increase in interagency coordination is evident and we are hopeful that these contacts will create an extended, long-term support system that will affect the ongoing transition of these persons in a positive manner. Our experiences, as well as data from numerous studies on the transition and life-long adjustment of persons with EBD, emphasize that these disorders are extremely durable and have long-term deleterious effects (Kazdin, 1987a, 1987b; Wolf et al., 1987). Services for adolescents and young adults, in many cases, should be conceptualized along the lines of a chronic disease model (Kazdin, 1987b) in which the individual is monitored and supported for long periods, perhaps over his or her entire life–far longer than we are able to achieve through a time-limited project such as Job Designs. Adolescents and young adults and young adults with EBD can become contributing members of our society. It is naive, however, to believe that such success will be achieved easily or quickly. Programs such as Job Designs represent only a piece of the service delivery system necessary to foster such positive achievements.

## REFERENCES

Azrin, N., & Besalel, V. (1980). *Job club counselor's manual.* Baltimore: University Park Press.

Bandura, A. (1977). Self efficacy: Toward a unifying theory of behavioral change. *Psychological Review, 84*, 191-215.

Blackorby, J., Edgar, E., & Kortering, L. (1991). A third of our youth? A look at the problem of high school dropout among students with mild handicaps. *Journal of Special Education, 25*, 102-113.

Bullis, M. (1992). *Project SERVE: Support for the emotional, residential, vocational, and educational needs of young adults with EBD.* Funded proposal, Rehabilitation Services Administration.

Bullis, M., Fredericks, H. D. Bud, Lehman, C., Paris, K., Corbitt, J., & Johnson, B. (1994). Description and evaluation of the Job Designs program for adolescents with emotional or behavioral disorders. *Behavioral Disorders, 19*, 254-268.

Bullis, M., & Gaylord-Ross, R. (1991). *Moving on: Transitions for behaviorally disordered.* Reston, VA: Council for Exceptional Children.

Burns, B. (1994). The challenges of child mental health services research. *Journal of Emotional and Behavioral Disorders, 2*, 254-259.

D'Amico, R., & Marder, C. (1991). *The early work experiences of youth with disabilities: Trends in employment rates and job characteristics.* Menlo Park, CA: SRI International.

DeStefano, L., & Wagner, M. (1992). Outcome assessment in special education: What lessons have we learned? In F. Rusch, L. DeStefano, J. Chadsey-Rusch, L. Phelps, & E. Syzmanski (Eds.), *Transition from school to adult life* (pp. 173-207). Sycamore, IL: Sycamore Publishing.

Edgar, E. (1987). Secondary programs in special education: Are many of them justifiable? *Exceptional Children, 53*, 555-561.

Edgar, E. (1988). Employment as an outcome for mildly handicapped students: Current status and future directions. *Focus on Exceptional Children, 21*(1), 1-8.

Edgar, E., & Levine, P. (1987). *Special education students in transition: Washington state data 1976-1986.* Seattle: University of Washington, Experimental Education Unit.

Garrett, C. (1985). Effects of residential treatment on adjudicated delinquents: A meta-analysis. *Journal of Research on Crime and Delinquency, 22*(4), 287-308.

Halpern, A. (1992). *Job experiences of students with disabilities during their last year of school.* University of Oregon: Transition Follow-along Project.

Hasazi, S. B., Gordon, L. R., & Roe, C. (1985). Factors associated with the employment status of handicapped youth exiting high school from 1979 to 1983. *Exceptional Children, 51*, 455-469.

Hobbs, N., & Robinson, S. (1982). Adolescent development and public policy. *American Psychologist, 37*, 212-223.

Kazdin, A. (1987a). *Conduct disorders in childhood and adolescence.* Beverly Hills, CA: Sage.

Kazdin, A. (1987b). Treatment of antisocial behavior in children: Current status and future directions. *Psychological Bulletin, 102*, 187-203.

Kortering, L. J. & Edgar, E. B. (1988). Vocational rehabilitation and special education: A need for cooperation. *Rehabilitation Counseling Bulletin, 31*, 178-184.

Marder, Wechsler, M., & Valdes, K. (1993). *Services for youth with disabilities after secondary school.* Menlo Park, CA: SRI International.

Massimo, J., & Shore, M. (1963). The effectiveness of a vocationally oriented psychotherapeutic program for adolescent delinquent boys. *American Journal of Orthopsychiatry, 4*, 634-642.

Neel, R., Meadows, N., Levine, P., & Edgar, E. (1988). What happens after special education: A statewide follow-up study of secondary students who have behavioral disorders. *Behavioral Disorders, 13*(3), 209-216.

Nosek, M., & Fuhrer, M. (1992). Independence among people with disabilities: I. Heuristic model. *Rehabilitation Counseling Bulletin, 36*, 6-20.

Patterson, G. R., Reid, J., & Dishion, T. (1992). *Antisocial boys.* Eugene, OR Castalia.

Shore, M. F., Massimo, J. L., & Mack, R. (1965). Changes in the perception of interpersonal relationships in successfully treated adolescent delinquent boys. *Journal of Consulting Psychology, 29*(3), 213-217.

Syzmanski, E. (1994). Transition: Life-span and life-space considerations for empowerment. *Exceptional Children, 60*, 402-410.

Thornton, H., & Zigmond, N. (1987). *Predictors of dropout and unemployment among LD high school youth: The holding power of secondary vocational education for LD students.* Pittsburgh, PA: University of Pittsburgh.

Thornton, H., & Zigmond, N. (1988). Secondary vocational training for LD students and its relationship to school completion status and post school outcomes. *Illinois Schools Journal, 67*(2), 37-54.

Valdes, K., Williamson, C., & Wagner, M. (1990). *The National Longitudinal Transition Study of Special Education Students: Volume 3, Youth categorized as emotionally disturbed.* Palo Alto, CA: SRI International.

Walker, H., & Bullis, M. (In press). Comprehensive interventions in the educational setting. In C. M. Nelson, B. Wolford, & R. Rutherford (Eds.), *Develop-*

*ing comprehensive systems that work for troubled youth.* Richmond, KY: National Coalition for Juvenile Justice Services.

Weber, J. (1987). *Strengthening vocational education's role in decreasing the dropout rate.* Columbus, OH: Ohio State University, Center for Research in Vocational Education.

Will, M. (1984). *OSERS program for the transition of youth with disabilities: Bridges from school to working life.* Washington, DC: Office of Special Education and Rehabilitation.

Wolf, M., Braukmann, C., & Ramp, K. (1987). Serious delinquent behavior as a part of a significantly handicapping condition: Cures and supportive environments. *Journal of Applied Behavior Analysis, 20,* 347-359.

Wolfgang, M., Thornberry, T., & Figilo, R. (1987). *From boy to man, from delinquency to crime.* Chicago: University of Chicago Press.

## APPENDIX A

## Overview of Service Delivery Agencies

a. *State Children's Services Division.* Many of the referrals for Job Designs come from this division. This agency provides financial resources for the group home and foster care elements that constitute part of the support network in this project. In addition to providing referrals, group home and foster care funding, this agency often provides funding for work clothing, start up costs for apartments, stipends for minors who are in the process of preparing to emancipate, and payment of fees for classes in areas of interest such as electronics or modeling.

b. *County Mental Health Division.* Job Designs receives referrals from the local mental health department and makes referrals directly to the division. Services provided include crisis counseling, and drug and alcohol evaluation and treatment.

c. *Local School District.* The school district refers students to Job Designs. Whenever possible program staff work with the school to design an individual program for the student that incorporates work experience and school credit. In addition to receiving credit for work experience students sometimes are able to receive English credit for keeping a diary of their work experiences and making a notebook consisting of relevant job search information. Job Designs staff participate in the transition planning process and advocate within the system for the student.

d. *Local Community College.* The college provides interest and aptitude surveys to Job Designs participants at no charge, provides G.E.D. preparation, and work experience placements for selected individuals.

e. *Social Security Administration.* A portion of the Job Designs participants receive or are eligible to receive social security benefits. The
   agency assists in accessing Social Security Incentive Programs, specifically Plans for Achieving Self-Support (PASS), and Impairment
   Related Work Expenses (IRWE). Job Designs also assists its participants to apply for benefits from Social Security.

f. *State Division of Vocational Rehabilitation.* Job Designs has had the
   opportunity to collaborate closely with the local office of Vocational
   Rehabilitation. The partnership has been very successful, and has
   provided a range of services such as work clothing and supplies,
   assistance with vocational planning, and independent living skills.

g. *JTPA.* The local JTPA program is known as the Community Services
   Consortium (CSC). This agency has proved to be invaluable to many
   of our participants. When an individual presents extreme service delivery challenges, we have been able to access CSC funding to pay the
   individual for hours worked. Job Designs provides the job development, training, and on the job supervision and facilitates the compliance with all of the regulations on the part of the employer and the
   participant. CSC has enrolled many of our participants in the "Learn
   to Earn" program in which participants are paid for attending study
   lab and making progress in academics.

h. *Low Cost Housing.* A low cost housing agency exists in each county
   in Oregon. Job Designs relationship with the local branch is that of a
   liaison between the agency and those individuals who need assistance
   to complete necessary paperwork and monitor ongoing benefits.

i. *Corrections System.* Many referrals come from the juvenile corrections system. The parole and probation officers take an active role in
   participants' daily activities. Compliance with the vocational program
   is sometimes written into the conditions of parole.

j. *Oregon Health Plan.* Job Designs assists in the completion of forms
   required for acceptance into the Oregon Health Plan which provides
   medical and dental benefits for participants with qualifying incomes.

k. *Adult and Family Services.* Issues food stamps and public assistance
   to low income participants. Program staff assist in the completion of
   necessary forms and with monthly reporting requirements.

l. *Job Corps.* Job Designs refers participants who wish to have further
   specialized training to the Job Corps. The Job Corp program can
   provide a smooth transition from home to independent living and
   allows for additional job training.

## APPENDIX (continued)

m. *Multi-Cultural Assistance Program.* Job Designs uses this agency to provide sources of support and translation services for participants who are Mexican-American.

n. *Senior and Disabled Services.* Senior and disabled services collaborates with many community agencies to provide treatment and funding necessary for persons to gain living independence. Job Designs worked closely with this agency to secure appropriate living arrangements for an individual moving to the area from the state mental hospital.

# Children and Adolescents Network:
# A Community-Based Program
# to Serve Individuals
# with Serious Emotional Disturbance

Carla Cumblad
Michael H. Epstein
Kimberly Keeney
Talitha Marty
Jennifer Soderlund

Northern Illinois University

**SUMMARY.** The prevalence and outcome data on children with serious emotional disturbance indicate that a significant number of them experience severe mental health, social, and educational problems. These problems are very costly to the child, the family, and the community both socially and financially. While many schools and

Address correspondence to: Michael H. Epstein, Department of Educational Psychology, Counseling, and Special Education, Northern Illinois University, DeKalb, IL 60115-2867.

The authors are grateful to Kevin Quinn and Sonya Peterson for their significant contributions in the development of Project CANDU and to Deb Holderness for her preparation of the manuscript.

Preparation of this manuscript was supported in part by a grant from the U.S. Department of Education, Office of Special Education (H237E20014). The opinions expressed herein are those of the authors and in no way represent positions of the U.S. Department of Education.

[Haworth co-indexing entry note]: "Children and Adolescents Network: A Community-Based Program to Serve Individuals with Serious Emotional Disturbance." Cumblad, Carla et al. Co-published simultaneously in *Special Services in the Schools* (The Haworth Press, Inc.) Vol. 11, No. 1/2, 1996, pp. 97-118; and: *Emerging School-Based Approaches for Children with Emotional and Behavioral Problems: Research and Practice in Service Integration* (ed: Robert J. Illback, and C. Michael Nelson) The Haworth Press, Inc., 1996, pp. 97-118. Single or multiple copies of this article are available from The Haworth Document Delivery Service [1-800-342-9678, 9:00 a.m. - 5:00 p.m. (EST)].

communities have opted to serve these children in restrictive, out-of-community settings, other communities have developed comprehensive programs to serve these children. The Children and Adolescents Network of DuPage County (Project CANDU) is a program providing comprehensive services to children with SED and their families. The project is based on several components essential to the development of a community-based system of care, including interagency collaboration, target population, principles of care, a needs assessment, individualized care services, and comprehensive evaluation. The rationale for each of these components and how they were implemented, data on the children and families served, and a case study are presented. *[Article copies available from The Haworth Document Delivery Service: 1-800-342-9678.]*

There are disturbing signs that our schools are unable to meet the often complex needs of students with serious emotional disturbance (SED). Recently published government documents, follow-up data, and national reports underscore the challenges. Summarized, these findings show that less than one-half of students with SED are currently educated in general education settings (U.S. Department of Education, 1992), their drop-out rate is over 40 percent (U.S. Department of Education, 1992), upon leaving school nearly one-third of these students are neither working nor receiving training for work (Neel, Meadows, Levine, & Edgar, 1988) and perhaps as many as 40 percent are likely to have a police record shortly after leaving school (Jay & Padilla, 1987). As these reports indicate, students with SED demonstrate specific problems in the areas of academic, social, vocational, and personal adjustment.

Unfortunately, however, the current system of service delivery is often unable to respond in a timely, coordinated, and comprehensive fashion to the multiple and interconnected needs of students with SED and their families (Nelson & Pearson, 1991). This is because traditionally, schools have worked largely in isolation, without systematically involving parents and community agencies as necessary supports to meet student needs (Knitzer, 1993; Knitzer, Steinberg, & Fleisch, 1990). Indeed, in the past, community mental health and child welfare agencies were involved in a largely hit or miss fashion. Moreover, parents were more often than not viewed as the cause of the problem, and therefore, their wants or needs regarding treatment goals, plans, or interventions were not sought or were ignored (Friesen & Koroloff, 1990). It is clear that if the challenging behaviors of students with SED are to be met adequately, school, parent, and public and private agency efforts will need to be carefully integrated (Nelson & Pearson, 1991).

In the past few years, a number of national, state, and local initiatives have been launched to address the challenging needs of children with SED and their families. The Child and Adolescent Service System Program (CASSP) funded by the National Institute of Mental Health (Stroul, 1985), the Robert Wood Johnson Foundation local community initiative (Beachler, 1990), the Alaska Youth Initiative (VanDenBerg, 1989), the Ventura County program (Jordan & Hernandez, 1990) and others have identified several components essential to the development of a community-based system of care. These components indicate that communities develop an interagency collaboration network, agree on a target population definition and principles of care statements, conduct a meaningful needs assessment, commit to providing individualized care services, and collect evaluation data (Epstein et al., 1993).

The development of a comprehensive system requires collaboration across professionals and agencies. *Interagency collaboration* involves a clearly defined arrangement among the primary child care agencies. This arrangement addresses such critical issues as agency responsibilities, financing of services, joint system planning, and collaborative programming (Duchnowski & Friedman, 1990). Another essential component affecting the development of an effective community-based system of care is reaching an agreement on a *definition of the target population* (Jordan & Hernandez, 1990; Magrab, Young, & Waddell, 1985). A third essential component is the extent to which policy makers reach agreement on *principles of care* that will establish a direction and a purpose for the community-based program. In developing a comprehensive, community-based system of care, it is necessary to understand the complex and diverse needs of children and youth and their parents, and the equally multifaceted *needs and resources* of service providers and social agencies (Arizona Department of Health, 1991; Friedman, 1988; Magrab et al., 1985). The general goal of a *needs assessment* is to obtain sufficient data to make informed decisions about the system of care. Also, agencies need to make a total commitment to provide services to the child and his/her family on an *individualized care basis*. The principles of individualized care central to a model program of services are unconditional care, intensive case management, individual planning, family involvement, flexible funding, and cultural competency. Finally, careful *evaluation* of services provided and the outcomes of children and families is essential to ensuring that a system of care be accountable, responsive, and effective. The evaluation should gather data that are functional in terms of children and family needs and outcomes, and the services delivery process.

The Partnership for Family Preservation in DuPage County, Illinois, with support from the U.S. Office of Education, began to develop an interagency approach to serving children with SED and their families that addressed each of the components of a system of care through the Children and Adolescents Network of DuPage County (Project CANDU). In the first 18 months, the Partnership developed the needed *infrastructure* for collaboration to occur. In the next 12 months, an *individualized care* approach was implemented and services began to be provided to children and families. In this paper we will describe the components of the system of care as they were implemented, describe the children and families that were served by the project, and present a case study.

## A COMPREHENSIVE SYSTEM OF CARE: THE INFRASTRUCTURE

### Target Site

DuPage County is located 30 miles west of Chicago, is comprised of 23 municipalities and 32 school districts, and has an estimated population of 800,000 of which 230,000 are children. In 1991, approximately 12,000 students were receiving special education services, 1,750 students were enrolled in programs for students with SED, 311 children had been psychiatrically hospitalized and 60 children were residentially placed via school funds.

### Interagency Collaboration

DuPage County has developed a tri-level interagency system of care for children with SED and their families. At Level 1, the *Council of Executive Directors* is the administrative organization comprised of the directors of the primary mental health, social, and educational agencies in the county and, where appropriate, representatives from state agencies. The Council holds meetings for two purposes: (a) to discuss interagency and service delivery issues, authorize interagency initiatives, and agree on local policy for serving children with SED and their families, and (b) to convey a sense of vision and commitment within their respective local agencies and state authorities. At Level 2, the *Partnership for Family Preservation* is a group formed to plan, develop, and monitor interagency collaboration efforts for children with SED. The membership of the Partnership includes parents, middle managers of public agencies, and private provider representatives. In addition, the private providers represent three constituent groups, counseling/therapy, substitute care, and private hospitals. At Level 3, the *Inter-*

*agency Child and Family Planning Teams* were formed by the Partnership to plan, write, and monitor unified service plans to serve children with SED. The teams are made up of the parent and child (when appropriate), natural supports for the parents (e.g., a family friend, a grandparent), an educator, a mental health worker, a social worker, a substance abuse counselor, a probation officer, or a rehabilitation counselor. Assigned to each team is a service coordinator whose primary tasks are to involve families, facilitate collaboration, and coordinate services.

## Target Population

A clear, concise definition of the target population has been viewed as an important first step in facilitating efforts across agencies (Jordan & Hernandez, 1990). A definition assists in developing criteria for identifying those children most in need of services and determining who will provide services. In DuPage County, a prototype definition was drafted by a subcommittee of the Partnership with representatives from the major public agencies that allowed each of the agencies input into identifying the parameters of those children who would be served. The subcommittee met on several occasions, reviewed definitions developed by other programs and agencies, and drafted and edited several versions of their own until one was submitted to the Partnership and Executive Directors for final review and approval (see Table 1).

## Principles of Care

The principles of care determine the context in which services are delivered within a community to children with SED and their families. Briefly, a subcommittee of the Partnership reviewed statements (e.g., Stroul & Friedman, 1986) from other communities, drafted several versions, and submitted a draft to the Partnership and Executive Directors for review and approval. In DuPage County the principles of care acknowledge that the system is to: (a) be child and family centered and community based; (b) provide assessments that identify a child's needs and strengths, that are sensitive to cultural differences, and that lead to individualized service and transition plans; (c) offer services that are comprehensive and reflect a best practices model and that foster self-reliance on the part of children and families; and (d) provide a system that protects and advocates for the rights of children and families. The principles of care have been agreed upon by the executive directors of each of the public agencies and now govern the collaborative activities in the county.

## TABLE 1. Target Population

A child or adolescent referred to the Partnership for Family Preservation is at major risk for failing to develop the emotional, behavioral, academic, and vocational skills required by society to become an independent, self-sufficient adult and whose service needs are complex, requiring service coordination and/or interagency collaboration to foster growth. The child or adolescent is one who:

A. is a DuPage County resident;

B. is 0-21 years of age, and is currently being served by an agency(s) represented by the Partnership for Family Preservation;

C. exhibits behaviors that:

    1. result in a serious diagnosis as measured by the current DSM III (R);

    2. fall into one or more of the following categories:

        a. severely impaired social, academic and self-care functioning (grossly inappropriate and bizarre behavior or emotional reactions which are frequently inappropriate to the situation);

        b. serious, long-term management problems or conduct disorders including extreme hyperactivity, impulsiveness, aggressiveness or substance abuse;

        c. serious discomfort from anxiety, depression, irrational fears and concerns including serious eating and sleeping disturbances, extreme sadness of suicidal proportion, maladaptive dependence on parents, persistent refusal to attend school or avoidance or nonfamilial social contact; or

        d. seriously impaired contact with reality (e.g., confused thinking);

D. has impaired functioning which has the duration of at least one year or is of short duration and high intensity or danger;

E. is currently in a restrictive school, living, or treatment environment, or is at-risk of being separated from home and/or community due to either:

    1. imminent placement in a more restrictive school, living, or treatment environment, or

    2. chronic family factors, e.g., a primary caretaker with mental illness, the family is unable to meet the child's basic and/or emotional needs, the child is threatened or in danger of being harmed, or documented child abuse or neglect;

F. has special service needs that may:

    1. include a history of multiple agency involvement over at least one year, or

    2. require the coordination of two or more service systems or agencies.

## Needs Assessment

A *needs and resources assessment* is a systematic examination of the system of care. A thorough needs and resource assessment affords communities the opportunity to: (a) identify the nature of their target population's service needs; (b) determine the current system's ability to meet those needs; (c) identify overlaps and gaps in the current service system; (d) prioritize goals for system development; and (e) create strategies for funding needed services (Epstein, Quinn, Cumblad, & Holderness, in press).

In an attempt to understand and improve the system of care, a comprehensive needs and resource assessment was implemented in DuPage County (Quinn, Epstein, Cumblad, & Holderness, in press). Three procedures for obtaining the data were included: (a) an archival review of case records of the children (N = 237) who met the target definition (Epstein, Cullinan, Quinn, & Cumblad, 1995); (b) surveys of direct service providers (N = 650) (Quinn, Epstein, & Cumblad, 1995) and parents (N = 220) (Cumblad, Epstein, Quinn, & Soderlund, in press); and (c) interviews with administrators (N = 12), direct service providers (N = 13), parents (N = 8), and children (N = 8). Based on the needs assessment data, the gaps and barriers to effective services were identified and an action plan to better serve children and youth and their families in DuPage County was developed. The action plan prioritized 15 service needs (see Table 2).

## Individualized Care

Individualized care is a critical feature of the provision of services in a comprehensive system of community-based care. The principles of individualized care central to the program in DuPage County are interagency collaboration, strength-based assessment, unified service plans, intensive service coordination, and family involvement.

## Evaluation

A comprehensive evaluation plan is essential to ensuring the effectiveness of the program. In DuPage County, the evaluation plan includes the use of quantitative (e.g., rating scale) and qualitative (e.g., interviews) data collection instruments. Functional information is being gathered in many areas including child status, family involvement, interagency collaboration, community-based services, consumer satisfaction, and demographic information. The specific questions that are guiding the evaluation are presented in Table 3.

TABLE 2. Priorities for System of Care Development

| | |
|---|---|
| 1. | Alternative Funding |
| 2. | Interagency Collaboration |
| 3. | Early Intervention |
| 4. | Emergency/Crisis Respite |
| 5. | In-Home Support |
| 6. | Service Coordination |
| 7. | Therapeutic Foster Care |
| 8. | Transition |
| 9. | Cross-Agency Training |
| 10. | School-Based Support |
| 11. | Vocational/Career Preparation |
| 12. | Recreation Services |
| 13. | Competency Training |
| 14. | Benefit Coordination |

## A COMPREHENSIVE SYSTEM OF CARE: PROVIDING SERVICES

### Referral

Any child in DuPage County is eligible for interagency services if they are identified as SED *and* they have special service needs that require the coordination of services from two or more agencies. Any parent, direct service provider, or administrator may request services for a child by referring the child to the clinical committee, a subcommittee of the Partnership for Family Preservation. The clinical committee is an interagency group composed of public and private service providers and parents. A primary purpose of the group is to determine whether a referral will or will not be accepted for interagency planning through the project. The decision is based on whether the child's behavior and situation matches the target population definition. To date, 43 children have been referred, 12 children have been denied services, and 31 have been accepted into the program. Once a child is accepted for services, they are assigned to a CANDU service coordinator whose tasks are to establish an interagency family planning team and to involve the family.

## TABLE 3. Evaluation Questions

1. **Child Status** (mental health/child placement)

   What is the mental health status of children and youth served in this project as perceived by their service coordinators/interagency treatment teams?

   AND

   What is the mental health status of children and youth served in this project as determined by the assessments of their families and teachers?

   AND

   Are the children and youth served in this project placed in less restrictive residential and educational placements?

2. **Family Status**

   What is the degree of adaptability, flexibility, and cohesion in the families served by this project? To what degree are these families able to adapt to the needs of their SED children?

   AND

   What is the effect these children have on their families?

3. **Interagency Collaboration**

   What are the views of service providers from the local agencies regarding the level of interagency collaboration and the services provided to the children and youth?

4. **Community-Based Services**

   To what extent has the local community's capacity for providing community-based services to children and youth changed over time?

5. **Client Satisfaction**

   What level of satisfaction do the parents have regarding the services provided to their children and youth through this project?

   AND

   What level of satisfaction do the children and youth have regarding the services provided to them through this project?

6. **Background Information**

   Who are the children, youth, and families served by this project?

### *Interagency Collaboration*

At the direct service level, interagency collaboration is operationalized via an *interagency child and family planning team.* Once accepted into the program, a child is assigned a service coordinator who assembles the team. The planning team is comprised of the parents, natural supports of the family in the community, and individuals representing the public and private community agencies that can provide services to the child and family. Planning meetings are structured to allow for the free exchange of ideas between the family, interagency representatives, and other participants. A planning meeting is held shortly after a child is accepted into the program and then every two to three weeks thereafter.

Interagency child and family planning teams perform two important functions: conduct *strength-based assessments* and write *unified service plans*. In strength-based assessment, the child and family are viewed as individuals with specific talents and skills as well as specific unmet needs. Therefore, instead of viewing a child as pathological, the planning team may identify the child's strength as being an athletic skill (e.g., basketball) or a specific hobby (e.g., play an instrument), or an interest (e.g., finding a job). These strengths are identified by the child, family members, and all those in attendance at the meeting. Also, an ecological perspective is taken in this assessment process whereby a child's and family's strengths are identified across several important life domains (e.g., school, family, living). These strengths are used throughout the planning process in developing unified service plans.

A unified service plan is written for each child in the program. A plan provides a framework for conceptualizing an idealized vision of the child and the family; in a sense, a plan is an extension of an IEP. A service plan has several important features. First, each plan has demographic information that includes such information as presenting behaviors, reasons for referral, agency involvement, family support, etc. Second, each plan has information on public (e.g., Medicaid status) and private (e.g., insurance) sources of funding. Third, each plan has an overall goal that indicates the life plan for the child. Fourth, each plan includes life domain planning in such areas as living arrangements, family relationships, educational experiences, psychological status, etc. Fifth, each plan has a set of service forms for each life domain considered. On these forms, a description of the services, the responsible persons and agencies, the funding sources, target dates, and review dates are indicated. Finally, each plan has a place for signatures.

## Service Coordination

The roles of a service coordinator are to facilitate the involvement of the family, develop a comprehensive treatment plan, network with direct service providers from other agencies, broker services necessary to meet treatment goals, and monitor intervention effectiveness. It is essential that the service coordinator foster and maintain positive interagency relationships with any and all potential sources of support for the child and family. The case load for the service coordinators is low, usually no more than seven children at any one time, reflecting the intensity and complexity of the service coordination activities required. The project presently supports three service coordinators.

The service coordinators play a significant role in the interagency planning staffings. Prior to meetings, the coordinators visit with families to introduce them to the interagency process, gather information from the family and records, collect baseline data, and identify the participants for an interagency team. At the planning meeting, the service coordinator establishes an agenda, chairs the meeting, facilitates the creation of service plans, establishes follow-up timelines, and schedules subsequent team meetings. After an interagency meeting, the service coordinator provides for an orientation to the services, follows up the service plan on a regular basis and establishes regular follow-up meetings with team members.

## *Family Involvement*

In the CANDU program, families are involved in all aspects of individualized planning and are encouraged to assume as much service coordination and management as they wish. The goal is to enable parents to become fully informed members of the interagency family planning team. Prior to any meetings, the service coordinator has many contacts with the family at locations that are convenient for the family. During these meetings, efforts are made to provide an orientation to the planning process, verify information, inform the families of their rights and responsibilities, make necessary arrangements for participation (e.g., transportation, translators), and make the family comfortable with the process (e.g., encourage the parents to invite others to the meetings). During the planning meetings, the service coordinator and other professionals view the family as a primary decision-maker regarding priorities for planning and service options. Throughout the meetings, families are encouraged to participate by identifying strengths and needs of the child, setting service priorities, and participating in follow-up activities.

Family involvement has also been achieved in the project via the establishment of a parent support group. The parent support group provides: (a) a resource network for parents about available community services; (b) a telephone network for parent-to-parent support; (c) educational opportunities for parents; and (d) a set of trained parent mentors who can guide parents through the service system and planning procedures. Also a *parent orientation* manual has been written with the intent to better inform families of their roles, responsibilities and rights. The parent group meets monthly and about 20 to 30 parents attend these sessions.

## DESCRIPTIONS OF CHILDREN AND FAMILY

As of April, 1995, 31 children had been referred and had received some services from the project. These referrals came from probation (N = 8), school (N = 4), child welfare (N = 8), mental health (N = 8), substance abuse (N = 1), and the community residential authority (N = 2). An additional 12 referrals were declined services for a number of reasons including family did not wish to participate (N = 6), agency did not want to support the child (N = 2), the child and family were referred to other services (N = 3) and the child did not meet the target population definition (N = 1).

### Child Characteristics

Demographic information at the time of intake was obtained on 21 children. A summary of this information appears in Table 4. The average age of the referred was 14 years, two-thirds were male, and 85% were white. Most of these children had experienced problems in school. Eighty percent of them had been identified by the schools as in need of special education services. The most frequent category was SED. These children also had a history of course failure (71.4%) and retention in grade (11.8%). Almost two-thirds of these children were taking medications to control their behavior. Over one-third had been adjudicated either because of contact with juvenile justice or child welfare. Over 60% of the children had been given a psychiatric classification.

At intake, the *Child Behavior Checklist* (CBCL; Achenbach, 1991) was completed by their parents. The CBCL contains 118 problem behaviors and respondents are asked to rate the presence or absence of these behaviors. For each child a Total Score, an externalizing problem score, and an internalizing problem score were calculated. Scores in excess of 63 are considered to be in the clinical range. The mean scores for the children were as follows: Total Score 72.41 (SD = 11.03), externalizing score 72.35 (SD = 10.66), and internalizing score 68.00 (SD = 13.09).

### Family Characteristics

A summary of the family characteristics appears in Table 5. Less than one half of these children came from intact families. Many of the parents were divorced (28.6%), widowed (14.3%), or separated (14.3%). At the time of intake, only one-third of these children lived with both parents. In over 20% of these families, guardianship of the child had been assumed by the state (17%) or the court (4.8%). Over one-third (36.8%) of the families were receiving some type of public assistance. A review of the records

TABLE 4. Characteristics of Referred Children

| Age in Years (100%) | | Medication (100%) | |
|---|---|---|---|
| Mean | 14 years | Yes | 61.9% |
| Range | 5 to 17 years | No | 38.1% |
| **Gender** (100%) | | **Adjudicated** (100%) | |
| Male | 66.7% | Yes | 38.1% |
| Female | 33.3% | No | 61.9% |
| **Race** (100%) | | **DSM Diagnosis** (61.9%) | |
| White | 85.6% | Yes | 61.5% |
| African American | 4.8% | No | 38.5% |
| Hispanic | 4.8% | | |
| Other | 4.8% | | |
| **Primary Educational Disability** (80%) | | | |
| Serious emotional disturbance | 80% | | |
| Learning disability | 20% | | |
| **Failed Courses** (66%) | | | |
| Yes | 71.4% | | |
| No | 28.6% | | |
| **Retained in Grade** (81%) | | | |
| Yes | 11.8% | | |
| No | 88.2% | | |

Note: Percentages in parentheses after each main entry indicate percentage of total N (21) for which data were available on this variable.

indicated that these families demonstrated significant histories that are likely to place children at risk for emotional and behavioral disorders.

## Service History

The children referred to this project had been frequent users of social services. At the time of intake these children were receiving an average of 1.95 social services (range 1-4). The primary agencies most involved with these children were mental health (81%), special education (76.2%), probation (42.9%), child welfare (33.3%), public aid (33.3%), and substance abuse (14.3%). The vast majority (81%) of these children had been placed outside their home on at least one occasion. The average out-of-home placements for these children was 3.7 separate placements.

## TABLE 5. Characteristics of Families of Referred Children

| Characteristics | % |
|---|---|
| Parent Marital Status (100%) | |
|     Married | 42.9 |
|     Divorced | 28.6 |
|     Widowed | 14.3 |
|     Separated | 14.3 |
| Child's Living Arrangement (100%) | |
|     Both parents | 33.3 |
|     Mother | 33.3 |
|     Parent and stepparent | 9.5 |
|     Group home | 9.5 |
|     Inpatient | 9.5 |
|     Residential | 4.8 |
| Guardianship of Child (100%) | |
|     Mother only | 42.9 |
|     Both parents | 33.3 |
|     State (child welfare) | 19.0 |
|     Court | 4.8 |
| Receiving Public Assistance (90%) | |
|     Yes | 36.8 |
|     No | 63.2 |
| Family Risk Factors (100%) | |
|     Mental illness | 28.6 |
|     Alcohol or drug abuse | 61.9 |
|     Criminal activity | 23.8 |
|     Family violence | 52.4 |

Note: Percentages in parentheses after each main entry indicate percentage of total N (21) for which data were available on this variable.

## CASE STUDY

### Child History

Franklin is a 14 year-old, African American boy who lives with his mother and older sister in a suburb of Chicago. He was referred to the CANDU Project just after his 13th birthday. At the time, Franklin had been involved with the juvenile justice system on 25 different occasions, with violations that included criminal damage to property, retail theft, battery, reckless conduct, and truancy. He had served time in the County Youth Home and in Audi Home, a locked detention facility, in Chicago. He had been hospitalized for psychiatric services on one occasion. He had been in special education for conduct and behavior problems since he was in third grade. When he was in fifth grade, he was placed in an alternative school for children with behavior disorders for approximately two years, where he was often truant and involved with criminal activities.

### Family History

Franklin's family life has been chaotic and unpredictable. When he was six years old, his parents separated due to the father's abusive treatment of all family members and his drug and alcohol problems. Consequently, his mother pursued long work hours and left Franklin in the care of older siblings. The family moved many times. They also experienced extreme financial difficulties that resulted in the mother filing for bankruptcy approximately one year prior to Franklin's admittance to the program. Franklin has two older brothers and a sister, all of whom have been involved with serious criminal activities and truancy. His sister has also been hospitalized for major depression.

Over the past year, many changes have occurred with this family. The father died from AIDS. The older brother moved to Chicago. The second oldest brother, at age 17, had a son of his own and moved in with his son's mother. His sister dropped out of school and became unemployed. The family moved several more times during the past year. During several family crises, the family members were all living in separate homes of friends or family members. They had no home of their own or means of transportation. Franklin was placed in an extended day school program where he demonstrated more aggression and hostile behaviors towards adults and peers. This aggression led to violations of his probation, and Franklin was placed again in the Youth Home. He was at imminent risk of placement in a residential care program.

### Family Strengths

Despite all their problems, Franklin and his family have significant strengths. Franklin is very engaging, likeable, and intelligent. He has started to pass courses in school. He has refrained from using drugs or alcohol or becoming involved with gangs. He is very concerned with and close to his mother and siblings. His mother also has many strengths, including her ability to find and keep work, her faith, her optimism, and her belief in her family. The other family members care a great deal for each other, are resourceful, and attend family meetings to try to improve their situation in life.

## Current Status

Currently, Franklin is living with his mother and his sister in an apartment. The family has a working, insured car, a telephone, furnishings, and food. Franklin has been doing well in school and is complying with all aspects of his unified service plan. A respite worker has started to assist him with recreation, supervision, and completion of his community service. He has been enrolled in a job training program for the summer. The family has been participating in family counseling, working on issues of personal boundaries and responsibilities. The mother has been employed in a stable job where she receives family benefits. Her financial status is better and she can provide for the family's home expenses, but she still has many significant legal obligations. The daughter has enrolled in school again. She has obtained pregnancy counseling and services as well as a part-time job. In addition, Franklin's brother and his family have been connected with young parenting programs and medical services.

## Collaboration

Over the course of the year, the child and family team met nine times. The team consists of Franklin, his mother, several family members, alternative school personnel, extended day school personnel, intensive probation workers, school family counselors, school individual counselors, school individual counselors, Franklin's individual counselor, and service coordinators from the CANDU Project. Additional community service providers have been contacted by family members or by service coordinators to assist the family. The additional services have included an African-American therapist for Franklin, food assistance through a local church, car repair assistance through a local church, financial counseling, housing assistance through Catholic Charities, connections for a car registration and personal licenses, medical appointments, legal and tax services, car insurance, medical insurance, banking, assistance with establishing Social Security Death Benefits, Veteran's Assistance, housing assistance, and assistance with furnishings/basic necessities.

## Funding

Funding for services has been obtained through the schools, mental health, and the juvenile probation department. (The mother will ultimately be responsible for what she can pay of the services provided by the probation department.) For non-categorical services, a local flexible fund assisted with transportation expenses, housing assistance, respite provision, and other types of "noncategorical expenses." Volunteer and charitable organizations also provided this family with support and assistance in many areas. To date, the costs of services for the year of community-based services have been approximately $44,500. Comparatively, if Franklin had been placed in a residential treatment facility, the costs would have been $61,300. Further, if Franklin had been placed out of community, no assistance would have been provided to other members of the family to meet their needs.

### Family Involvement

The family has been involved with the interagency process for about a year. As could be expected, the stress in the home contributed to chaos in planning. It was difficult to create meaningful plans in the midst of turmoil where follow-through by adults was next to impossible. A turning point came when a juvenile judge ordered that the mother's finances be turned over to the CANDU Project so that stable housing could be obtained. At that time, the staff were able to make important contributions and establish trust with the entire family. The family still has many issues that are unresolved and crises seem to be a family pattern. However, with time and support, these problems will be fewer and the family will be able to sustain itself.

*Service coordination.* This family demonstrates the "above and beyond" aspects of service coordination and family advocacy. Without the efforts of the CANDU Project in assisting the family with housing, Franklin would have been residentially placed for juvenile offenders. The service coordinators established a relationship with a family who were at first very unwilling to trust anyone from "the system." Further, the service coordinators were able to deliver basic needs and essential services for this family so that the mother could continue to work and provide for her family. The mother was so overwhelmed by what was needed to overcome her problems, she simply could not do it by herself. Further, the service coordinators advocated for Franklin and his family, in the face of mounting criticism and concern about Franklin and his behavior and the family's ability to supervise him. Finally, the service coordinators continued to hold meetings with key personnel to establish family-based goals for Franklin and his family, so that the service system could support the family in achieving their goals. Achieving balance within the context of multiple professional agendas has been a difficult, but essential element of service coordination for this family. An example of Franklin's unified service plan appears in Figure 1.

## DISCUSSION

The Children and Adolescents Network in DuPage (CANDU), within a relatively short period of time, has developed several of the components necessary to serve children with SED in community-based settings. For example, the collaboration across agencies at the executive directors, supervisors, and direct service providers levels facilitates the coordination of services for children. Second, the agreement on the target population definition and principles of care makes clear who is to be served by the project and how they are to be served. Third, the needs assessment data provided the county's policymakers with a rich source of information. The data identified (a) the emotional and behavioral challenges these children present to the system of care, (b) the major barriers to providing comprehensive services, and (c) the personnel and service needs required to work with the children and families in community settings. These data were used by community stakeholders to develop a strategic plan and an infrastructure that allows children with SED and their families to be served in community settings.

The intake data identified the multiple and complex needs evidenced by the children and their families. Specifically, over 60% were taking behavior controlling medication, almost 40% had been adjudicated, over 60% had a DSM-III R diagnosis, the vast majority of these children had had at least one out-of-home placement, and the children averaged almost four out-of-home placements. Moreover, almost all of the children came from broken homes and homes with significant histories of family and adult risk factors. These data are comparable to descriptions of children and families that receive services in other community-based programs (e.g., Epstein, Cullinan, Quinn, & Cumblad, 1994; Landrum, Singh, Nemil, Ellis, & Best, in press; Rosenblatt & Attkisson, 1992).

Although this project is not completed and child and family outcome data have not yet been collected, there is evidence to suggest that when a community provides intensive support, children with SED, even those with a history of out-of-home placements, can be treated in their own schools, homes, and communities. We believe that the success is related to three factors. First, the degree of collaboration on a system-wide basis and a case-by-case basis has allowed service needs and barriers to be identified and for coordinated resources and staff to address these needs and barriers to be forthcoming. Second, the service coordinator position fulfills a sig-

FIGURE 1. Example of Franklin's Unified Service Plan

## OPTIONS PLANNING FORM

Name: ___Franklin___                                                    Date: ___March 15, 1995___

Goal(s): _____

| Option | Description of Option | Responsible Person Agency | Funding | Target Dates | Transportation Costs |
|---|---|---|---|---|---|
| Housing | 2 bedroom with rent no higher than $630 | CANDU/Mother | Mother/Catholic Charities/Veterans Administration | Find by 4/30/95 | No charge |
| Community Service | Safety Town Community Center | CANDU/Probation | No charge | Locate site by 3/20/95 | No charge—Can walk to both |
| SSI—Death Disability | Get paperwork for mother to fill out; establish eligibility | CANDU/Mother | No charge | Forms filled out by 3/31/95 | No charge |
| Therapy | Individual & Family Therapy | Individual—Through Center Family—Through School | Flexible Fund School/Probation/ Health Dept. | 1 per week for 3 months starting 3/17/95 | No charge |
| Respite Care | Provide Franklin with positive role model to do activities with | Staff—Hired by CANDU | Flexible Fund | 6 hours per week for 3 months starting 3/20/95 | $30 per month |

Signature _____                                             Signature _____

115

nificant role in providing comprehensive services. These individuals are responsible for assuring that the needs of the children and families are met from a wide spectrum of public and private agencies. In this way, the service coordinators provide a unique perspective that helps to identify school and community resources and service barriers on a case-by-case basis. Finally, and most importantly, we believe that a major factor accounting for the project's success is the clear and specific commitment to the involvement of families in the planning and decision-making process. From an individualized care perspective, the child is considered to be at the center of a family unit and the family's needs and strengths should determine, in part, the priorities and selection of services.

The staff of the CANDU Project and the policymakers and service providers in DuPage County have participated in a systems reform effort that views services for children with SED as being community based, coordinated across agencies, and family centered. A number of significant milestones have been passed and several more are in sight on the horizon. The next step will be collecting and analyzing the 12 month outcome data on the children and families served. These data will indicate the effectiveness of this type of treatment approach.

## REFERENCES

Achenbach, T. M. (1991). *Manual for the child behavior checklist.* Burlington: University of Vermont, Department of Psychiatry.

Arizona Department of Health Services. (1991). *State of Arizona children's behavioral health services needs and resources assessment.* (A.R.S. Section 36-3421 and A.R.S. Section 36-3431-35). Arizona: Author.

Beachler, M. B. (1990). The mental health services program for youth. *The Journal of Mental Health Administration, 17,* 115-121.

Cumblad, C., Epstein, M. H., Quinn, K. P., & Soderlund, J. (in press). Parent's perceptions of services for children and youth with emotional and behavioral disorders. *Journal of Community Practice.*

Duchnowski, A. J. & Friedman, R. M. (1990). Children's mental health: Challenges for the nineties. *The Journal of Mental Health Administration, 17*(1), 3-12.

Epstein, M. H., Cullinan, D., Quinn, K. P., & Cumblad, C. (1994). Characteristics of children with emotional and behavioral disorders in community-based programs designed to prevent placement in residential facilities. *Journal of Emotional and Behavioral Disorders, 2,* 51-57.

Epstein, M. H., Cullinan, D., Quinn, K., & Cumblad, C. (1995). Personal, family, and service utilization characteristics of young people served by an interagency community-based system of care. *Journal of Emotional and Behavioral Disorders, 3,* 55-63.

Epstein, M. H., Nelson, C. M., Polsgrove, L., Coutinho, M., Cumblad, C., & Quinn, K. (1993). A comprehensive community-based approach to serving students with emotional and behavior disorders. *Journal of Emotional and Behavioral Disorders.*

Epstein, M. H., Quinn, K., Cumblad, C., & Holderness, D. (in press). Needs assessment of community-based services for children and youth with emotional or behavioral disorders and their families: Part 1. A conceptual model. *Journal of Mental Health Administration.*

Friedman, R. (1988). Strategies for conducting needs assessments based on system of care models. In P. Greenbaum, R. Friedman, A. Duchnowski, K. Kutash, & S. Silver (Eds.), *Children's mental health services and policy: Building a research base* (pp. 52-58). Tampa: Florida Mental Health Institute.

Friesen, B. J., & Koroloff, N. M. (1990). Family centered services: Implications for mental health administration and research. *Journal of Mental Health Administration, 17,* 13-25.

Jay, D. E., & Padilla, C. L. (1987). *Special education dropouts.* Menlo Park, CA: SRI International.

Jordan, D. D., & Hernandez, M. (1990). The Ventura planning model: A proposal for mental health reform. *The Journal of Mental Health Administration, 17,* 26-47.

Knitzer, J. (1993). Children's mental health policy: Challenging the future. *Journal of Emotional and Behavioral Disorders, 1,* 8-17.

Knitzer, Steinberg, Z., & Fleisch, B. (1990). *At the schoolhouse door: An examination of programs and policies for children with behavioral and emotional problems.* New York: Bank Street College of Education.

Landrum, T. J., Singh, N. N., Nemil, M. S., Ellis, C. R., & Best, A. M. (in press). Characteristics of children and adolescents with serious emotional disturbance in systems of care. Part II: Community-based services. *Journal of Emotional and Behavioral Disorders.*

Magrab, P. R., Young, T., & Waddel, A. (1985). *A community workbook for: Developing collaborative services for seriously emotionally disturbed.* Washington, DC: Georgetown University Child Development Center.

Neel, R. S., Meadows, N. V., Levine, P., & Edgar, E. B. (1988). What happens after special education. A statewide follow-up study of secondary students who have behavioral disorders. *Behavioral Disorders, 13,* 209-216.

Nelson, C. M., & Pearson, C. A. (1991). *Integrating services for children and youth with emotional and behavioral disorders.* Reston, VA: The Council for Exceptional Children.

Quinn, K. P., Epstein, M. H., & Cumblad, C. (1995). Developing comprehensively individualized community-based services for children and youth with emotional and behavior disorders: Direct service providers' perspectives. *Journal of Child and Family Studies, 4,* 19-42.

Quinn, K. P., Epstein, M. H., Cumblad, C., & Holderness, D. (in press). Needs assessment of community-based services for children and youth with emotional and behavioral disorders and their families: Part 2: Implementation in a local system of care. *Journal of Mental Health Administration*.

Rosenblatt, A., & Attkisson, C. (1992). Integrating systems of care in California for youth with severe emotional disturbance. III. Answers that lead to questions about out-of-home placements and the California AB377 project. *Journal of Child and Family Studies, 2*(2), 119-141.

Rosenblatt, A., & Attkisson, C. C. (1992). Integrating systems of care in California for youth with severe emotional disturbance. I. A descriptive overview of the California AB377 evaluation project. *Journal of Child and Family Studies, 1*, 93-113.

Stroul, B. (1985). *Child and adolescent service system program (CASSP) system change strategies, a workbook for status.* Washington, DC: CASSP Technical Assistance Center at Georgetown University.

Stroul, B. A., & Friedman, R. M. (1986). *A system of care for seriously emotionally disturbed children and youth.* Washington, DC: CASSP Technical Assistance Center.

U.S. Department of Education. (1992). *Fourteenth annual report to Congress on the Implementation of Public Law 94-142.* Washington, DC: U.S. Government Printing Office.

VanDenBerg, J. (1989). *The Alaska youth initiative.* Anchorage, AK: Department of Mental Health.

# School-Linked Services in Context: A Formative Evaluation of Linkages to Learning

Peter E. Leone
Sean A. Lane
Nancy Arllen

University of Maryland, College Park

Haifa Peter

Department of Social Services
Montgomery County, Maryland

**SUMMARY.** This paper describes a formative evaluation of a school-linked service delivery system for immigrant and low income families in a large suburban county in Maryland. Initially we discuss local needs that prompted the development of the program and we place problems with services for children and families with multiple needs in a broad context. Next we discuss the methods and results of the evaluation. Findings indicate the program provides a range of appropriate services to intended beneficiaries but that lack of infrastructure and articulated understandings among participating orga-

Address correspondence to: Peter Leone, Department of Special Education, University of Maryland, 1308 Benjamin Building, College Park, MD 20742.

The authors give special thanks to Dr. Carlos Mandulay, Ms. Agnes Leschner, parents, teachers, and LTL program staff for their cooperation and assistance in conducting the evaluation.

[Haworth co-indexing entry note]: "School-Linked Services in Context: A Formative Evaluation of Linkages to Learning." Leone, Peter E. et al. Co-published simultaneously in *Special Services in the Schools* (The Haworth Press, Inc.) Vol. 11, No. 1/2, 1996, pp. 119-133; and: *Emerging School-Based Approaches for Children with Emotional and Behavioral Problems: Research and Practice in Service Integration* (ed: Robert J. Illback, and C. Michael Nelson) The Haworth Press, Inc., 1996, pp. 119-133. Single or multiple copies of this article are available from The Haworth Document Delivery Service [1-800-342-9678, 9:00 a.m. - 5:00 p.m. (EST)].

nizations present potential problems. *[Article copies available from The Haworth Document Delivery Service: 1-800-342-9678.]*

Youth in the United States are at great risk, physically, and otherwise. In 1991, 21.8% of children under the age of 18 in the U.S. were living in poverty (Child Welfare League of America, 1992) and in 1992 over 2.9 million children were reported to Child Protective Services offices nation-wide as alleged victims of child abuse and/or neglect, with a substantiation rate of approximately 40% (McCurdy & Daro, 1993). Many youth are also at risk educationally. Less than 70% of youth who entered high school in 1986 graduated in 1990 (Annie E. Casey Foundation, 1993).

Knitzer (1982) estimated that of the approximately three million children in the United States with emotional difficulties, two-thirds are not receiving services. Others estimate that 14 to 20 percent of children ages birth to 18 have some type of mental health disorder and that three to five percent have a serious disorder (Stroul, 1993). While problems associated with emotional or behavioral difficulties challenge the capabilities of any family, minority families who are poor and have children with disabilities face monumental challenges, are vulnerable to systematic discrimination, and because they lack some material and social supports, are most devastated by these experiences. Those families, particularly the ones who have recently immigrated, often face an additional difficulty–"they do not speak the language of the school" (Harry, 1992, p. xiii).

This paper describes a formative evaluation of Linkages to Learning, a school-linked service delivery program based at an elementary school in a large suburban county in Maryland. After discussing needs of children and families in the county, we place the program in the context of similar programs and initiatives developed in recent years. We discuss the formation of the program, negotiations associated with the evaluation process, and describe methods and findings from our evaluation. We conclude with a discussion of the politics of program evaluation and school-linked services and emerging concepts in program evaluation.

## CHANGING FAMILIES, CHANGING NEEDS

Low income and immigrant families often have many service support needs. In meeting the needs of those families, it is critical to view the child in the context of the family and families in the context of their culture, community, and unique experiences. Programs which break from traditional bureaucratic roles and modes of service delivery while demonstrating cultural sensitivity, respect, and service flexibility, can meet the needs of those families (Schorr, 1989; Harry, 1992).

The challenges facing low income and immigrant families exist within a broad social context. Analysis of U.S Bureau of the Census data indicates that the relative poverty of children in the United States (as measured in relation to median family income) declined from the 1940s through the 1960s. After 1969, poverty rates for children increased to a level in 1988 that equaled rates of the late 1940s. Examining income inequality, the gap between children living in luxury and those in poverty increased dramatically in the 1980s (Hernandez, 1993). These data suggest that fewer material resources are available to the current generation of children than were available to previous generations.

While many existing programs for children and families have been developed during the past 20 years, they have not always responded in a manner sensitive to individual family needs. The federal government spent nearly 60 billion dollars in FY (fiscal year) 1989 on over 340 different programs serving children, while at the same time, state and local governments spent three times that amount. Typically, each program has its own eligibility criteria, and though families may need, and be entitled to, assistance from several programs, they are forced to deal with separate bureaucracies, file separate applications, and are evaluated multiple times in order to secure help (National Commission on Children, 1991).

Some children and families, in addition to experiencing emotional or other disabilities of a family member, may also wrestle with other difficulties, including poverty, abuse and neglect, malnutrition, and language or cultural barriers (Child Welfare League of America, 1992; Children's Action Alliance, 1990; Harry, 1992; National Commission on Children, 1991). In turn, those children and their families often interact with many different parts of the human services system. There has been substantial discussion in the literature of fragmented human service delivery and its inherent inefficiencies (Dryfoos, 1990, 1994; Huntze, 1988; National Commission on Children, 1991; Weissman, 1978). Families with multiple needs clearly require assistance from collaborative interagency programs (Katz-Leavy, Lourie, Stroul, & Zeigler-Dendy, 1992; Stroul, 1993).

Recently, in Montgomery County, Maryland, the number of low income and immigrant families has increased dramatically. The percentage of low income families receiving Aid for Families with Dependent Children (AFDC) increased 21% from 1990 to 1992, and the number of families receiving food stamps increased 35% during that same period. Further, average monthly enrollment in the Women's, Infant's, and Children's (WIC) program increased 48% from 1991 to 1992 and the number of applications for Housing Crisis Intervention was up nearly 50% from 1992 to 1993. In addition, Montgomery County has seen tremendous growth in the number of immigrant youth. According to Montgomery County Public Schools data, the enrollment of Asian students has increased almost 250% since 1980 and the Hispanic student population has more than tripled during that same period. Census data from 1990 show that Montgomery County residents who are Hispanic are younger, have lower incomes, and are more likely to have minor children living at home compared to all other racial or ethnic groups in the county (Montgomery County Government, 1993).

## DEVELOPMENT OF LINKAGES TO LEARNING

In 1991, the Montgomery County Council's Education Committee held hearings related to children at risk and their families. Findings from the hearings reported that children at risk in the county face many obstacles to academic success, such as poverty, poor health, physical or emotional abuse, and home conditions where foreign languages and cultures isolate their families from community resources. In November 1991, the Council urged the creation of three pilot programs focused on developing family preservation services and providing resources, including mental health services, for at risk children and their families. Furthermore, the Council advocated for the pilot sites to provide non-educational services through a school-based interagency collaboration model.

Linkages to Learning (LTL) was launched in early 1993 in response to the County Council's recommendations. The program has served over 400 families and almost 1000 children since its inception (Linkages to Learning, nd). According to an LTL brochure, "Linkages to Learning provides services to students and their families to improve the student's performance in the school, home, and community." LTL program sites include two elementary schools and a health services center at the International Student Admissions Office. Sites were selected based on location in an area where many of the students and their families are transient, immigrants, and English is not the language primarily spoken in the home. Through a flexible service delivery system, the program is designed to provide social services (including financial and food assistance), counseling, physical and mental health care, translation, and educational support. Agencies collaboratively serving LTL families and their children include the Montgomery County Public Schools and the Departments of Health; Addiction, Victim, and Mental Health Services; Social Services; Family Resources; Kensington Wheaton Youth Services; and the Community Psychiatric Clinic. While interagency collaboration seems the logical approach to address the complex needs of families, there is limited information on the efficacy of programs such as Linkages to Learning. Before discussing the formative evaluation of Linkages to Learning, we briefly examine other evaluations of school-linked services.

## EVALUATION OF SCHOOL-LINKED AND COMMUNITY-BASED SERVICES

A variety of models have been developed to offer comprehensive flexible services for children and their families in partnership with service agencies such as mental health, juvenile justice, education (Dryfoos, 1994; Gomby & Larson, 1992; Illback, 1993). Some are based in schools or within close proximity to schools, whereas others are offered elsewhere within the community while still maintaining a connection to the school (Behrman, 1992). While there is great intuitive appeal in comprehensive school-linked service models that address the myriad needs of students and their families, it is necessary to assess the effectiveness, efficiency of programs, and client satisfaction with new service arrangements (Larson, Gomby, Shiono, Lewit, & Behrman, 1992). The breadth of programs (single site, community-wide, or state-wide initiatives) and the diversity of services provided complicate an examination of school-linked evaluations.

An emerging literature base exists concerning school-linked services and community-based programs that serve students and their families through comprehensive and collaborative multiagency involvement (Gomby & Larson, 1992). At the present time, however, limited information exists on the evaluation of those programs (Barfield et al., 1994). Additionally, the goals of evaluation may differ over the course of a program (e.g., formative, summative) (Gomby & Larson, 1992), and desired outcomes of school-linked collaborative ventures (e.g., adopting truly collaborative philosophies) may take years to unfold (Barfield et al., 1994). Also, trends toward more comprehensive multi-agency collaborations with multiple outcomes (e.g., improved academic performance, coordinated provider relationships) may restrict the availability of evaluation data (Gomby & Larson, 1992). All of these considerations impede a comprehensive overview of evaluations of school-linked programs.

Many of the evaluations of school-linked programs are published locally and do not appear in professional journals or monographs. Some of these evaluations are described in *Partnerships for Care* (Cole & Poe, 1993) and *School-Linked Human Services* (General Accounting Office,

1993), documents describing the range of programs that exist and synthesizing findings from preliminary evaluations. Despite the small number of evaluations of comprehensive, school-linked services that exist, findings indicate several positive short-term results associated with new collaborative service systems (GAO, 1993; Philliber Research Associates, 1994). Evidence suggests that the placements of students in more restrictive settings (outside of the home, community, and state) are decreasing (Comprehensive Services Act, 1992) and the number of students living with their families is increasing in programs providing school-linked services (Cole & Poe, 1993). A number of other benefits that have been identified with school-linked programs include an increase in the stability of children's placements (students experiencing only one rather than multiple placements), decrease in the use of residential treatment or inpatient hospitalizations, fewer inpatient days, a lower number of hospital admissions, and an increase in the number of students fully integrated into public school programs (Cole & Poe, 1993).

Another benefit reported by evaluations of school-linked programs is improved academic achievement (GAO, 1993). An evaluation of the Walbridge Caring Community (St. Louis, MO) compared the reading performance (percentage change in reading grades) of intensively served Walbridge students with other Walbridge children and with a comparison group in another school. Results indicate that intensively served students made a significant improvement in comparison to the other groups (Philliber Research Associates, 1994). The Texas Communities in Schools project utilized school records to measure changes in grades and results reflected almost half of the students who were failing math or English prior to the project's implementation earned passing grades over the course of the study. Evaluations of other programs (e.g., Hillsdale County Elementary Success Program, Hillsdale County, MI; Project Pride, Joliet, IL; Focus on Youth, Los Angeles, CA) however, reflect nominal or inconclusive results with respect to academic performance (GAO,1993).

An objective of almost all comprehensive programs is an increase in family involvement and stakeholders' satisfaction with services. Several programs reflect greater degrees of family participation (Family Mosaic, CA), increased parent support and satisfaction (IMPACT, KY), and youth satisfaction with support services (New Directions, VT) (Cole & Poe, 1993).

While initial evaluations of school-linked programs are positive, more rigorous, systematic evaluations of these emerging service delivery options are needed. At the present time, each program serves distinct populations, defines outcomes differently, and consequently findings cannot be generalized to all school-linked multiservice programs (GAO, 1993).

## EVALUATION METHODOLOGY

Evaluation of school-linked services like Linkages to Learning requires methodology that is responsive to the characteristics of the children and families served. For the present study, the newly developed service system was still evolving and the methods used needed to focus on program implementation. The formative evaluation presented here has its roots in naturalistic inquiry, a field-based approach to systematic, qualitative investigations of educational and social services programs and social phenomena (Lincoln & Guba, 1985).

The team that conducted the evaluation reported here was approached by program staff for assistance in program evaluation. During a series of meetings, the purposes of an evaluation were negotiated between the University staff (the evaluation team) and the agencies participating in Linkages to Learning. In May 1994, a memorandum of understanding among the parties was drafted and signed by administrative heads of agencies participating in LTL and the evaluation team. The memorandum identified six broad questions to guide the evaluation process:

- To what extent does LTL provide the services identified in documents authorizing the creation of the program?
- To what extent does LTL serve the families that it was designed to serve?
- How satisfied are parents with the services they have received through LTL?
- What administrative structures within and across the cooperating agencies in Montgomery County facilitate or inhibit the services provided by LTL?
- How do teachers, support personnel, and administrators in the school perceive the work of LTL?
- How do students whose families receive services through LTL fare in school?

A primary purpose in conducting this evaluation was to determine the extent to which Linkages to Learning provided the services and met the needs of clients it was designed to serve. As a formative evaluation, the study attempted to examine the process through which services were provided, determine client and staff satisfaction with the program, and identify areas where more effective or efficient means of operating might be warranted. Because Linkages was still in its formative stages, questions such as, "Does Linkages have a positive effect on the academic performance of children whose families are served?" could not be definitively answered at that time. That question and others that attempt to investigate causal links between program practices and client outcomes can be answered through summative program evaluations and different research methods at a later date.

The primary field research activities included file reviews, individual and small group interviews, and "member check" meetings. Consent forms and interview protocols were translated into Spanish to provide informed and active participation of all families. The data collection and analysis was a cooperative endeavor in which information was shared regularly between the evaluators and program staff, and program staff were continually involved in the evaluation process.

### Participant Selection

In order to recruit student and parent participants, the evaluation team, with the assistance of LTL staff, sponsored an informal pizza dinner at the elementary school in June 1994. Following dinner, the staff explained to parents the purposes of the evaluation, the parent and child interviews, and file reviews that were part of the study. All parents and/or guardians who were interested in participating were included in the evaluation.

### File Review

After obtaining permission from parents or guardians, student files were reviewed to develop a profile of the students served by the program. Data were retrieved on demographic characteristics, attendance, retention, compensatory services such as special education, Title I enrollment, and free and reduced lunch status.

### Interviews

Data were collected from interviews with students, parents, staff, teachers, and administrators involved with Linkages. Most interviews were conducted at the school by two evaluation team members. Field notes were reviewed at the end of each interview session and preliminary findings were discussed at "member check" meetings with separate groups of parents, teachers, and the leadership team. These meetings were held to validate information obtained through interviews, clarify preliminary findings, and possibly obtain new information.

## Triangulation and Member Check

Triangulation is a procedure to improve the validity of findings and interpretations. Through multiple sources of information, an evaluation team attempts to confirm practices and understand differing perspectives. Member check is a method of reviewing findings and interpretations with members of the group who were involved as sources for information. It allows evaluators to clarify their interpretations and findings so that their work more clearly reflects the "realities" of the respondents. Members of the group can immediately clear up misinformation or misinterpretations and frequently this "playback" of information may spawn further information not discussed initially (Lincoln & Guba, 1985).

In October, 1994, a meeting between the evaluation team and parents involved with Linkages was held to discuss and clarify preliminary findings from parent interviews. Twenty parents participated in this meeting at the elementary school. Similarly, a meeting between teachers and evaluation team members was held in early November, 1994 to discuss and clarify findings from teacher interviews. Sixteen teachers volunteered their time to participate in the meeting. A similar meeting was held with the Leadership Group in September and served as a "member check" for this group.

## Data Analysis

Data analysis involved reviewing interview notes, program documents, aggregate data on student characteristics and student performance from the school systems' Department of Educational Accountability (DEA), and data retrieved from individual student's files. Interview data were reviewed to identify common themes, understandings, and beliefs of participants. The member check process, discussed briefly above, was used to confirm preliminary findings and elicit new information from respondents.

## FINDINGS

The findings from the evaluation centered around three broad areas of interest: (a) the services delivered by the program and the recipients of those services; (b) student, family, and staff satisfaction with the program; and (c) the structural and organizational aspects of the program that affect service delivery.

## Program Services and Recipients

The goal of Linkages to Learning (LTL) as described in program documents is to provide services or assist families and students in obtaining services that promote successful experiences for children in school, at home, and in the community. File reviews and interviews revealed that Linkages provided counseling, social services, health care, and educational support for children and families. For many families, initial contact involved securing medical assistance. Often families sought other services including English classes, general guidance and support from Linkages' staff, and child counseling. An area of concern voiced in several interviews was that Linkages had difficulty meeting the demand for child and family mental health services. By and large, information from interviews confirmed that LTL was providing the range of services it was created to provide.

Documents developed and distributed by Linkages define the target population for LTL intervention as children and their families who have "multiple risk factors." These include, but are not limited to, cultural/ethnic isolation, school failure, poverty, and lack of access to health care. Parent and student interviews and review of school and system records indicated that Linkages serves students and their families who closely resemble the target population. An examination of the records of 613 students enrolled in the school at the start of the 1993-1994 school year showed that almost two-thirds of the students were minorities and over half of the student body received free or reduced lunch. Additionally, over one-third of the students were receiving Title I services and about one in six students were attending ESOL classes. Review of a sample of files of students whose families receive LTL services revealed that Linkages-involved students were more likely to be enrolled in entitlement programs such as ESOL and free or reduced lunch than their classmates at the school. The one exception was students receiving Title I services where slightly fewer LTL students were enrolled. Absenteeism rates were virtually identical between the sample of Linkages-involved students and their classmates. Further, according to LTL reports, about two out of three Linkages-involved families receive some program assistance in securing medical assistance.

### Satisfaction with the Program

Nearly all who were involved with Linkages to Learning had positive things to say about the program and believed that it was responding well to the needs of the community. The parents interviewed believed that Linkages was a valuable asset to the school and the community. Parents described LTL staff as honest, hard working, and respectful. Most parents used the school as the source for gaining access to, or finding out about,

Linkages, while others reported inquiring about Linkages on their own or were referred to LTL by a friend.

Evaluation team members also spoke with several students whose families received assistance from Linkages to Learning. When asked about Linkages, the students also responded with positive comments about the program. One student commented that the Linkages staff member with whom he worked is "good with family problems" and "helps people with problems." In addition, there appeared to be no stigma attached to receiving services from LTL. Students apparently viewed Linkages as part of their school experience.

Linkages to Learning received high marks from school staff and program staff for its "cut the tape to make it happen" philosophy. Overall, the teachers interviewed see Linkages as a positive addition to the school and the community at large. Teachers spoke of improved parent involvement in school and more freedom to focus on instruction rather than on "social work" issues.

### Structure and Organization of the Program

While Linkages to Learning provides a range of services to its intended beneficiaries and is very well received by the community, the structure and organization of the program reflects the difficulty of developing school-linked services. Interviews with direct care staff indicated that the ability of LTL to serve clients is hampered at times by a lack of central decision-making and fiscal autonomy. Staff reported that parent or participating agencies requested documentation which required duplication of efforts. Often staff were required to provide identical data to agencies on different forms. There appeared to be no Memorandum of Understanding among agencies and departments participating in Linkages to Learning. While implicit expectations and *ad hoc* relationships have developed during the first two years of the program, lack of clarity about the roles of the various agencies and departments contributing to the development of Linkages inhibits the program's ability to provide direct services. Recently, following the presentation of the evaluation report, members of the Leadership Group scheduled a meeting to draft a Memorandum of Understanding.

Another structural concern that we noted in our interviews and file reviews, was that LTL has no operating budget and staff must go 'hat in hand' to parent agencies for even the most basic office supplies. LTL has no clerical support and has experienced lengthy delays in receiving requested materials from participating agencies. The discretionary monies that Linkages does have are strictly used for client support.

Many respondents discussed communication between school and program staff. Many teachers expressed a desire to know more about Linkages' involvement with a student and the family after a teacher initiates a referral. Linkages and school personnel see confidentiality, scheduling conflicts, and a lack of clear school policy as factors that inhibit communication among LTL staff and teachers.

## DISCUSSION

Children and families whose needs transcend the boundaries and eligibility criteria of traditional educational, health, social service, and mental health agencies can be difficult to serve effectively. The evidence suggests that Linkages to Learning, developed by several departments and agencies of the Montgomery County Government, the Montgomery County Public Schools, and private agencies, is a well integrated, school-linked, service delivery system for children and their families. Those participating in this evaluation were almost unanimous in their praise for Linkages' ability to reach families, meet their needs, and get many things done in an expeditious manner.

Linkages' staff were cited for creative problem solving, sensitivity and honesty in working with families, and persistence in responding to difficult situations. School staff felt that with the support from LTL, parents were more inclined to become involved in their child's education and in turn, be more supportive of the school's efforts.

Several concerns were identified during the course of the evaluation. The role of the Leadership Group, fiscal and administrative support for Linkages' staff, and communication between Linkages' staff and the teaching and support staff at the school were all problem areas. The Leadership Group, instrumental in getting Linkages' off the ground, needs to define a role for itself that is supportive of Linkages' activities without micro-managing the program. Uniform data collecting and reporting requirements for all participating departments and agencies need to be developed. Program staff require an operating budget and decision-making authority. Leadership and greater resources are needed in providing mental health services to children and their families.

Improved communication between Linkages' staff and the school staff is needed. LTL staff should increase their participation and visibility in school meetings and activities. In turn, the school staff need to provide additional information about Linkages in teacher handbooks, at school functions, and school, newsletters. In particular, parents of all children at the elementary school, including those not receiving services, need to be made aware of the program. While some efforts have been made to publicize Linkages, staff reported that families new to the school were unaware of Linkages' existence. With regard to sharing information about particular students and/or families, Linkages' staff and the school staff need to develop guidelines to promote the flow of appropriate information and at the same time ensure that they protect students' and families' rights to privacy. Under current practices, some teachers are unaware of who is being served and how they might be able to help.

Some of the problems we noted in this report are to be expected when programs involving professionals from different agencies collaborate to develop a new service delivery system. At this preliminary stage in the evolution of school-linked services in Montgomery County, Linkages to Learning is an innovative service delivery system. Evidence suggests that the program is doing a good job of responding to the needs of the school's students and their families. Continued administrative support, greater resources for mental health services, and improved communication among all parties will ensure the continued success of the Linkages to Learning program.

### A Final Note

School-linked services and programs, like Linkages to Learning, require a common philosophy among all participating agencies and service providers. Local government officials, agency heads, and direct care staff must subscribe to a shared responsibility for providing assistance for low income and immigrant students and their families. Programs such as Linkages to Learning are an integral part of cost avoidance and secondary prevention. When incipient problems and needs among elementary school children and their families can be identified and appropriate services provided, subsequent difficulties including school failure and medical crises can be averted.

Linkages was created by reassigning staff and reallocating resources among agencies to create the new service delivery system. The only new monies allocated for the program involved a small pool of discretionary monies for client support.

While the evaluation team received wide-spread support in conducting our work and presenting our findings, one major stakeholder had concerns about the validity of our findings. Recommendations contained in our evaluation report were viewed as a threat to one of the participating agencies. Through a process of negotiation with this stakeholder, the evaluation team was able to present findings to local government officials in a manner that didn't threaten the security of a key player.

New ways of doing business require new ways of thinking about clients, how to serve them, and our relationships to them and other professionals. Those concerned with the welfare of children and families experiencing difficulties in an increasingly complex and technical society, need to work together, listen to the children and families with whom we work, and carefully evaluate both the means of providing services and the outcomes experienced by our clients.

## REFERENCES

Annie E. Casey Foundation, Center For The Study of Social Policy. (1993). *Kids count data book.* Washington, DC: Author.

Barfield, D., Brindis, C., Guthrie, L., McDonald, W., Philliber, S., Scott, B. (1994). *The Evaluation of New Beginnings.* San Diego: Department of Social Services.

Behrman, R.E. (1992). Introduction. *The Future of Children: School linked services,* 2(1), 4-5.

Child Welfare League of America. (1992). *Building partnerships: Schools and agencies advancing child welfare practices.* Washington, DC: Author.

Children's Action Alliance. (1990). *A framework for child welfare reform in Arizona.* Phoenix, AZ: Author. (ERIC Document Reproduction Service No. ED 334 005)

Cole, R.F., & Poe, S.L. (1993). *Partnerships for care: System of care for children with serious emotional disturbances and their families.* Washington, DC: Washington Business Group on Health.

*Comprehensive Services Act for At Risk Youth and Families: A Report to the Governor and General Assembly.* (December, 1992). Richmond, VA.

Dryfoos, J.G. (1990). *Adolescents at risk.* New York: Oxford University Press.

Dryfoos, J.G. (1994). *Full service schools: A revolution in health and social services for children, youth, and families.* San Francisco: Jossey-Bass.

Gomby, D.S., & Larson, C.S. (1992). Evaluation of school-linked services. *The Future of Children: School Linked Services,* 2(1), 68-84.

Harry, B. (1992). *Cultural diversity, families, and the special education system.* New York: Teachers College Press.

Hernandez, D.J. (1993). *America's children: Resources from family, government, and the economy.* New York: Russell Sage Foundation.

Huntze, S.L. (1988). Cooperative interface of schools and other child care systems for behaviorally disordered students. In M.C. Wang, M.C. Reynolds, and H.J. Walberg (Eds.), *The handbook of special education: Research and practice (Vol. 2).* (pp. 195-217). Oxford, England: Pergamon.

Illback, R.J. (1993). *Formative evaluation of the Kentucky family resource and youth service centers: A descriptive analysis of program trends.* Louisville, KY: R.E.A.C.H. of Louisville, Inc.

Katz-Leavy, J.W., Lourie, I., Stroul, B., & Zeigler-Dendy, C. (1992). *Individualized services in a system of care.* Washington, DC: CASSP Technical Assistance Center, Georgetown University.

Knitzer, J. (1982). *Unclaimed children.* Washington, DC: Children's Defense Fund.

Larson, C.S., Gomby, D.S., Shiono, P.H., Lewit, E.M., & Behrman, R.E., (1992). Analysis. *The Future of Children: School Linked Services, 2*(1), 6-18.

Lincoln, Y.S., & Guba, E.G. (1985). *Naturalistic Inquiry.* Newbury Park, CA: Sage.

McCurdy, K., & Daro, D. (1993). *Current trends in child abuse reporting and fatalities: The results of the 1992 annual fifty state survey.* Chicago, IL: National Committee for Prevention of Child Abuse.

Montgomery County Government. (1993). *Trends in Youth Population in Montgomery County* (1993). Rockville, MD: Department of Family Resources, Division of Children, Youth, and Families, Author.

National Commission on Children. (1991). *Beyond rhetoric: A new American agenda for children and families: Final report of the National Commission on Children.* Washington, DC: Author.

Philliber Research Associates, (1994). *An Evaluation of the Caring Communities Program At Walbridge Elementary School.* St. Louis, MO.: Author.

Schorr, L. (1989). *Within our reach: Breaking the cycle of disadvantage.* New York: Doubleday.

Stroul, B. (1993). *Systems of care for children and adolescents with severe emotional disturbances: What are the results?* Washington, DC: CASSP Technical Assistance Center.

United States General Accounting Office. (1993) *School-linked human services: A comprehensive strategy for aiding students at risk of school failure* (GAO/HRD-94-21). Washington, DC. Author.

Weissman, H. H. (1978). *Integrating services for troubled families.* San Francisco: Jossey-Bass.

# Restructuring Schools Through the Wraparound Approach: The LADSE Experience

Lucille Eber

La Grange (IL) Area Department
of Special Education

**SUMMARY.** The La Grange Area Department of Special Education's (LADSE) Wraparound Project (WRAP) is a five year school-based systems change initiative for students with emotional and behavioral disabilities (EBD) and their families. WRAP is focused on improving outcomes for these students and their families by converting the existing categorical special education and mental health services into a more integrated and flexible system (Eber, 1993). This systems change initiative culminated in the restructuring of special education programs into the LADSE EBD Network beginning with the 1994-95 school year. This network embodies the wraparound approach and integrates mental health, education and other family-focused services in a comprehensive school-based model. This article describes the progressive development of wraparound pilots and projects and the resulting restructured education service network which has been developed in the LADSE community. Evaluation data, which has been used to shape decision-making throughout the development of the LADSE EBD Network, is discussed in the context of the systems change process. Implications for the field are also considered. *[Article copies available from The Haworth Document Delivery Service: 1-800-342-9678.]*

---

Address correspondence to: Lucille Eber, LADSE, 1301 West Cossitt Avenue, La Grange, IL 60525.

[Haworth co-indexing entry note]: "Restructuring Schools Through the Wraparound Approach: The LADSE Experience." Eber, Lucille. Co-published simultaneously in *Special Services in the Schools* (The Haworth Press, Inc.) Vol. 11, No. 1/2, 1996, pp. 135-149; and: *Emerging School-Based Approaches for Children with Emotional and Behavioral Problems: Research and Practice in Service Integration* (ed: Robert J. Illback, and C. Michael Nelson) The Haworth Press, Inc., 1996, pp. 135-149. Single or multiple copies of this article are available from The Haworth Document Delivery Service [1-800-342-9678, 9:00 a.m. - 5:00 p.m. (EST)].

Wraparound approaches have gained recent attention as a means to improve services and outcomes for students with EBD and their families (Burchard, Burchard, Sewell & VanDenBerg 1993; Cole & Poe, 1993; Lourie, 1994; Stroul, 1993). Mental health and child welfare have been the more usual points of entry for this approach which involves individualized services for specific needs of students. Family Preservation Initiatives, CASSP Projects, Robert Wood Johnson sites and others embarking on this new way of organizing and providing services have expressed concerns and sometimes frustrations about their attempts to partner with education in this process. Education, mental health, social service and other providers are struggling with lack of agreement on prioritized target populations, financial challenges, liability and coordination of resources (Eber, Osuch & Redditt, under review).

In communities where systems of care principles are functioning well, there is marginal and cautious involvement with education (Lourie, 1994). Education's involvement has been described as ". . . limited to one school," ". . . last to join the partnership," ". . . never been full partners" and ". . . not directly involved in systems change" (Lourie, 1994). Although schools in these communities frequently refer students to interagency systems, they reportedly have not coordinated their own programs with the interagency system. Education tends to see these interagency efforts as merely a process they can tap into ". . . to get help with bothersome children" (Lourie, 1994).

The current debate on school inclusion for all students with disabilities (Fuchs & Fuchs, 1994) reinforces as well as complicates the incorporation of the wraparound approach into systems providing services for students with emotional or behavioral disabilities (EBD). The emphasis on more inclusive school options for all students has heightened educators awareness that more natural environments with specialized supports can be beneficial for students with EBD (Bullock & Gable, 1994). However, students with EBD often are the last group considered when inclusive school options are discussed and planned for at the school building level (Guetzloe, 1994; Maroney, 1994; Price, 1994).

A report of community-based individualized treatment programs raises questions about school administrators and teachers receptivity to implementing the strategies and interventions needed for these students in natural school settings (Clarke, Schaefer, Burchard & Welkowitz, 1992). Educators have articulated concerns about the unconditional care and natural environment tenets of wraparound. They fear that wraparound may force school inclusion for a population of students many educators currently are not prepared to accept in integrated settings. Furthermore, federal special education mandates make educators anxious about liability and fiscal responsibility for providing services in the full array of life domain services identified in wraparound planning. These issues create challenges for the comprehensive and sometimes nontraditional aspects of wraparound in the educational system.

## WRAPAROUND WITHIN LADSE

### The LADSE Community

LADSE is a special education cooperative providing services to 16 school districts in the southwest suburbs of Chicago. The member school districts include 54 school buildings and approximately 24,000 students. The districts represent a range of socio-economic levels from upper-middle class to lower-middle class. Minority representation in LADSE districts is varied, but overall, low. Several districts have small (maximum 15%) African American or Hispanic representation. About 1.5% of the total student population is identified as EBD. This EBD classification is equivalent to the federal special education category of severe emotional disturbance (SED) defined by the Individuals with Disabilities Act (IDEA).

LADSE schools have a history of inclusion for students with disabilities, as no separate centers or schools ever have been established. Self-contained classrooms have been the most restrictive option for students with disabilities in the public schools. Private day school settings have been accessed for some students. Historically, the high schools have used this type of placement at a greater rate than the elementary schools.

### Program Development

For the past 4 years, LADSE has implemented school and community-based wraparound approaches through projects that are integrated into the larger local and state special education, mental health, and social service systems. LADSE's Wraparound Project (WRAP) evolved from the initial 1990-91 pilot which began by integrating mental supports for students and families through school programs. During the 1990-91 pilot, a Coordinating Council was formed, consisting of policy makers, service providers, families and community representatives. WRAP progressed to an interagency systems change process by expanding the Council into the Wraparound Interagency Network (WIN) through a grant awarded to LADSE by the U.S. Department of Education in November, 1991. A coalition of families and public/private providers from the fields of education, mental health, social services, and juvenile justice, came together through WIN to assist in the development and implementation of comprehensive community-based wraparound plans for students and families. In July, 1993, WRAP expanded by initiating the Wraparound in Schools (WAIS) component with a grant from the Illinois State Board of Education (ISBE). WAIS brought the wraparound approach directly into schools where students with EBD were placed in self-contained special education programs.

The experiences of these initiatives led to a restructured educational system for students with EBD in the LADSE schools at the beginning of the 1994-95 school year. Based on WAIS experiences, a new configuration of supports and services was developed by LADSE as a response to schools' and families' requests for more comprehensive options. This newly structured delivery system is called the LADSE EBD Network and represents the integration of the wraparound approach into school service options for students with EBD and their families. The LADSE EBD Network facilitates wraparound planning and implementation for students in self-contained EBD classrooms as well as students with EBD who are included in their home schools.

### Conceptual Foundations

Implementation of wraparound through the LADSE WRAP Project and the resulting EBD Network is based on principles defined by the International Initiative on the Development, Training and Evaluation of Wraparound Services (1992). Network (WRAP) teams facilitate strength-based plans between school and home, support and advocate for parents, and develop new resources for students. Table 1 summarizes how these principles of wraparound are prioritized and applied in the development and implementation of comprehensive wraparound plans for students and their families.

WRAP teams focus on student/family strengths while developing plans that typically require providing services *differently* in contrast to the traditional approach of providing progressively more *restrictive* services. The wraparound planning process encourages flexible use of resources and freedom to go beyond the barriers of the traditional system. The goal is to actualize Knitzer's (1993) concept of "rethinking intensity" by creating effective networks of supports around students and families in more natural settings. Students have been deflected or returned from residential placements and others have been included more effectively in natural school settings (including regular education classes). Prevention of special

TABLE 1. Principles of Wraparound as Prioritized and Implemented by WRAP

| PRINCIPLES OF CARE | IMPLEMENTATION CHARACTERISTICS |
|---|---|
| BUILDING PARENT PARTNERSHIPS | Parent-driven planning process<br>Relationship that is parent focused, not problem focused<br>Respect parents as equal partners<br>Earn trust of parents<br>In-home parent support<br>Supports to parent in meeting his/her own needs<br>Parent to parent services<br>Families have home phone number or pager number of FSF |
| STRENGTHS FOCUSED | Strengths of child & families identified & used as integral piece of wraparound planning<br>Support to prepare & empower parents at WRAP meetings<br>Continuous reframing of parent/professionals intent/abilities<br>Model strength focus, not problem/deficit focus<br>Reframe negative statements into positive strength based statements |
| INDIVIDUALIZED PLANNING | Culturally competent planning & implementation of plans in 3 or more life domains<br>Facilitate communication between parent & school<br>Consultation & wraparound of planning facilitation<br>Facilitate mental health support to school teams<br>Observation in classroom to support student in development of wraparound plan<br>Intensive care facilitation<br>Interagency modeling & encouraging coalition/team building<br>Resource development |
| NATURAL ENVIRONMENTS | Facilitate school inclusion & additional school services<br>Facilitate increased community recreation participation<br>Access to art, drama, tutoring, etc.<br>Assistance to obtain jobs<br>Assistance to families in accessing medical services needed<br>Advocate with parents to secure any publicly provided services |
| UNCONDITIONAL CARE | Never give up<br>Empowering with knowledge<br>Training in normal child development, training in youth's disability, training in youth's diagnosis<br>Trying plan after plan, sticking with child/family through unsuccessful interventions, analyzing & learning from these, & revising plans as needed<br>Seeing plan as failing/not the child<br>Advocacy support<br>Viewing crises as opportunity for family & student needs to be met<br>Develop agency counterparts to be teammate for each family |
| FLEXIBLE FUNDING | Paid parent partners, youth buddies, recreational coaches<br>Purchase services or resources needed by family |

education placement has also been achieved for some students (Eber, Osuch, Redditt, under review).

## The LADSE EBD Network

One year of WAIS implementation in three schools clearly illustrated that strength-based wraparound planning promoted more creative and effective supports and interventions for students in self-contained EBD classes. New partnerships with families and new roles for personnel in schools were having a positive impact. Fourteen out of 19 students in the 1993-94 WAIS research cohort moved to or were maintained successfully in less restrictive school settings. Similar success with less restrictive environments also were noted for the WIN students (Eber, Osuch, Redditt, under review).

As a result of these WIN and WAIS experiences, LADSE restructured its special education program to offer wraparound approaches and supports for students identified with or at-risk of EBD. LADSE resources and positions for the 1994-95 school year were reorganized to support this new approach for students with EBD in a variety of school settings, including regular education. Concurrently, WIN began merging into the local area networks (LANs) formed throughout Illinois as part of a system of care reform plan. Two LANs began accepting referrals for interagency wraparound-based service plans in February, 1995.

The 1994-95 LADSE EBD Network includes three levels of service with the flexibility to create services across a variety of school settings. Intensity of service or complexity of student disability does not dictate level of restrictiveness of placement through the Network. The Network provides supports to students in regular education, resource and inclusion settings. It is interesting to note that students served through the Network are similar in clinical functioning to those who entered the LADSE WRAP Project through WIN because of return from or at-risk of out-of-home placements. A review of clinical measures of students involved in the LADSE Network and restrictiveness of their placements as well as those involved in the WIN research cohort indicated that type of educational placement is not associated with emotional and behavioral functioning.

The EBD Network allows for the integration of wraparound approaches and new types of services through a variety of school settings. Individually designed wraparound plans focus on interventions that maximize natural school resources and supports while also addressing family needs and community functioning. Table 2 illustrates the variety of services delivered through the Network during 1994-95. These services are similar to

TABLE 2. LADSE EBD Network–Examples of Services Provided Through School-Based Wraparound Plans

| Student Services | School Services | Family Services | Community Services |
|---|---|---|---|
| Develop behavior change programs | Coverage for in-school to prevent out-of-school suspensions | Home visits | Recreational coaching |
| Develop transition plans for high school | In-school respite: | Accompany parents & students to court | Develop transition plans for high school |
| Medication management |   lunchrooms | Facilitate the completion of needed neurological and psychiatric evaluations | Business partnerships: |
| Secure peer buddies |   PE class | Facilitate communication between home and school |   Subway Sandwiches |
| After school tutoring |   recess | Support for families in crisis |   Brookfield Zoo |
| Develop home/school homework plans |   computers | Provide transportation to needed appointments |   Bank One |
| Develop transition plans into regular ed |   library | Secure before school child care |   Target Store |
| |   art | Accompany parents & students to doctor's |   Sign Source |
| | Technical assistance: | Referral to the LANs | Community Service liaison to provide: |
| |   Changing roles of school-based staff | Develop home behavior plans |   Christmas tree & gifts |
| |   Inclusion of EBD students | |   Rent waiver to avoid eviction |
| |   Clinical consultation | |   Funds to pay utilities |
| |   Case review opportunities | |   Drug screening |
| |   Behavioral programming | |   Recreation activities |
| |   Dealing with resistance | |   Mentoring by police |
| |   Developing school wraparound plans | |   Mental health agencies |
| | Provide substitutes to assure teacher participation at meetings | | Develop Community Resource Directory |
| | Crisis intervention at school | | |
| | Individual observations and behavior programming | | |
| | Academic testing | | |
| | Coordinate out-of-school supports | | |

services provided through the community-based WIN Network, especially with regard to families.

The EBD Network was implemented by restructuring roles of special educators. Examples of these new roles include:

- Special education teachers, supervisors and coordinators beginning to function as *wraparound facilitators and school-based case managers* to coordinate individual wraparound plans inside schools.
- The availability of mobile *team teachers* provides support for special education and regular classroom teachers as they form teams around students and develop and implement more inclusive wraparound plans for the school day. The availability of team teachers allows for planning time and co-teaching, assistance with classroom observations, development of behavior intervention plans, co-teaching in regular education classes, modeling of intervention and instructional strategies.
- Special education social worker positions were restructured into *family service facilitators*. The family service facilitator role is designed to assist school personnel in brokering services and creating true partnerships with families. Family linkages with community services have been critical to effective school-based wraparound.
- Teacher assistants take on the more mobile and flexible role of *in-school respite workers*, moving around the school to support teachers and students in more integrated settings. In-school respite workers are flexible to assist with transitions or support students and teachers in classroom settings. In addition to individual behavior supports in regular education settings, respite workers facilitate information sharing among team members throughout the school, coordinate effective peer support plans, and provide academic tutoring or other services needed to implement an individual wraparound plan.

An overall focus of LADSE's EBD Network is to help school teams stay focused on student strengths and normalized needs. This can allow school teams to pursue innovative strategies using more natural supports and settings. The Network team can provide the extra hands-on support needed as teachers transition from their categorical positions into more flexible roles needed to facilitate comprehensive wraparound plans for students and families.

### Ongoing Program Evaluation

The evaluation process is an ongoing attempt to review the impact of the developing system of care and provides a view of the program development changes which have occurred. Beginning in 1993-94, standardized data collection on Project WRAP began as part of a statewide evaluation of school-based systems change projects conducted through LADSE. WIN and WAIS students were entered into the database during 1993-94. Students in the LADSE EBD Network who were not previously in WIN or WAIS began entering the data base in September, 1994. Currently, 57 students are in the LADSE data base.

A format for charting services was used during the 1993-94 school year. This procedure was refined from 1991-93 WRAP evaluation procedures (Eber & Osuch, 1994). Services were classified retrospectively by examining the student and family wraparound plan. Twenty-seven services were classified into four categories: respite, teacher supports, family supports and referral and coordination of community resources. Table 3 lists the 1993-94 services by category. Continued review provided through application of the wraparound process led to useful restructuring strategies as the EBD Network was developed. A March, 1995 review of EBD Network students indicated that 85% are involved with community mental health providers and 95% of the school-based wraparound plans include supports for families.

The Child Behavior Checklist (CBCL), the Teacher's Report Form (TRF), the Child and Adolescent Functional Assessment Scale (CAFAS), and Demographic Risk Factors are used to assess students' level of behavioral and emotional functioning. Twenty-one of the 47 LADSE EBD Network students were included in a preliminary analysis of a statewide evaluation which included five other sites in Illinois. Thirty-five students served by WIN and WAIS pilots during 1993-94 also are included. Seventy percent of the LADSE students in this statewide evaluation scored in the clinical range for Internalizing Behavior and 81.5 percent scored in the clinical range for Externalizing Behavior on the CBCL. Seventy-four percent of the students were in the clinical range for Internalizing Behavior and 90 percent were in the clinical range for Externalizing Behavior on the TRF. The clinical presentation of this sample seems to be similar to those of students in the statewide evaluation as well as those reported by other studies of students involved in wraparound (Duchnowski, Johnson, Hall, Kutash, & Freidman, 1993).

Educational placements are recorded for students at time of referral and at six month intervals thereafter. Placement options range from the most restrictive (psychiatric hospital and residential) to the least restrictive (regular education). Educational data from 1993-94 for WIN and WAIS students at Time 1 (referral ) and Time 2 (1994) indicate that six students had moved to "more restrictive" settings (e.g., regular education to self-con-

TABLE 3. Percent of Cases Receiving Various Services for 1993-94

| Service Type | % |
|---|---|
| **Family Supports** | |
| Home/School communication | 94.6 |
| Support parents at school meetings | 94.6 |
| Reframe families at school meetings | 91.9 |
| Meet family needs | 83.8 |
| Crisis interventions | 27.0 |
| Parent to parent services | 27.0 |
| Family advocacy | 18.9 |
| Parent network | 18.9 |
| **Referral and Coordination** | |
| Reframe students at school meetings | 97.3 |
| Mental health services | 59.5 |
| Inclusion in regular ed classes | 37.8 |
| Community-based tutors | 13.5 |
| Resource development | 10.8 |
| **Respite Services** | |
| Recreation coaching | 43.2 |
| Regular ed class support–behavior | 32.4 |
| Respite–project funded | 27.0 |
| After school tutoring–at home | 21.6 |
| In-school tutoring | 21.6 |
| Respite–agency funded | 21.6 |
| Regular education support–academic | 13.5 |
| In-home community respite | 13.5 |
| In-home project respite | 10.8 |
| After school tutoring–at school | 10.8 |
| **Teacher Supports** | |
| WRAP planning with school team | 86.5 |
| Implement WRAP plan | 78.4 |
| Class coverage for WRAP planning | 48.6 |
| Class coverage for teacher planning | 32.4 |
| Team teaching in regular education | 5.4 |

tained class), 18 students had moved to "less restrictive" settings (e.g., self-contained class to regular education) and 17 students showed "no change" in their placements (one student dropped out and two students moved). The number of students in regular education at Time 2 nearly tripled and the number of students in LD resource doubled. Of the 17 students whose level of restrictiveness did not change, five were in regular education, four were in EBD classrooms, three were in cross-categorical classrooms, three were in LD resource, one was in day treatment and one was in a classroom for students with developmental disabilities.

The 1994-95 LADSE EBD Network includes 19 students in Level 1 (self-contained) and 27 students in Level 2. The Level 2 students include 22 receiving resource support and 5 receiving other special education program support. A preliminary analysis of placements in March, 1995 indicated that students in the Network had zero days of hospitalization and zero days of homebound instruction.

## IMPLICATIONS

The experiences of one school system's efforts to use system of care concepts and wraparound practices suggests new directions for schools. Additionally, application of wraparound through a school-based approach offers insights that can extend beyond the educational arena. LADSE's WRAP experiences have policy and program development implications that may be useful for other school systems and communities involved in changing system responses and outcomes for children with EBD and their families.

*Schools and communities need to adopt specific strategies for moving from using wraparound as a crisis response (i.e., when institutional place-ments have occurred or are imminent) to using wraparound as an ap-proach for preventing the escalation of EBD and out-of-home placements.* Many of the services provided to students with significant EBD through LADSE, including respite, in-home family supports, community mentors, advocacy, classroom assistance, and teacher support should be provided earlier to prevent acceleration of EBD and movement to more restrictive placements. This prevention capacity is suggested by the evaluation of students who received wraparound through the WAIS component of WRAP during 1993-94. Mental health providers can offer a variety of types of respite, in-home family services and school-based services along with traditional therapy and out-patient services. Special education may want to consider more flexible use of teachers, classroom assistants, and school social workers so that individual needs can be met in more natural settings based on the strengths of the child. Wraparound plans that address multiple life domains, existing resources, and natural supports creatively have become standard practice for all children evidencing emotional and behavioral difficulties. Comprehensive plans that address the school day, including academic strategies, teacher supports, and behavior interven-tions are important components of the wraparound plan.

*System of care leaders, including educators, need to recognize the importance of including parents as active partners and develop strategies that address the challenge inherent in this shift to more family-focused planning and service delivery.* System of care models that proactively engage families are reporting more effective outcomes for children (Cole & Poe, 1993; Stroul, 1993). An evaluation of eleven school-based system change wraparound projects in Illinois showed significant improvement in adaptability and cohesion as measured by the Family Adaptability and Cohesiveness Evaluation Scale (II) (FACES) (Olson, Porter, & Bell 1985) for families receiving wraparound support. The data on variety and frequency of services provided to families through LADSE's WRAP Project also indicate that family-driven services positively impact hospitalizations, out-of-home placement, and child/family functioning. Service provider feedback suggests that this is the aspect of wraparound that feels most different than what they have been doing. However, LADSE experienced a constant need to focus on role changes and the discomfort reported by service providers when parents are put in leadership and decision-making roles. This further confirms the need for focused attention in this area. Acceptance of this challenge to move to a new way of partnering with families seems to be critical to improving outcomes for students with EBD.

*School inclusion for students with EBD requires a wide variety of supports for students, teachers and families.* The wraparound planning process, based on strengths and needs, can lead to creative use of school-based supports and ensure more effective inclusion experiences. This involves moving the process away from developing plans based on what school programs traditionally have offered to plans based on what the child actually needs. New roles for special education teachers may include facilitation of school wraparound plans, team teaching in regular classrooms, and providing technical assistance support for regular education teachers. Development of in-school respite options can include classroom-based supports as well as non-punitive options that remove students from certain settings for short time periods. Peer support systems that require coordination from school counselors, teachers, or social workers may become an integral part of a school-based wraparound plan. Tutoring, during or after school, sometimes is a more effective option for a student with EBD than placement in a remedial program or a special education setting with lower-functioning students. Community mentors and mental health providers may also play active roles in implementing effective options in natural school settings.

*Schools need to prioritize staff development and ongoing technical assistance for all teachers to effectively intervene with and support students with or at-risk of EBD.* School personnel consistently report concerns about their capacity to effectively manage students with emotional and behavioral problems (Braaten, Kaufman, Braaten, Polsgrove, & Nelson 1988). The data on WIN and WAIS suggests that students with EBD are found in various educational settings and that a greater variety of school settings can become effective intervention sites. Providing teachers with consistent training and support for integrating strategies into their classrooms can positively impact their responses to students with, or at-risk for, EBD. The high level of classroom-based and teacher supports called for in school-based plans indicates a need for more directed assistance to teachers. The programmatic flexibility offered through in-school respite, team teachers, and the support provided by Family Service Facilitators resulted in stabilized placements in less restrictive settings for many students.

A review of supports provided to teachers and feedback from consultants who observed in classrooms and met with teachers during the 1993-94 WAIS pilot indicated specific training and technical assistance needs for regular and special education teachers. These include training in more proactive interventions such as life-space interviewing, reality therapy applied in classrooms, and social interaction-networking. Supporting teachers through efforts to enhance the "learning life" of students with EBD through strengthened curricula and a greater range of interesting and innovative instructional strategies also was recommended (Jane Knitzer, personal communication, March 20, 1994). The need for greater awareness of the language deficiencies of students with EBD and proactive instructional and behavioral support strategies in regular and special education classes also were cited (Zina Steinberg, personal communication, March 11, 1994).

*It may be prudent to carefully monitor how services and supports for implementing wraparound are developed so that the availability of specific services does not dictate wraparound planning.* Experiences with one child/family frequently offers insights for service planning for others and, as experienced by WRAP, can lead to the development of new service options. However, it is important to be mindful that even innovative service options can result in new categorical slots and inflexible plans if they are not truly individualized and driven by student needs. For example, in-school respite can be a valuable support for several students. One student's plan may require assistance for the science teacher during lab activities where chemicals and equipment may be involved. Another student's plan may call for a covert back-up person for PE class to prevent physical altercations during competitive games. But if applied to all identified children in a given school, respite can become a new categorical approach. This could result in all students with EBD suddenly having respite workers following them around. Or, respite resources may become bundled into one position that begins functioning like another teacher's aide attached to the self-contained program. This could diminish the impact and flexibility of wraparound planning.

*Special projects and initiatives can result in systems change, especially if the project keeps changing as the impact of the project is experienced by the various stakeholders.* A constant focus on evaluating project experiences and outcomes is critical to effecting pervasive system change. This requires flexible attitudes of key staff and an acceptance that long term change is needed. When implementation of special projects bring the barriers in the current system to the forefront, there must be a willingness to discuss these barriers openly and change direction when indicated.

LADSE's WRAP Project represents a model for replication for communities throughout Illinois and other states in which individualized systems of care for the benefit of children with EBD are being organized. The ongoing evaluation of issues faced during this four year systems change initiative have guided program development, training and policy development across various elements of the system. Evaluation of child/family outcomes and placement trends over time and comparison of this data to experiences of other communities in Illinois and other states is expected to provide further opportunity for system enhancements.

## REFERENCES

Braaten, S., Kaufman, J., Braaten, D., Polsgrove, L. and Nelson, D.C. (1988). The regular education initiative: Patent medicine for behavioral disorders. *Exceptional Children*, 55 (1), 21-27.

Bullock, L. & Gable, R. (Eds.)(1994). *Monograph on Inclusion: Ensuring appropriate services to children and youth with emotional/behavioral disorders.* Hartford, CT: Council for Exceptional Children.

Burchard, J. & Burchard, S., Sewell, C. & VanDenBerg, J. (1993). *One kid at a time: Evaluative case studies and description of the Alaska Youth Initiative Demonstration Project.* Juneau, AK: State of Alaska Division of Mental Health and Mental Retardation.

Clarke, R. T., Schaefer, M., Burchard, J. D., Welkowitz, J. W. (1992). Wrapping community-based mental health services around children with a severe behavioral disorder: an evaluation of project wraparound. *Journal of Child and Family Studies*, 1 (1) 241-261.

Cole, R. & Poe, S. (1993). *Systems of care for children with serious emotional disturbances and their families: Partnerships for Care.* Interim report of the Mental health Services Program for Youth. Washington Business Group on Health, Washington, DC.

Duchnowski, A., Johnson, M., Hall, K., Kutash, K. & Friedman, R. (1993). The alternatives to residential treatment study: initial findings. *Journal of Emotional and Behavioral Disorders,* 1 (1) 17-26.

Eber, L. (1992). Evaluation and summary of the 1990-91 Wraparound Pilot, La Grange Area Department of Special Education, La Grange, IL.

Eber, L. (1993). *LADSE's WRAP Project. Linking School and Mental Health Services: Research Findings from Model Programs.* NIMH and U.S. Department of Education Sponsored Symposium: The Third Annual Virginia Beach Conference. Virginia Beach, VA.

Eber, L. & Osuch, R. (1994). *Evaluation school-based system change initiatives.* Conference Proceedings from the Seventh Annual Research Conference. Tampa, FL: University of South Florida.

Eber, L., Osuch, R., Redditt, C. A. (1995). *Restructuring Service Models and Shifting Roles: An Approach for Systems Change.* Conference Proceedings for the 7th Annual Research Conference for Children's Mental Health. Tampa, FL.

Eber, L., & Osuch, R. (1995). *School-Based Wraparound: How Implementation and Evaluation Can Lead to System Change.* Presentation at the 8th Annual Research Conference for Children's Mental Health. Tampa, FL.

Eber, L., Osuch, R., & Redditt, C. (under review). *Illinois School WRAP.* Special edition of the *Journal of Child and Family Studies* Special Issue on Children's Wraparound Services Research.

Fuchs, D. & Fuchs, L. (1994). Inclusive schools movement and the radicalization of special education reform. *Exceptional Children,* 60 (4), 294-308.

Guetzloe, E. (1994). Inclusion of students with emotional/behavioral disorders: The issues, the barriers, and possible solutions. In L. Bullock & R. Gable (Eds.), *Monograph on Inclusion: Ensuring appropriate services to children and youth with emotional/behavioral disorders* (pp. 21-24). Hartford, CT: Council for Exceptional Children.

Knitzer, J., Steinberg, Z., & Fleisch, B. (1990). *At the school house door.* New York: Bank Street College of Education.

Lourie, I. (1994). *Principles of local system development for children, adolescents and their families.* Kaleidoscope, Chicago, IL.

Maroney, S., (1994). Welcoming back students with emotional/behavioral disorders into the least restrictive environments appropriate. In L. Bullock & R. Gable (Eds.), *Monograph on Inclusion: Ensuring appropriate services to children and youth with emotional/behavioral disorders* (pp. 29-31). Hartford, CT: Council for Exceptional Children.

Olson, D. H., Portner, J., & Lavee, Y. (1985). Family adaptability and cohesion scale. Family social science. St. Paul, MN: University of Minnesota.

Price, J. (1994). Promoting inclusive education for students with emotional/behavioral disorders. L. Bullock & R. Gable (Eds.), *Monograph on Inclusion: Ensuring appropriate services to children and youth with emotional/behavioral disorders* (pp. 25-38). Hartford, CT: Council for Exceptional Children.

Stroul, B. A. (1993). *Systems of care for children and adolescents with severe emotional disturbances: What are the results?* Washington, DC: CASSP Technical Assistance Center, Center for Child Health and Mental Health Policy.

# Memphis City Schools Mental Health Center: A Comprehensive Integrated Service Program

Judy Faris
Gerry T. Nichol
Memphis City Schools Mental Health Center

SUMMARY. This article describes a nationally recognized integrated service program in operation since 1969 within the Memphis (TN) City Schools. Memphis City Schools Mental Health Center represents a comprehensive model for the delivery of integrated mental health and substance abuse services to children and youth with a wide range of problems. Notably, the model incorporates elements of primary and secondary prevention and community outreach into service delivery, components that may be under-emphasized in programs that are oriented toward specific clinical populations (e.g., SED). Program components are discussed in detail to demonstrate both unique and inter-related program features, reflecting the complex needs of the children and families being served. Future directions and challenges are also considered. *[Article copies available from The Haworth Document Delivery Service: 1-800-342-9678.]*

The present article describes the structure and operation of a nationally recognized integrated service program that has been in operation since

---

Address correspondence to: Judy Faris, Memphis City Schools, 2597 Avery Avenue, Memphis, TN 38112.

[Haworth co-indexing entry note]: "Memphis City Schools Mental Health Center: A Comprehensive Integrated Service Program." Faris, Judy, and Gerry T. Nichol. Co-published simultaneously in *Special Services in the Schools* (The Haworth Press, Inc.) Vol. 11, No. 1/2, 1996, pp. 151-167; and: *Emerging School-Based Approaches for Children with Emotional and Behavioral Problems: Research and Practice in Service Integration* (ed: Robert J. Illback, and C. Michael Nelson) The Haworth Press, Inc., 1996, pp. 151-167. Single or multiple copies of this article are available from The Haworth Document Delivery Service [1-800-342-9678, 9:00 a.m. - 5:00 p.m. (EST)].

*151*

1969 within the Memphis (TN) City Schools. The program is not geared exclusively to serving children with serious emotional and behavioral difficulties (SED), but rather represents a comprehensive model for the delivery of integrated mental health and substance abuse services to children and youth with a wide range of problems. Notably, the model incorporates elements of primary and secondary prevention (Hawkins and Catalano, 1989; Cowen and Work, 1988) and community outreach into service delivery, components that may be under-emphasized in programs that are oriented toward specific clinical populations (e.g., SED). Following a discussion of the history and development of the program, each of the program components is discussed in more detail to demonstrate both unique and inter-related program features, reflecting the complex needs of the children being served.

## HISTORY AND DEVELOPMENT OF THE PROGRAM

Established on the premise that children's mental health services are best provided from a systems perspective, the Memphis City Schools Mental Health Center (MCSMHC) has maintained a focus on healthy school adjustment for every child through the encouragement of positive classroom environments, broad-based prevention efforts, and timely, effective response to students with behavioral, emotional, and learning difficulties. With a staff of 162 mental health professionals, MCSMHC provides comprehensive mental health services to Memphis City Schools' students and their families. An administrative component of the largest school system in Tennessee, the sixteenth largest school system in the nation, the MCSMHC serves a district of 162 schools and 108,000 students. Memphis City Schools' racial composition is primarily African American (82%); over 60% of the students' families have incomes at poverty level. In addition to providing services to individual students, MCSMHC staff work closely with classroom teachers, guidance counselors, and special education personnel to encourage students' success and to foster a healthy learning environment. Working from three satellite centers, masters and doctoral level psychologists, social workers, and alcohol and drug counselors, serving as mental health teams, offer a core program of mental health services and an array of specialty, prevention and treatment programs to address the needs of students and their families. (See MCSMHC organizational chart, Figure 1.)

Funding is from local sources and through contracts with Tennessee Department of Human Services and the Tennessee State Department of Health. The MCSMHC is also the recipient of the system's Drug Free

FIGURE 1. Organizational Chart of the Memphis City Schools Mental Health Center

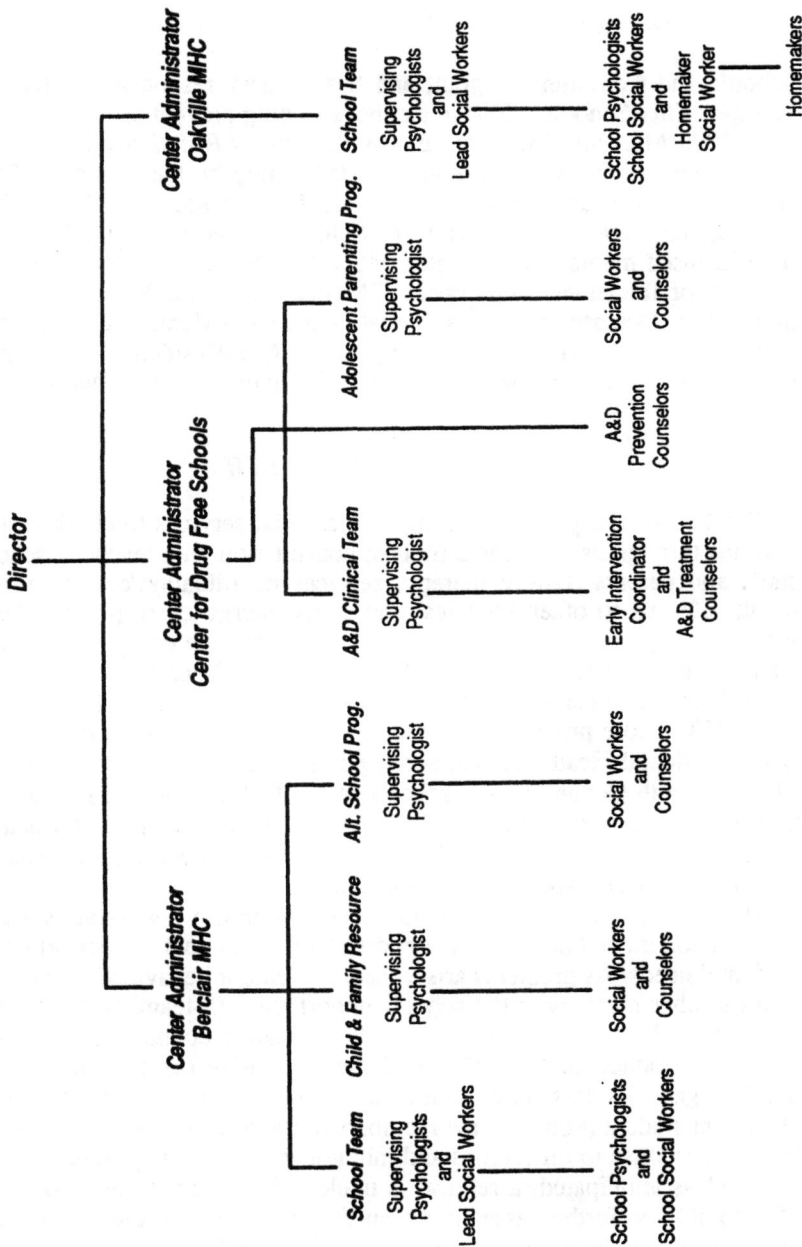

Schools and Communities grant and has primary responsibility for the Memphis City Schools' effort in alcohol and drug prevention.

In 1982 MCSMHC received the first *Award of Excellence for School Psychological Services Programs* awarded jointly by the American Psychological Association–Division of School Psychology (APA-Division 16) and the National Association of School Psychology (NASP). As a state licensed mental health center, MCSMHC holds licenses granted by the State of Tennessee, Department of Mental Health and Mental Retardation and the Department of Health, that include: (1) Mental Health Outpatient Facility, (2) Alcohol and Drug Abuse Non-Residential Treatment Facility, and (3) Alcohol and Drug Abuse Early Intervention Facility.

## CORE MENTAL HEALTH

The MCSMHC provides a range of essential services to children and families through assessment activities; consultation with teachers, school staff, and parents; family therapy; services coordination/case management; referrals to other agencies; and crisis/emergency response. These services are provided by six mental health teams each composed of nine staff members that rotate through the schools. Other teams focus on completion of special education re-evaluations. An outreach program, MCSMHC's core program is provided by staff from two satellite centers, Berclair Mental Health Center, serving in North Memphis, and Oakville Mental Health Center serving schools in South Memphis. In addition to traditional mental health services offered by these school mental health teams, staff also offer social skills training groups, divorce issue groups, grief issues groups, and anger management.

Through a pre-referral consultation and screening system established in each school, mental health staff support school personnel in responding to students' needs. As problems arise, academic and/or behavioral, the classroom teacher meets with the school support team (S-team) that includes the principal (or his/her designee); the guidance counselor; a special education teacher; and mental health representative (usually the school psychologist). Parents are often included. Meeting weekly to stay abreast of current student problems, the members of the S-team develop interventions in response to difficulties and monitor results. If the problem is not resolved as anticipated, a referral is made, with parental permission, to MCSMHC for further assessment and/or treatment. A typical S-team meeting may include not only student problems related to learning difficulties but also conduct issues, symptoms of depression and anxiety, family stress, and follow up on previously handled emergencies. There has been recent interest in establishing a requirement that a parent be present for the initial S-team meeting to encourage parent involvement and cooperation.

MCSMHC handles over 10,000 referrals each year combining carry-over cases and new referrals. During 1993-94, over 5,000 students received psychological assessments (including initial assessments and special education re-evaluations). Treatment cases requiring individual, family, and group counseling are handled both in the schools and at the centers. The range of problems is wide and forces school mental health staff to be generalists.

## SPECIALIZED SERVICE PROGRAMS

In addition to the core services of MCSMHC, a range of specialized services targeted toward specific populations with diverse needs is provided. A sample of programs includes: (1) services for abused and neglected children; (2) alcohol and drug early intervention program; (3) adolescent parenting program; (4) substance abuse prevention program; (5) violence prevention program; and (6) prevention programs with a multiple behavior focus. Prevention program are based on the "Communities That Care" model (Developmental Research and Programs, Inc., 1993). It can be seen that the needs of children with serious emotional disabilities are met in a comprehensive fashion through this program model at individual, school, family, and community levels, and in relation to a broad array of problems and issues.

### Services for Abused and Neglected Children

Through funding provided by contracts with the Tennessee Department of Human Service (TDHS), MCSMHC offers treatment services to MCS students who are identified by TDHS as abused and/or neglected. Because of the severity of these cases, multiple contacts with the student and their families are often necessary, and extensive collaboration with other agencies is required. Specific populations served include physically and/or emotionally abused children, sexually abused children, and students who have been placed in foster care because of abuse or neglect.

With the goal of providing supportive services to families that are receiving protective services for children, MCSMHC and the Tennessee Department of Human Services (TDHS) initiated the Homemaker Program. Ten homemakers assist and monitor the progress of parents in nutrition, budgeting, grooming, child care and parenting skills, and housekeeping in up to 50 households identified by TDHS as abusive or neglectful.

Another initiative designed for this population is the foster care counseling program in which a MCSMHC social worker provides individual and group counseling and parent/school consultation to ten MCS children who are in custody of the Tennessee Department of Human Services. This outreach program, which involves home and school visits, facilitates the child's adjustment in the foster home, and enhances chances for successful permanent placement or adoption through continuity of treatment during what is often a highly emotional transition period. Efforts to achieve goals may include individual and group therapy, home visits, parent consultation (both biological and foster parent, if needed), and school consultation as required. Each treatment plan is the result of staffing between the Department of Human Services' foster care case worker and MCSMHC staff. Interagency communication and coordination are emphasized.

### Alcohol and Drug Early Intervention Program

Alcohol and drug (A&D) early intervention groups are an important part of Memphis City Schools' alcohol and drug abuse effort. The A&D staff includes a doctoral level psychologist, eight master's level alcohol and drug counselors and an early intervention coordinator. Services provided by the team include: (1) assessment for alcohol and other drug related problems as part of the discipline process for students who receive board suspensions for A&D related offenses; (2) early intervention counseling/educational services for students who receive board suspensions for A&D related offenses and their parents; (3) early intervention counseling/educational services for students who are "high risk" to develop A&D related problems, but who have not yet received a board suspension for an A&D related offense; (4) assessment for alcohol or other drug related problems for students referred by parents, the school, or self-referrals; (5) individual, family, and group outpatient therapy for students who meet DSM IV diagnostic criteria for Psychoactive Substance Abuse or Dependence; and (6) relapse prevention counseling for students returning to school after a period of residential or inpatient treatment for a substance abuse problem.

Early intervention groups serve as a major component of the school system's alcohol and drug abuse prevention effort. Board policy states that any student using or possessing any alcohol, marijuana, or other illicit drug must be given a board suspension. An assessment is conducted of the student's alcohol and other drug use. As a condition of returning to school, the student is required to attend an early intervention group of eight sessions. A concurrent parent group is available for the student's parents. Additional individual and/or family counseling is available as needed. Early intervention groups are also provided in selected schools for students at risk for A&D related problems. Outpatient individual, family, and group therapy for substance abuse and dependency are available to students enrolled in the MCS who meet criteria for DSM IV diagnosis of Psychoactive Substance Abuse or Dependence. Students who receive board suspensions and meet treatment criteria are required to attend a treatment group in lieu of the early intervention group.

## *Adolescent Parenting Program*

A mental health team serves the Adolescent Parenting Program, a collaborative program for approximately 125 pregnant, parenting Memphis City Schools' students at the Comprehensive Pupil Services Educational Center. In addition to providing services at the school for pregnant teenagers, the team also consults with principals and guidance counselors throughout Memphis City Schools regarding pregnant students, offering services as appropriate. Goals for pregnant students include high school graduation, development of parenting skills, delay of second pregnancy, and career initiatives. Services offered by the mental health team include individual, family, and group counseling. Regularly scheduled student enrichment periods are held focusing on such topics as stress management, personal goal setting, African American issues, self-concept, and anger management.

## *Substance Abuse Prevention*

The core of the substance abuse prevention program is the Mendez Too Good For Drugs (Mendez Foundation, 1988) tobacco, alcohol, and other drug abuse prevention curriculum. Teachers in grades K-12 have been trained by Center for Drug Free Schools' (CDFS) staff to teach the curriculum and have been provided support by prevention counselors assigned to school sites in the form of consultation and the provision of supplementary activities.

The Drug Abuse Resistance Education (Los Angeles Unified School District, 1994) program is a recent addition to the basic curriculum and is a collaborative effort between MCSMHC and the Memphis Police Department to have uniformed officers provide additional information and skill building to students in the fifth or sixth grade of their elementary school. Eighteen schools are participating in a piloting of the program this year. A CDFS prevention counselor with a background in curriculum and instruction was trained in the curriculum with the officers and assists in the school selection process, the introduction of the program to principals and faculty, and the provision of consultation as needed to officers and teachers.

A second area of student programming is the creation of drug free peer groups and opportunities for participation. The Parent Resource Institute for Drug Education (PRIDE) program has achieved high visibility in 19 secondary schools within MCS. Every secondary school has the option of requesting this program of training students to communicate drug free messages to peers and younger students through songs and skits. To become members of PRIDE, students must commit to staying drug free. Practices held weekly at school sites serve to develop a closely knit peer group with similar values, strengthening resistance to negative peer pressure in the larger school community. Students may elect to participate on the community PRIDE team which travels to train other students within the state and at the annual international conference.

Just Say No Clubs, while in place at all grade levels, are most popular in the elementary school setting. Activities are made available throughout the year which promote the establishment of peer groups which value being healthy and drug free. A collaboration with the MCS Adopt-A-School program enables monthly awards to be given to schools demonstrating exemplary efforts. CDFS staff train the coordinators of these programs and for consistency provide a structure for monthly recognition of those schools with the most active programs.

The student program with the most potential for impacting the entire school population is the leadership training program. At the secondary level, each school selects a mixture of formal and informal leaders to be trained at a city wide workshop in the fall. The students are addressed by a well respected leader in the community and are presented a series of hour-long sessions/programs describing drug and violence prevention programs they might choose to implement in their school. Each team then creates an action plan that has goals and objectives addressing drug and/or violence prevention, and more broadly, school climate. CDFS prevention counselors train the school program coordinators and regularly monitor each team's progress in reaching their goals. A spring conference allows the teams to report on the success of their action plans and to review any obstacles or new ideas resulting from the execution of their plans. At the elementary level, training is conducted at the school site, and the focus of meetings is to develop leadership skills among the members, with school projects of secondary importance.

Another student program that often attracts members of PRIDE and the leadership team is the Cross Age Peer Program (CAPP). Research has shown that when compared with teacher interventions, peer interventions in social influence resistance training have resulted in greater reduction of drug use (Klepp et al., 1986; McAlister, 1983; Murray et al., 1984). In CAPP, students are trained by CDFS personnel and their school sponsor to teach lessons from the upper elementary drug prevention curricula. They then arrange to visit elementary schools to teach these lessons. The elementary students enjoy the attention and interest of the older students and take the opportunity to ask questions about high school life and how to resist peer pressure. Other activities of CAPP include mentoring and individual tutoring of elementary age students. The most at risk elementary students are selected to have regular contact with the positive role models provided through CAPP.

In addition to student-focused programs, CDFS is regularly engaged in collaborative activities within the Memphis community. Staff attend the monthly meeting of the Prevention Network, a coming together of all the community agencies and organizations engaged in drug prevention. Information about programs is disseminated and collaboration is encouraged on new projects. CDFS staff collaborate with the regional coordinator for the Governor's Alliance for a Drug Free Tennessee and the Memphis Alcohol and Drug Council to conduct a one week summer camp for at risk adolescents (Tennessee Teen Institute). Other community collaborations are designed to raise community awareness.

The Parent to Parent video-based workshop series produced by PRIDE 1990 has been utilized as the primary strategy for providing parents the knowledge and skills they need to raise drug free children. Two prevention counselors conduct three facilitator training workshops annually. To date, a cadre of facilitators has been trained, comprised of guidance counselors, teachers, MCSMHC staff, the business community, parents, and church representatives. Sites for parent trainings are most frequently schools and churches to maximize attendance. Facilitators have utilized opportunities to present the eight session workshop to suspended students' parents, who are already bringing their children to group counseling twice a week. Sessions have also been initiated in a number of schools having early childhood programs, where parents are required to participate one day per week.

## Violence Prevention

MCSMHC is playing a key role in Memphis City Schools' response to Goal Seven of the National Education Goals (1994): *By the year 2000, every school in the United States will be free of drugs, violence, and the unauthorized presence of firearms and alcohol and will offer a disciplined environment conducive to learning* (p. 11). To this end, the superintendent called for the creation of the School Violence Task Force co-chaired by the director of the MCSMHC. The task force met to examine issues related to youth violence and to propose initiatives to deal with these concerns. Within subcommittees, members (parents, students, school personnel, representatives of community agencies) reviewed the reports of other local task forces and examined the literature on youth violence. Violence prevention initiatives have focused on: (1) assessing the safety of each school and tailor interventions accordingly; (2) taking a strong public stand in commitment to the personal safety of students and staff, and publicizing specific prevention initiatives; (3) increasing parental commitment to and support of schools; (4) equipping staff to foster a non-violent climate in Memphis City Schools; (5) preparing students to deal with conflict non-violently; (6) clarifying and enforcing policies regarding student behavior; and (7) encouraging community awareness of school issues in a positive way.

In September, 1992, the entire MCSMHC staff attended a two day workshop in conflict resolution skills training (Grace Contrino Abrams Peace Foundation, 1992) provided by the Drug Free Schools' grant. At risk students were identified by staff at numerous schools to participate in group counseling focused on training the students in these skills the remainder of the year. Demand for the training increased to the point that requests were made to train entire classrooms and grades. A pilot program was begun the following year that trained seventh graders through English classes at one school. A dramatic difference in the number of discipline referrals made to the office, comparing trained and untrained students, led to an expansion of the program to three additional schools for the 1994-95 school year. An innovative strategy of the program has been the utilization of high school leadership students to train seventh grade students.

The district wide safety committee's Training Subcommittee in Spring, 1994, purchased a variety of conflict resolution training materials for every school in the system. Training in the use of the materials was provided by CDFS staff to all school guidance counselors, who then developed a plan to either teach classes themselves or assist teachers in using the materials. Training of entire school populations is being planned for the 1995-96 school year by providing intensive training directly to teachers.

The peer mediation pilot program has received a very positive reception by students and school staff. Consultants were brought in to train the prevention staff, two coordinators from each of eleven schools and students in October, 1994. Professional mediators from the community were also included in the training and provided assistance in supervising the students in role play activities. Upon returning to school, the mediators, coordinators, and prevention counselors, trained 14 additional mediators to provide a sufficiently large cadre to handle referrals without missing class an inordinate amount of time. One community mediator is assigned to each school to meet with the student mediators once a month to provide consultation on difficult mediations and skill review.

Because research shows that young students who are excessively aggressive have a high probability of exhibiting violent behavior as adolescents (Kellam and Brown, 1982; Loeber, 1988), the Interpersonal Cognitive Problem Solving Program (Shure, 1992) curriculum for Grades K and 1 was piloted in 42 schools. CDFS scheduled training for guidance counselors serving those schools and six prevention counselors in use of the curriculum. The guidance counselors then trained the K and Grade 1 teachers, who began training their students in the development of a vocabulary to identify feelings in themselves, to acknowledge differences between themselves and others, and to generate ideas for solving problems. The six prevention counselors serve as consultants to the program and assist in the program evaluation.

A major student-focused collaborative effort with the Memphis Police Department (M.P.D.) is the coordination of the Gang Resistance Education and Training (City of Phoenix, 1994) program. One thousand five hundred seventh graders from eight schools are participating in the pilot project designed to have specially trained police officers present information on setting goals, resisting pressures, learning how to resolve conflicts without violence, and understanding how gangs and youth violence impact the quality of their lives. CDFS staff carry out program evaluation, recommend schools for selection, and function in a consultation and coordination role.

Comprehensive violence prevention strategies not only are directed toward students, but also toward principals, teachers, and other school staff. Twelve prevention counselors have been trained along with twelve assistant principals and twenty-four guidance counselors to provide teachers with techniques to verbally de-escalate potentially violent situations involving students through a program entitled Non-violent Crisis Intervention (Crisis Prevention Institute, 1980). All principals and assistant principals have received the training, and by the end of the school year, seventy-two schools will have had the six-hour workshop presented at their sites for faculty and other staff. Two trainings have been conducted for mental health center staff. Response to the training has been very favorable with schools and mental health center staff expressing greater confidence in being able to handle volatile situations and feeling they have learned skills to protect themselves.

A related aspect of preparing school staff to handle potentially violent situations is training in gang awareness. In a collaborative effort with the Memphis Police Department's Organized Crime Unit, two MCSMHC psychologists presented workshops designed to increase knowledge about gangs, including history, use of colors, graffiti, and behavior. Strategies for preventing youth involvement in gang activities were also discussed. The two psychologists then prepared other MCSMHC personnel to make the presentation, increasing availability of the workshop to school faculties.

A major collaborative project was begun in Fall, 1994, as a result of MCSMHC receiving a federal planning grant for youth gang prevention. Among the major collaborators are the Memphis Police Department's Organized Crime Unit, United Way, University of Tennessee Prevention Center, and Memphis Housing Authority. The grant has a strong community focus involving ethnographic interviewing of adults and youth residing in a three elementary school area in south Memphis. A needs assessment is being developed from interview responses and two public hearings in the community. Residents will be involved in a strategic planning process addressing the reduction of community, family, school, and individual risk factors. An advisory board comprised of key leaders, business owners, collaborators, local gang experts, and school principals will assist in the development of a five year implementation plan based on the "Communities That Care" model.

In addition to the use of the Parent To Parent program, CDFS staff are currently examining The Parent Project (Alternative Resources, 1995), a sixteen-week parent training program designed to help parents who need assistance in managing their strong-willed or "out of control" children. Because of the severity of the behavior, parents many times cannot find strategies that enable them to intervene successfully. This program combines multimedia instruction, small group practice, problem-solving, and collective learning experiences to provide parents with practical skills and emotional support in facilitating teaching their children responsibility, mature decision-making, and self-discipline. Memphis City Schools' need is great for this type of program in working with parents of substance abusers, severely emotionally disturbed students, and students at its alternative school.

## Programs with a Multiple Behavior Focus

The Student Assistance Program (SAP) offers special training to a team of ten faculty members and other school staff in responding to at risk students. One prevention counselor trained in SAP coordinates the three day training of five schools in identifying community resources for referrals, development of an action plan, and the structure for returning to their schools to develop a crisis response plan for a variety of school emergencies which might arise. Solutions to many problems can be found within the school building through staff collaboration. Twenty-two schools have been trained in SAP and are provided continuing support by the training coordinator and another prevention counselor well versed in SAP.

The Urban Initiative (UI) Program is perhaps the best example within MCS of collaborative efforts in addressing students' needs. Schools requesting this training are brought together for a three-day training. Each school brings a team of ten members representing school staff, parents, business owners from the community, religious leaders, law enforcement officials, and other community agency representatives. The team carries out a needs assessment of the school and the surrounding community. Training is provided in the "Communities That Care" model and its use in developing an action plan designed to address the needs chosen by the team to be targeted.

Team building is also an important part of training. The prevention counselor assigned to that school as well as the UI prevention counselor specialist follow up with the team once it has returned to the school and provide consultation. Thirty-four school/community teams have been trained over the past five years. A particularly unique and innovative strategy presented itself when four neighboring schools requested training. The elementary school, junior high school, senior high school, and vo-tech center all serve the same population of students and decided to develop their action plans together to promote coordination of school/community activities to prevent drug use and violence among students. Communication among the school staffs has significantly increased, and the transitioning of students from one campus to the next has improved greatly. Activities in the community have been conducted on a larger scale and are better coordinated.

In August, 1994, MCSMHC received an AmeriCorps grant through the Corporation for National and Community Service. The purpose of the grant is threefold: (1) to provide a means for MCS graduates and other members of the community to gain understanding and the experience of community service; (2) to enable workers to receive an educational award to attend college at the completion of service; and (3) to provide needed services to children during the school day as well as in after-school programs. Community collaborators in the grant are the Memphis Park Commission, which operates the after school programs; WKNO, the local educational television station; and Rhodes College, a local higher education institution. During the school day tutoring and mentoring are provided by 40 full and part-time service workers under the supervision of two CDFS prevention counselors (a project leader and site manager). The focus of the after-school program is also tutoring and mentoring, with the addition of drug prevention activities, conflict resolution skills training, educational television workbook activities, arts and crafts, and recreation. Service workers also collaborate with other agencies in the community to provide assistance to their projects, such as being docents at the National Civil Right Museum and packing lunches for the homeless at the city's interfaith association. CDFS staff provide much of the training for the service workers and provide technical assistance in the evaluation of the objectives of the program.

The Center for Drug Free Schools is the primary collaborator in another grant with the Memphis Alcohol and Drug Council. Thirty members of the community PRIDE team were selected to participate in this community service project, also awarded by the Corporation for National and Community Service. Students provide tutoring in their schools, assist the MCSMHC AmeriCorps program in carrying out drug and violence prevention activities in the after-school program, collaborate with the Memphis Police Department's Boys' Choir in performing drug and violence prevention messages through songs and skits at community events, and assist the Memphis City Beautiful Commission by participating in their citywide projects as well as developing beautification projects at their own schools. These activities not only build collaboration between the school and community, but also strengthen the bond between these students and their school and community, an important protective factor in prevention.

Another initiative of MCSMHC has been the Rites of Passage program, (Okwumabua, 1994) designed to prepare African American youth for the assumption of adult roles and responsibilities by involving them in 16 major areas of study: (1) knowing Africa; (2) knowing self and others; (3) family history; (4) the history of African people; (5) sexuality and sexual education; (6) spirituality; (7) personal grooming and etiquette; (8) housekeeping and finances; (9) values clarification and goal setting; (10) conflict resolution and violence prevention; (11) creativity; (12) life management: time, school work, and leisure; (13) communication; (14) assertiveness and leadership; (15) AIDS/HIV, drugs, and other life threats; and (16) career development. The Rites of Passage program typically runs from six to nine months, beginning with a simple initiation ceremony. One hour group meetings are held weekly either during the school day or at a community-based site after school. Often, groups are co-facilitated by individuals in the community who are good role models and demonstrate a particular interest in helping youth. The training culminates with an overnight retreat or recognition ceremony. Family and friends are invited to a closing ceremony where, in addition to receiving gifts, the participants are formally presented to their community.

Finally, for two summers, the Center for Drug Free Schools' staff have provided supplemental social and living skills training to students making the transition from elementary to junior high school. In collaboration with the Division of Instructional Support, two prevention counselors developed and conducted group sessions with students who had been retained at least twice and who had displayed some interpersonal and/or conduct problems. Practical activities such as reading a school map, opening combination locks, and asking adults for assistance are used as the context for addressing problem-solving skills, self-esteem issues, resistance of peer pressure, and coping with new situations.

## FUTURE DIRECTIONS

Taking a leadership role in the School Violence Task Force and the district wide safety committee, as well as in the application for grants, has accelerated MCSMHC's involvement in community collaboration. These activities have established well-defined reasons for initiating contacts with community organizations and agencies. The greater potential for effecting positive changes through the utilization of community-wide resources has both been exciting to envision and fruitful in our early endeavors. The synergy present has been obvious and has contributed to the building of greater rapport between the school system and the community. Turf-oriented, competitive relationships break down in favor of cooperative, comprehensive strategies for addressing the needs of the community's youth. The collaborations have also served to decrease the public's common perception of "the school" as the single responsible organization for solving the problems presented by youth. The needs of youth become the focus rather than the needs of a particular organization.

As a result of the greater familiarity with specific community agencies gained through working together, MCSMHC's goals are to build upon existing collaborations and expand efforts to initiate additional collaborations with other community agencies. Consistent with the African adage that "it takes a whole village to raise a child," MCSMHC's philosophy is that it takes community-wide collaboration to address the needs of Memphis' youth. Advisory boards for grants MCSMHC has received include representatives of the collaborating agencies and serve to continue collaboration well beyond the grant application process. Areas to receive priority in new collaborations are parent/family outreach and training, continued expansion of violence prevention programs, and extension of services into the community.

MCSMHC is taking a leadership role in encouraging collaboration among divisions within the school system itself. The size of MCS has unfortunately contributed, at times, to divisions viewing themselves as independently functioning entities. Consequently, there has been unintended duplication in service delivery and inadequate knowledge of other divisions' programs. Concerned about this issue, MCSMHC staff approached the school system's grants and compliance coordinator, who then set up a series of meetings of the various divisions, including programs such as Chapter I and II, research, bilingual education, vocational education, instructional support, special education, and alternative education. Representatives from these divisions have now organized themselves by service categories (e.g., parent training, early childhood education, at risk prevention/intervention programs, staff development). Collaboration among divisions will not only enhance service delivery, but also strengthen resources and capabilities in developing grant proposals.

The funding of public education and its supportive programs presents an ongoing challenge to school administrators. Available federal, state, and local monies are becoming more scarce, creating a competitive funding atmosphere. Increasingly, funding sources are requiring school/community collaboration in the formulation of program proposals. MCSMHC is committed to the continuation and expansion of effective programs and will continue to seek new funding opportunities that support MCSMHC program directions, encourage innovation, and invite collaboration to provide children and their families a comprehensive array of services that are coordinated and integrated.

## REFERENCES

Alternative Resources. (1995). *The parent project: A parenting skills program for parents with strong-willed or out-of-control children.* Ontario, CA.

City of Phoenix (1994). *Gang resistance education and training (G.R.E.A.T).* Phoenix, AZ.

Cowen, E. & Work, W. (1988). Resilient children, psychological well, and primary prevention. *Journal of Community Psychology, 16,* 591-607.

Grace Contrino Abrams Peace Education Foundation, Inc. (1992). A series of facilitator guides and activity books for students K-9 in building conflict resolution and mediation skills. Miami Beach, FL.

Hawkins, J.D. & Catalano, R.F. (1989). *Risk and Protective Factors for alcohol and other drug problems in adolescence and adulthood. Implication for substance abuse prevention.* Available from Social Development Research Work Group, School of Social Work, University of Washington, Seattle, WA.

Kellam, S.G. & Brown, H. (1982). *Social adaptational and psychological antecedents of adolescent psychopathology ten years later.* Baltimore, MD: Johns Hopkins University.

Klepp, K., Halper, A., & Perry, C.L. (1986). The efficacy in peer leaders in drug abuse prevention. *Journal of School Health,* 56, 407-411.

Loeber, R. (1988). Natural histories of conduct problem, delinquency, and associated substance use: Evidence for developmental progressions. In B.B. Lahey and A.E. Kazdin (Eds.), *Advances in clinical child psychology* (Vol. 11, pp. 73-124), New York, NY: Plenum Press.

Los Angeles Unified School District (1994). *Drug abuse resistance education* (D.A.R.E. America), Los Angeles, CA.

McAlister, A.L. (1983). Social-psychological approaches. In T.J. Glynn, C.G. Leukefeld, & J.P. Ludford (Eds.). *Preventing adolescent drug abuse: Intervention strategies* (pp. 36-50). NIDA Research Monograph No. 47, Washington, D.C.: U.S. Government Printing.

Mendez Foundation (1988). *Too good for drugs.* A drug prevention curriculum developed by the C.E. Mendez Foundation, Inc., in cooperation with the Hillsborough County Public Schools. Tampa, FL: Fidelity Printing.

Murray, D.M., Johnson, C.A., Luepker, R.V., & Mittlemark, M.B. (1984). The prevention of cigarette smoking in children: A comparison of four strategies. *Journal of Applied Social Psychology,* 14, 274-288.

National Crisis Prevention Institute, Inc. (1980). *CPI nonviolent crisis intervention training.* Brookfield, WI.

National Education Goals Panel (1994). *The National Education Goals Report.* Washington, D.C.: U.S. Government Printing.

Okwumabua, T.M. (1994). *"Let the circle be unbroken": A facilitator's handbook and model curriculum for "Rites of Passage."* Memphis City Schools Mental Health Center, Memphis, TN: Unpublished manuscript.

PRIDE Parent Training. (1990). *Parent to Parent Prevention Workshop.* An eight session video-based program designed to train participants in skills, attitudes, and abilities to get their children through adolescence without alcohol or drug use.

Shure, Myra A. (1992). *An Interpersonnel Cognitive Problem Solving Program.* Research Press. Champaign, IL.

# Designing Supportive School Environments

## J. Ron Nelson

Eastern Washington University

## Geoff Colvin

University of Oregon

**SUMMARY.** There is no question that all students, especially those with serious emotional disturbance, benefit from a predictable, consistent, well-organized, and safe school environment. The purpose of this paper is to describe and illustrate an effective approach that has had positive results in achieving such a school environment. Specifically, the paper describes how to achieve effective ecological arrangements and common area routines across the school environment. In addition, we present a case study with preliminary results. *[Article copies available from The Haworth Document Delivery Service: 1-800-342-9678.]*

What role can the school play in preventing serious emotional disturbance (SED)? We can identify children who have extreme behavioral

---

Address correspondence to: J. Ron Nelson, Department of Applied Psychology, Eastern Washington University, Cheney, WA 99004.

Preparation of this manuscript was supported in part by grants (#H237D20011 and #H029K10092) from the U.S. Department of Education, Office of Special Education Programs. Opinions expressed do not necessarily reflect the position of the U.S. Department of Education, and no endorsement should be inferred.

[Haworth co-indexing entry note]: "Designing Supportive School Environments." Nelson, J. Ron, and Geoff Colvin. Co-published simultaneously in *Special Services in the Schools* (The Haworth Press, Inc.) Vol. 11, No. 1/2, 1996, pp. 169-186; and: *Emerging School-Based Approaches for Children with Emotional and Behavioral Problems: Research and Practice in Service Integration* (ed: Robert J. Illback, and C. Michael Nelson) The Haworth Press, Inc., 1996, pp. 169-186. Single or multiple copies of this article are available from The Haworth Document Delivery Service [1-800-342-9678, 9:00 a.m. - 5:00 p.m. (EST)].

problems early in their educational careers, but if no attempts are made to support their coping and resiliency, they are likely to have poor educational and career outcomes (Edgar & Levine, 1987; Kauffman, Cullinan, & Epstein, 1987; Neel, Meadow, Levine, & Edgar, 1988). The time has come to make our schools supportive environments that promote children's social development. There is no question what types of environments promote the social development of children. The worst outcomes are achieved in environments that are either harsh and punitive in nature, or inconsistent in their expectations of child behavior and its consequences. The best outcomes are achieved when the environment is predictable, consistent, well-organized, and safe.

Unfortunately, across America, the predictable, consistent, well-organized, and safe school environment of earlier decades is past (Morrison, Furlong, & Morrison, 1994). In all too many cases, schools have become disorderly, unsafe, and disruptive to the teaching and learning process. This is unfortunate because developing a predictable, consistent, well-organized, and safe school environment is not only a low-cost, long-term, and highly effective way for schools to manage their common disciplinary and behavior problems, but is also fundamental to the development of children's psychological competencies, learning functions, and motivations (Gilbert, 1993). Such a school environment is both preventative and restorative in nature. A predictable, consistent, well-organized, and safe school environment is preventative, in that it does not provide the context in which behavioral problems arise or become more entrenched. Such a school environment also is restorative in that it provides the structure necessary to remediate problem behavior.

Two primary interrelated elements must be considered to achieve a predictable, consistent, well-organized, and safe school environment: (a) ecological arrangements; and (b) common area routines. The focus of the first element is physical arrangements and the scheduling and use of space. The focus of the second element is the common area routines. Entering, exiting, and feeding hundreds of students, for example, are extremely complex activities requiring a great deal of planning. Unfortunately, we have found that schools typically have ineffective ecological arrangements and common area routines. The institutionalized ecological arrangements and common area routines used by schools have been derived historically with little thought given to their effectiveness. Poorly designed ecological arrangements and common area routines can result in high levels of disciplinary and behavior problems.

The purpose of this paper is to describe and illustrate an approach that has had positive results in achieving a predictable, consistent, well-organized, and safe school environment which promotes the social development of children. In addition, we present a case study with preliminary results. This approach is based on work conducted in a number of elementary schools serving high numbers of students with SED and those who are at risk for developing SED. The schools are all located in low socioeconomic neighborhoods (over 70% of the students qualify for free or reduced lunches).

The development and implementation of effective ecological arrangements and common area routines is a relatively time-consuming process. However, taking the time to develop such arrangements and routines within the school not only will result in a predictable, consistent, well-organized, and safe school environment conducive to learning, but also will enhance staff morale, reduce stress and burnout, and improve community relationships. We have identified five steps for developing and implementing effective ecological arrangements and common area routines: (a) establishing a committee to guide the development, implementation, and maintenance of the ecological arrangements and common area routines; (b) conducting a needs assessment of the ecological arrangements and common area routines; (c) revising the ecological arrangements; (d) establishing common area routines including responses to problem behavior; and (e) implementing the revised ecological arrangements and common area routines.

## ESTABLISHING A COMMITTEE

The first step is to establish a committee to direct the development, implementation, and maintenance of the ecological arrangements and common area routines. Although the committee will direct and guide the process, it needs to be a joint venture with staff at all levels working together. Achieving consensus on the ecological arrangements and common area routines is essential to insure their implementation and maintenance.

The following factors should be considered when forming a committee. First, the composition of the team should be considered. Efficient teams generally are comprised of eight members (or less) who are representative of the entire staff. Broad representation is necessary to help achieve consensus among the school staff, and because each staff member will bring important information necessary for the development of effective ecological arrangements and common area routines. For example, it is difficult for teachers to understand fully all of the factors associated with the school lunch program without input from a staff member who is involved intimately with that program. Other factors to consider when establishing a committee to develop effective ecological arrangements and common area routines include the length of term for team members and how team members will be selected. Because the ecological arrangements and common area routines are continually refined, a 2- to 3-year term is recommended with a proportion of the team members rotating off each year to insure continuity from year to year. There are a number of options for selecting team members. The particular process used for selecting team members should match standard practices for establishing other building teams. Some options for selecting members of the committee include: (a) administrative appointments; (b) call for volunteers; (c) staff nominations; or (d) election of team members.

The overall responsibility of the committee is to direct the development, implementation, and maintenance of ecological arrangements and common area routines. The responsibilities and general activities of the committee include: (a) attend all planning meetings; (b) identify current ecological arrangements and common area routines; (c) evaluate effectiveness of current ecological arrangements and common area routines; (d) revise/establish ecological arrangements and common area routines; (e) field-test revised or new ecological arrangements and common area routines that are being considered for implementation; (f) actively communicate with staff members regarding the activities of the committee; and (g) conduct staff meetings to ensure and evaluate the implementation and maintenance of ecological arrangements and common area routines. In addition, it is important for the committee members to be persistent. Effecting school change is extremely intense and will result in many heated exchanges. Committee members must push through these exchanges in a positive manner.

## CONDUCTING A NEEDS ASSESSMENT
## FOR THE COMMON AREAS

A needs assessment is used to assess current ecological arrangements and common area routines. The needs assessment not only will provide school staff with a more accurate picture of current practices, but also will insure a variety of perspectives regarding them. The most accurate picture of what is happening with current ecological arrangements and common area routines can be obtained by: (a) collecting and analyzing data from multiple sources; and (b) involving all relevant parties such as students, parents, teachers, and support staff.

Methods for collecting the above information include surveys, interviews, observations, and reviews of records. Regardless of the method of data collection, the staff needs to understand how their responses will be treated, including the level of confidentiality. The following examples highlight possible approaches to collecting information to assess current ecological arrangements and common area routines:

1. *Survey instruments.* Surveys/questionnaires can be used to assess current practices and to establish development priorities. These may be open-ended or structured instruments.
2. *Interviews.* Individuals can be invited to participate in individual or group interviews to discuss current practices and their suggestions as well as to clarify or expand on responses to a survey.
3. *Observations.* Areas of the school can be observed by members of the committee. Observation data provide information about what is working well, in addition to identifying practices that need improvement.
4. *Reviews of records.* Archival school data can be reviewed to provide information on how well current practices are working, and the need for revising the record keeping system.

Figure 1 presents a checklist for determining the adequacy of the existing ecological arrangements, and Figure 2 presents a checklist for determining the adequacy of the common area routines.

## REVISING ECOLOGICAL ARRANGEMENTS

Numerous opportunities for ecological arrangements will contribute to the productive management of the common areas of the school. Although the effective design and use of the constructed environment can reduce the incidence of problem behavior in the school, there is a tendency to overlook obvious ecological solutions to problems. Based on the results of the needs assessment, modifications may need to be made to the ecological arrangements in the common areas of the school: (a) eliminating or adjusting unsafe physical arrangements; and (b) improving the scheduling and use of space.

### Eliminating or Adjusting Unsafe Physical Arrangements

Eliminating or adjusting unsafe physical arrangements involves actual structural changes and adjustments in the use of the space. Changes such as removing foliage, using barricades, or changing the designated use of an area (e.g., relocating gathering locations to areas with high levels of

FIGURE 1. Checklist for Determining the Adequacy of Existing Ecological Arrangements

Yes   No   1.   Unsafe physical arrangements are eliminated or adjusted.

     ✔ Objects or other structures that obstruct supervision are removed.
     ✔ Barricades are used to limit access to areas that are not easily observed or that are off-limits to students.

Yes   No   2.   The density of students (numbers and space/distance) is reduced as much as possible.

     ✔ All entrances and exits to a given area are utilized.
     ✔ The age spread of students (balance of younger students with older ones) is increased as density increases to more fully utilize a given area.
     ✔ Space/distance between groups/lines/classes are adequate (10′-15′).

Yes   No   3.   The travel distance and wait time is reduced as much as possible?

     ✔ Entrances and exits to a given area reduce travel distance.
     ✔ The density of students is decreased as travel distance increases (e.g., staggered start times).
     ✔ Wait time is short.

Yes   No   4.   Clear and stable signals are developed for behavioral expectations.

     ✔ Physical signals for expected positioning of students (e.g., indicators where to line up).
     ✔ Visual signals for expected behaviors (e.g., exit/entrance signs, posters depicting expected behaviors for a given area).
     ✔ Auditory signals for expected behaviors (e.g., bells).

supervision and natural surveillance) can often be made on the school grounds. School grounds problems relate to the overall site plan. Although each site plan will be unique, the following are examples of the four most common problems. First, campus borders often are poorly defined. Even when fencing is used, sometimes it is obscured by foliage that shields the campus from natural surveillance. Second, undifferentiated campus areas (e.g., a hidden corner of the playground) present opportunities for informal gathering areas that are out of sight from supervision. These areas not only may be used for prohibited activities, but also may increase the incidence of problem behavior and victimization. Third, building layout and design often will produce isolated spots (e.g., end of the hallway) where students will gravitate and either commit prohibited activities or expose themselves to victimization. Finally, bus loading areas often are in direct conflict with traffic flow or may create conflict and congestion with

FIGURE 2. Checklist for Determining the Adequacy of Existing Common Area Routes and Practices

Yes   No   1.   Are the behavioral expectations for each area of the school established?

     ✓   There is consensus among staff/community on behavioral expectations.
     ✓   Behavioral expectations are stated objectively.
     ✓   Behavioral expectations are reasonable and limited in number.

Yes   No   2.   Is there an implementation plan to insure staff, students, and parents understand the behavioral expectations?

     ✓   Behavioral expectations are written down.
     ✓   Teaching plans for the behavioral expectations are developed
     ✓   180 day implementation plan is established to insure that students understand and can perform the common area routines.
     ✓   Staff understand their responsibility in insuring students and parents understand behavioral expectations.

Yes   No   3.   Is there adequate supervision?

     ✓   Supervisors are trained.
     ✓   Ratio of supervisors to students is adequate to promote positive social behavior.
     ✓   There are established patterns of supervision.
     ✓   Natural supervision is utilized (e.g., natural flow of parents, staff, etc., are used to promote positive student behavior).
     ✓   Students are reinforced for exhibiting appropriate behavior.

Yes   No   4.   Are there effective reactive strategies in place to address minor problem behavior?

     ✓   Reactive strategies are reasonable, decisive (limited warnings), and provide students an opportunity to try again.
     ✓   Reactive strategies reduce opportunities for students to manipulate or engage staff.
     ✓   Strategies are designed to reduce the need for record keeping and communication.
     ✓   Continuum of structures is in place to address chronic minor problem behavior.
     ✓   Efficient record keeping and communication system is established to monitor chronic minor problem behavior.

Yes   No   5.   Is there a continuum of structures in place to address serious or challenging problem behavior?
     ✓   Behaviors warranting office referral are delineated.
     ✓   Efficient record keeping and communication system is established to monitor serious or challenging problem behavior.
     ✓   Progressive levels of discipline that are focused on increasing levels of support for the student and staff.

automobile parking areas. These zones also can be in direct conflict with the flow of students leaving the school grounds or entering for extra-curricular activities. Congestion created by traffic and student flow may provide an occasion for undesirable interactions between students.

### Improving Scheduling and Use of Space

One of the most effective strategies for promoting positive social behaviors centers around improving the scheduling and use of space. For instance, it takes longer to get groups through the lunch line because of congestion. The congestion may provide occasions for more undesirable interactions between students. For example, one class may be passing through a doorway to exit the cafeteria while another class may be entering the cafeteria at the same time. Separating the cafeteria entrance and exit by space, or staggering the start and end of the lunch period can help define movement in and out of the area. Although there are no set rules for scheduling and using space, the following guidelines are recommended: (a) reduce the density of students by using all entrances and exits to a given area, increasing the space between groups/lines/classes, and increasing the age spread of students as the density of students increases; (b) insure that wait time is kept at a minimum; (c) reduce travel time and distance as much as possible; (d) use physical signs to control movement such as clearly marked transition zones that indicate movement from a less controlled to a more controlled space or to indicate behavioral expectations for the common areas of the school; and (e) insure that the sequence of events in the common areas are designed to facilitate the type of behavioral momentum desired (e.g., going to recess before lunch rather than going to lunch before recess results in students being better prepared for instruction).

## ESTABLISHING COMMON AREA ROUTINES

The second major area examined for common areas in a school are the routines. Many school staff presume that students know the common area routines. We have found that these routines need to be systematically designed and taught. Based on the needs assessment, the building team identifies common area routines that promote positive social behavior and minimize problem behavior. The process of establishing effective common area routines includes: (a) identifying specific routines; (b) task analyzing the routines; (c) teaching and maintaining routines; and (d) responding to problem behavior.

## *Identifying the Routines*

Determining what school staff want to accomplish is the first step in establishing effective routines for the common areas of the school. The critical step is to identify the purpose of a given common area and then create a routine to achieve it. Routines for the common areas of the school typically evolve around three areas: (a) transitions; (b) administrative procedures; and (c) setting/activity requirements. Figure 3 presents some examples of routines that fall under each of these areas.

## *Task Analysis of the Routines*

A task analysis of the routines for the common areas is used to specify, in a precise manner, the behavior required by students in the common areas. These behaviors should be discrete, sequential, and observable. Before writing up the task analyses for the common area routines, committee members should look at information gained from the needs assessment as well as try the common area routines a few times themselves. Committee members should become aware of different ways the common area routines can be done. Think about the needs of the staff and students, then select the behaviors that work best for each. Note that the level of detail in the task analysis depends on the kinds of problems that have been identified, the age of the students, and the size of the group. Figure 4 presents an example of a problem area identified in the needs assessment and the associated revised routine.

## *Teaching and Maintaining Routines*

Teaching common area routines is much the same as teaching an academic concept or classroom routine. The more time spent teaching stu-

FIGURE 3. Routines for Common Areas of the School

| Transitions | Administrative | Setting/Activity |
|---|---|---|
| • Arrival<br>• Dismissal<br>• Hallways<br>• Bicycles<br>• Lining up | • Fire drill<br>• Office communication<br>• Procedures if sent to office<br>  for misbehavior | • Cafeteria<br>• Recess (indoor and<br>  outdoor)<br>• Restroom<br>• Safety Patrol<br>• Extracurricular<br>• Assemblies<br>• Bus |

dents the common area routines the better the students will do. Typically, teachers develop a lesson plan to teach a skill that involves explanations, modeling, practice, correction procedures, feedback, and review (Walker, Colvin, & Ramsey, 1995). Figure 5 outlines the major teaching elements included in a teaching or lesson plan for common area routines. The teaching elements parallel those used to teach an academic lesson, and require a well-developed lesson plan.

After teaching plans have been developed for each of the common areas of the school, instructional planning is the next step in establishing common area routines. This plan sequences which routines are taught on the first day of school, the second day of school, etc. Instructional planning includes: (a) prioritizing the routines with regard to how critical they are in maintaining a proactive positive school climate; and (b) developing a calendar plan for school staff to follow.

Identifying the desired behaviors in the common areas and teaching them does not guarantee that the students will demonstrate them throughout the year. There are no short cuts to effective and efficient common area routines. School staff must not only actively plan and teach students the common area routines, they must develop a 180-day maintenance plan to insure that students will continue to follow the common area routines. A 180-day maintenance plan includes three phases. In the first phase, students are taught the routines with high levels of supervision. This supervi-

FIGURE 4. Task Analysis of Routine for Students Coming in from Recess

---

<u>Problem Area Identified in Needs Assessment</u>

When the students come back from recess they rush to the classroom door, talk loudly, and many of the students are pushing and hitting each other. Teachers find it takes several minutes to get the students settled down in the classroom before they can start teaching.

---

<u>Task Analysis of Routine for Students Coming in from Recess</u>

The teacher meets the class at the door and signals to the students to line up.
Students form a single line with space between each student (no touching).
Students stay in their space for a brief second.
The teacher signals the students to enter the school.
The students enter the school walking quietly.
Students enter the classroom and go to their desk or assigned area.
Teacher gives students feedback on the extent to which they met the expectations.
Students begin work on assigned activity.

FIGURE 5. Elements in a Lesson Plan for Teaching Common Area Routines

| Teaching Element | Description |
|---|---|
| 1. Objectives | A statement that articulates to students what they will be able to do at the end of the lesson. |
| 2. Rationale | A statement that clearly explains to students the importance of learning a skill, including personal benefits and relevance. |
| 3. Modeling and Concept Teaching | Techniques utilizing a clear, explicit, and appropriate range of examples and non-examples through multiple demonstrations. Shows students what the behaviors look like. |
| 4. Role Playing | A procedure to provide practice through simulation. |
| 5. Rehearsal | Verbal or nonverbal procedure to provide practice under controlled conditions. |
| 6. Practice | Guided and independent activities to minimize errors and build learning. Gives students a chance to demonstrate their understanding of the common area routine. |
| 7. Coaching | A process to provide immediate and specific feedback on the students' performance. |
| 8. Feedback | Descriptive information regarding students' correct and incorrect performance of the routine. |

sion must continue through the first two to three weeks of school, and should include high rates of social reinforcement and corrective feedback if necessary. The second phase involves conducting periodic reviews during the first two months of the school session (e.g., systematic review every Monday) with reduced levels of supervision. "Booster sessions" are conducted throughout the remainder of the year in the third phase (e.g., as needed and after holidays).

### *Responding to Problem Behavior*

Teaching common area routines at the beginning of the year, and actively working to maintain them encourages appropriate behavior. However, students occasionally will exhibit problem behavior in spite of this proactive strategy. Thus, it is important for the committee to develop effective strategies for both minor and challenging problem behaviors. Although it is beyond the scope of this paper to fully describe a potential continuum of strategies for these behaviors, some factors should be considered when developing such strategies.

The basic response to problem behavior should be corrective in nature. That is, staff should respond to the student in a constructive and positive manner so that the problem behavior is identified and the students are directed to follow the routine. Overall, school staff respond to problem behavior quickly and directly. This implies that supervision needs to be active. Effectively implementing a continuum of responses to problem behavior in the common areas of the school begins with insuring that school staff are aware of what is going on at all times. Staff must be able to supervise one group of students while monitoring the rest. The ratio of supervisors to students must be adequate to promote positive social behavior. It is extremely difficult for staff who are supervising a common area of the school to be aware of what is going on if the ratio of staff to students is low. Establishing patterns of supervision enables staff to provide a more complete and balanced coverage of the common areas. Staff also need to be clear on behaviors warranting office referrals and which behaviors they should manage themselves. Staff will need to be given systematic training in the supervision of common areas and in implementing constructive responses to problem behavior.

Although schools should emphasize positive procedures, aversive interventions are a necessary part of a continuum of responses to problem behavior. It is important to note, however, that schools (and society) tend to rely on aversive interventions far too much. Nevertheless, aversive interventions help to deter problem behavior. Unfortunately, many of the typical aversive interventions used by schools (e.g., detention) are ill-designed, and may promote problem behavior rather than deter it. Aversive interventions should be designed to insure that they achieve their intended effect. The major issues to consider include: (a) insure that the aversive intervention is developed on the basis of its effect on students and not on the basis of its effect on school staff; (b) delineate and actively teach students what behaviors warrant the use of the aversive interventions; and (c) develop an informed-consent process such as a parent manual and/or individual communication structures.

## Implementing and Maintaining Ecological Arrangements and Common Area Routines

A six-step review, revision, adoption, and evaluation process is used to implement and maintain the ecological arrangements and routines for the common areas of the school. The first step involves the development of a draft proposal. The draft proposal should contain a description of the current ecological arrangements and common area routines and a description of the revised arrangements and routines, including a discussion of the rationale for the changes (pros and cons).

In the second step, the draft proposal is presented to all staff for discussion. The committee should explain the process that the staff will use to review, revise, and adopt the ecological arrangements and common area routines. Staff should be given copies of the draft proposal a few days prior to the formal presentation of the proposal. This will allow staff adequate time to fully assess the implications of the revised ecological arrangements and common area routines, and to provide useful feedback and recommendations. In addition, it is important that the committee spend time explaining the development phase, especially a discussion of the design considerations and rationale that were used to develop the ecological arrangements and common area routines. Staff members will understand more fully the proposed ecological arrangements and common area routines if they are aware of those things that were considered in their development.

In the third step, the proposal is revised based on staff feedback and recommendations. Some ecological arrangements and common area routines may require major revisions, while others will be approved quickly. Quite often this is dependent upon the culture of the school and the process used for other school-wide matters. The review, revision, and adoption meetings should have an established agenda that is followed. This will enable the committee to move through the entire process in a timely manner. The second and third steps are repeated until consensus is achieved.

The fourth step involves presenting the final proposal to all staff for approval, including a staff development plan to insure the implementation of the ecological arrangements and common area routines. Staff development actually begins with the review, revision, and adoption process. Staff will begin to develop a common knowledge base as they consider, discuss, and finally adopt the ecological arrangements and common area routines. This process will provide them with an understanding of the design considerations, rationale, and fundamental changes in the ecological arrangements and common area routines. After this point, the committee should arrange the necessary staff development activities that will insure the successful implementation of the ecological arrangements and common area routines.

Fifth, a conceptually sound and properly implemented supervision system for school staff is a vital component of the effective implementation of the ecological arrangements and common area routines. Regardless of how well the ecological arrangements and common area routines have been designed, they are only as effective as the people who implement them. In other words, effective personnel insure effective ecological arrangements and common area routines.

The final step is evaluation. Four key points are critical to the evaluation of the ecological arrangements and common area routines. First, evaluation must be based on a variety of formal and informal information. Second, the evaluation information should be compared to baseline information collected during the needs assessment and subsequent evaluation data. Third, the evaluation findings must be shared with the entire school staff. Finally, the ecological arrangements and common area routines should be adjusted based on the results of the evaluation.

## CASE STUDY AND PRELIMINARY FINDINGS

We will present some preliminary findings to illustrate the effects that establishing effective ecological arrangements and common area routines has on the social behavior of students. The findings are based on work conducted in a number of large elementary schools ($n = 700$) serving a low socioeconomic neighborhood (over 80% of the students receive free or reduced lunch). A typical recess lunch period will be used to illustrate the effects of effective ecological arrangements on the social behavior of students. Office referral data collected over a two-week period (a software package was used to track office referral data) in the school indicated high rates of problem behavior during the lunch recess period. Approximately 35 office referrals per week were made during the lunch recess. Close inspection of the office referrals indicated that a majority of them were made in response to students' behavior immediately prior to entering the school rather than during the lunch recess period itself. Observations revealed that students were required to line up two minutes prior to their teachers picking them up to return to the classroom. The wait time was reduced to 30 seconds. This resulted in a 98% reduction in office referrals during the lunch recess period.

Two typical common area routines will be used to illustrate the effects of well constructed routines on the social behaviors of students. Two primary dependent measures were used to assess the effects of well-constructed common area routines: (a) social behavior (positive and disruptive behavior during the breakfast and before school settings); and (b) disciplinary actions for the common areas of the school. (Optimal ecological arrangements were established prior to the implementation of the common area routines.) Figures 6 and 7 present the percentage of intervals scored as positive behavior

FIGURE 6. Percentage of Intervals Scored as Positive Behavior

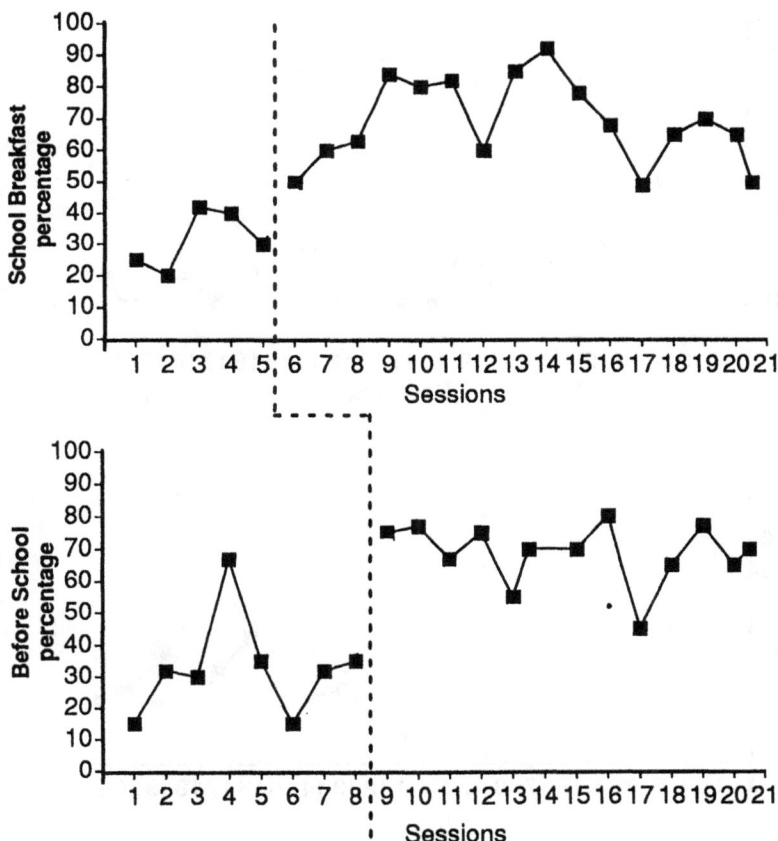

and disruptive behavior in the school breakfast and before school settings, respectively. The rates of positive behavior increased in both of these settings following the implementation of the school-wide program (see Figure 6). In contrast, the rates of disruptive behavior decreased in both the school breakfast and before school settings following the implementation of the school-wide program (see Figure 7).

The average number of referrals per day to the office for disciplinary action during baseline conditions for the common areas of the school was approximately 5 (range 1 to 11). Following the implementation of the school-wide program, the average number of referrals to the office for

FIGURE 7. Percentage of Intervals Scored as Disruptive Behavior

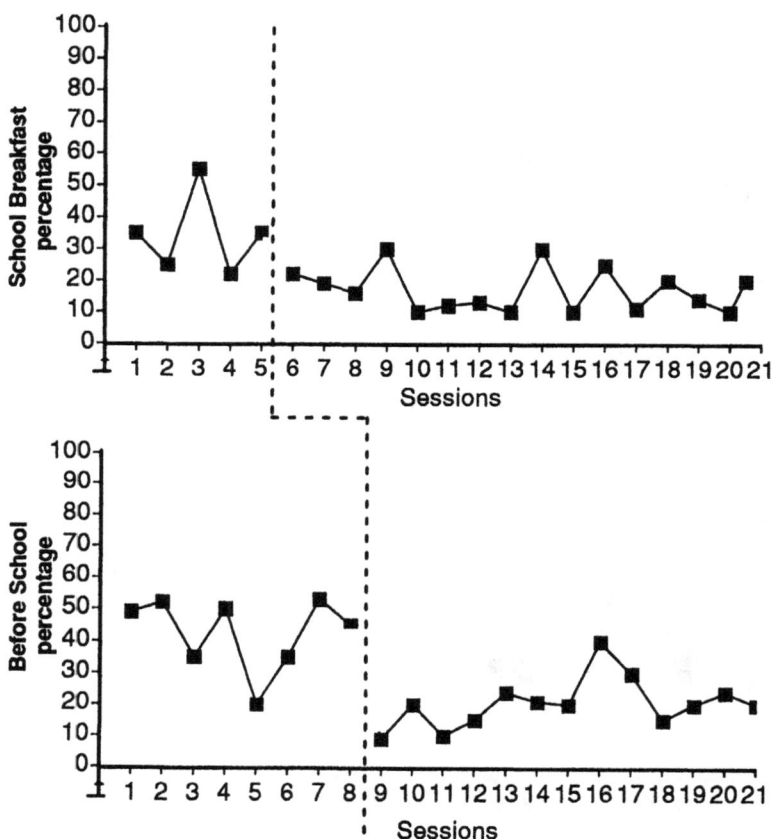

disciplinary action decreased. The average number for the common areas of the school was approximately 1 (range 0 to 5).

## CONCLUSION

Developing supportive school environments are critical to the success of all students including those with SED. This is especially critical because the management of problem behavior or the "lack of discipline" has been identified by the public as the most persistent and possibly the most troublesome issue facing schools (Center & McKittrick, 1987; Cotton, 1990; Elam, Rose, & Gallup, 1992; Jones, 1993). Increasingly, public school personnel are facing problem behavior that occurs more frequently and that significantly affects staff and student safety (Greenbaum & Turner, 1989). Further, significant shifts in patterns of poverty and in family characteristics occurring in the demographic makeup of the United States will add to this problem. In short, our nation's schools must reconceptualize their fundamental approach to addressing the more complex patterns of social behavior that confront them. A basic part of this reorientation will center on reconceptualizing school-wide discipline practices. The purpose of this paper was to describe an approach designed to achieve effective ecological arrangements and routines in the common areas of the school.

Clear and salutary changes in social behavior occurred for students when the ecological arrangements and common area routines were introduced. The rates of positive child social behavior increased and the rates of negative child social behavior decreased. These rates maintained throughout the experimental condition. The introduction of the program also reduced the rates of negative adult social behavior and increased the rates of positive adult social behavior. These findings suggest that ecological arrangements and routines in the common areas of the schools play a role in the social behavior of students.

Converging evidence for the effectiveness of achieving effective ecological arrangements and common area routines comes from previous work conducted on the disciplinary actions taken with junior high school students (Colvin, Sugai, & Kameenui, 1994). In this study, a similar comprehensive instructional approach to school-wide and classroom management was implemented at a junior high school. The findings indicated that the approach significantly reduced disciplinary actions. For example, there was a 50% decrease in office referrals for problem behavior. Notable decreases also were observed in office conferences, suspensions, detentions, and parent meetings.

Finally, the process of designing a supportive school staff also benefits the entire staff. The design and implementation process requires that staff work together and develop consensus on a wide range of discipline issues. As a result of this process, staff report that the working environment of the school is more supportive and collegial. In addition, staff report that they are more satisfied with their jobs and that they are more confident in their ability to work with children with challenging behavior.

## REFERENCES

Center, D. B., & McKittrick, S. (1987). Disciplinary removal of special education students. *Focus on Exceptional Children, 20*(2), 1-9.

Colvin, G., Sugai, G., & Kameenui, E. (1994). Reconceptualizing school-wide discipline. *Education and Treatment of Children, 16,* 361-381.

Cotton, K. (1990). *School improvement series, close-up #9: School wide and class-room discipline.* Portland, OR: Northwest Regional Educational Laboratory.

Edgar, E., & Levine, P. (1987). *Special education students in transition: Washington State data 1976-1986.* Seattle: University of Washington, Experimental Education Unit.

Elam, S. E., Rose, L. C., & Gallup, A. M. (1992). The 24th annual Gallup/Phi Delta Kappa poll of the public's attitudes toward public schools, *Kappan, 74*(1), 41-53.

Gilbert, P. (1993). Defense and safety: Their function in social behaviour and psychopathology. *British Journal of Clinical Psychology, 32,* 131-153.

Greenbaum, S., & Turner, B. (Eds.) (1989). *Safe schools overview: NSSC resource paper.* Malibu, CA: U.S. Department of Justice, U.S. Department of Education and Pepperdine University.

Jones, V. (1993). Assessing your classroom and school-wide student management plan. *Beyond Behavior, 4*(3), 9-12.

Kauffman, J. M., Cullinan, D., & Epstein, M. H. (1987). Characteristics of students placed in special programs for the seriously emotionally disturbed. *Behavioral Disorders, 12,* 175-184.

Morrison, G. M., Furlong, M. J., & Morrison, R. L. (1994). School violence to school safety: Reframing the issue for school psychologists. *School Psychology Review, 23,* 236-256.

Neel, R., Meadows, N., Levine, P., & Edgar, E. (1988). What happens after special education: A statewide follow-up study of secondary students who have behavioral disorders. *Behavioral Disorders, 13*(3), 209-216.

Walker, H., Colvin, G., & Ramsey, E. (1995). *Antisocial behavior in school: Strategies and best practices.* Pacific Grove, CA: Brooks/Cole.

# SYSTEMS CHANGE TOWARD INTEGRATED SERVICES

## Involving Families in Change: Challenges and Opportunities

Barbara J. Friesen

Portland State University

Trina W. Osher

Federation of Families for Children's Mental Health

**SUMMARY.** In this article, a range of matters are considered that have to do with involvement of families with children with severe behavioral and emotional disorders in change. Family participation on education and system change is reviewed, while principles of family participation are enumerated. *[Article copies available from The Haworth Document Delivery Service: 1-800-342-9678.]*

Public education, at all levels, is the subject of much public criticism at the same time that it is undergoing constant reform. Although the ap-

---

Address correspondence to: Barbara J. Friesen, Research & Training Center on Family Support and Children's Mental Health, 1912 SW 6th, Portland State University, Portland, OR 97207-0751.

[Haworth co-indexing entry note]: "Involving Families in Change: Challenges and Opportunities." Friesen, Barbara J., and Trina W. Osher. Co-published simultaneously in *Special Services in the Schools* (The Haworth Press, Inc.) Vol. 11, No. 1/2, 1996, pp. 187-207; and: *Emerging School-Based Approaches for Children with Emotional and Behavioral Problems: Research and Practice in Service Integration* (ed: Robert J. Illback, and C. Michael Nelson) The Haworth Press, Inc., 1996, pp. 187-207. Single or multiple copies of this article are available from The Haworth Document Delivery Service [1-800-342-9678, 9:00 a.m. - 5:00 p.m. (EST)].

proaches to reform are as diverse as the children, families, schools and communities of this country, increased family involvement is an important aspect of most change efforts. Taking up the initiative of the nation's governors, bipartisan Congressional leadership established a vision for reform of public education today that is expressed in the Goals 2000: Educate America Act (U.S. Department of Education, 1994). Don Davies (Davies, 1994), a noted scholar of school reform, observed that, "significant changes at the school level are most likely to happen when there is consumer demand for change and when the reform effort includes families and communities in partnership with educators" (p. 44). Davies suggests that those interested in reform should work hard to "light up the fires of consumer demand" (p. 34) and create new roles for family and community members within our school systems.

Support for including families in the reform effort is expressed in Goal 8 of Goals 2000: "Every school will promote partnerships that will increase parental involvement and participation in promoting the social, educational, and academic growth of children" (U.S. Department of Education, 1994). Discussing the new Family Involvement Initiative, Secretary of Education Riley (1994) made the following appeal to teachers and to schools, "In my mind, a good parent is a national treasure, and we need to make parents and families partners with their children's teachers and principals in the process of education. By reaching out to parents, schools can encourage parental support for learning" (p. 12). Although the language in Goals 2000 refers to "parents," our use of the word families is purposeful, because not all primary care givers are parents. In addition to birth, foster, or adoptive parents, many children are raised by older siblings, grandparents, aunts or uncles, or partners of any of the above. Furthermore, extended family members of all children have talents and skills that can be tapped to enrich schools.

Not only does the current policy emphasis on family participation reflect beliefs about the importance of families in the lives of children, it is also supported by a large body of research. Study findings in both general and special education provide strong support for a link between parent involvement with their children's education and academic achievement, attendance, attitudes, and satisfaction (Dwyer & Hecht, 1992; Greenwood & Hickman, 1991). As stated in *Strong Families, Strong Schools* (U.S. Department of Education, 1994), "Thirty years of research shows that greater family involvement in children's learning is a critical link to achieving a high quality education and a safe, disciplined learning environment for every student" (page iii). Providing opportunities for families to get involved in and make a contribution to school improvement presents opportunities and challenges for all schools and all families.

Clearly, public schools need support to continue doing what they do well and to make changes where indicated. Satisfied families are the best advocates the public education system and the personnel who work in it can possibly have. Families must be sought out and encouraged to provide leadership and have meaningful policy input at all levels of decision making in the public school system as this is the way to have real influence in the educational process. If schools are to satisfy families, school staff must reach out and learn what their primary customers want from schools. They also need to communicate frankly about the system's strengths and weaknesses and seek genuine community input on the options and solutions being considered. Improving family involvement in schools is a jointly shared responsibility. Family members must make the effort to get involved in making decisions about their child's education. Family organizations must become knowledgeable about and actively seek involvement in the functioning and reform of the system as a whole.

Emphasizing the meaningful participation of all families should also increase the schools' capacity to respond to the diverse needs of children and families. It can also help promote culturally relevant educational experiences. This capacity will be increasingly important as "minority" students are projected to account for over 50 percent of the school-aged population by the year 2000 (Harry, 1992a). And diversity includes a wide variety of characteristics and qualities beyond race, such as cultural background, language, religious beliefs, income, education, age, gender, family composition, and employment status. Each of these differences may have implications for involving family members in the educational process. For example, Dauber and Epstein (1993) found that parents who worked were less likely to participate at school, but were as likely to be involved with their children's education at home as those who were not employed. Harry (1992) suggests that positive views of African American families and of children's learning needs must replace current perspectives to promote the participation of African American parents in the special education process. And Chavkin and Williams (1993) found variation in parents' preferences for types of school involvement across ethnic groups.

In addition to factors associated with cultural, social, and economic diversity, families whose children have emotional, behavioral, or mental disorders may face other barriers to school involvement. This group of family members is still highly stigmatized, and some family members may be reluctant to become involved with their child's school because of their fear of being blamed for their child's problems (Friesen & Koroloff, 1990;

Shea & Bauer, 1991). Family members may also be wary of interactions with school personnel because of past negative experiences with schools or other parts of the service system (Knitzer, Steinberg & Fleisch, 1990; Schulz, 1987). And families struggling with troubling behaviors on the part of their children and those with small children at home may lack time and energy for participation without specific support.

Despite these potential barriers, however, there is reason for considerable optimism. Family members from a broad cross-section of racial, economic, and social circumstances express an interest in being more involved in their children's education ( Chavkin & Garza-Lubeck, 1990; Chavkin & Williams, 1985;1989;1993). Further, reports from a number of programs designed to increase family participation in the educational process suggest that a wide variety of strategies are effective (Brinckerhoff & Vincent, 1986; Chavkin & Garza-Lubeck, 1990; Comer & Haynes, 1991; Chavkin & Williams, 1989; Dauber & Epstein, 1993).

## FAMILY PARTICIPATION IN EDUCATION AND SYSTEMS CHANGE

Public Law 94-142, (Education for All Handicapped Children Act of 1975) and its successor, the Individuals with Disabilities Education Act (IDEA) (1990), clearly mandate family involvement in the special education process by requiring that parents or other guardians be invited to participate in the process of developing and reviewing the Individual Educational Plan (IEP). Despite this mandate, and despite literally hundreds of books and articles devoted to the topic of parent involvement, the participation of family members in special education planning appears to be uneven and somewhat disappointing (Brinckerhoff & Vincent, 1986; Coughlin, 1989; Harry, 1992a; Katsiyannis & Ward, 1992; Palfrey, Walker, Butler & Singer, 1989; Schulz, 1987). Many authors emphasize strategies to encourage family members to participate in and with the schools, some featuring specific interventions to prepare and support families in the IEP process. Much of the literature addressing family involvement in general education contains a similar emphasis, including strategies to promote school-home communication and collaboration (Berger, 1991; Dwyer & Hecht, 1992).

In contrast with P.L. 94-142's focus on educational planning for children with disabilities, Part H of the Education of the Handicapped Act Amendments (1986) (PL. 99-457), recognizes the importance of providing support for families whose children under three years of age have disabilities. Through a plan that addresses the needs of the entire family, the Individualized Family Service Plan (IFSP), an interdisciplinary approach to addressing complex problems, PL. 99-457 provides a model for a more holistic approach to children and families, foreshadowing the "integrated services approach" addressed in this volume.

For children with emotional, behavioral, or mental disorders and their families, an important factor in promoting both parent participation in service planning and an integrated service approach has been the leadership of the federal government through the Child and Adolescent Service System Program (CASSP). Funded by Congress in 1984 through the National Institute of Mental Health, the CASSP initiative provided grants to states to stimulate interagency service coordination, the development of community-based services, family participation in all aspects of service planning and delivery, and a variety of financing and service delivery innovations. These reforms have also been stimulated by foundation support, notably the Robert Wood Johnson and Annie E. Casey Foundations (Stroul, 1995).

The development of two new national family organizations, the Federation of Families for Children's Mental Health, and the Child and Adolescent Network of the National Alliance for the Mentally Ill (NAMI-CAN), is evidence of the extent to which parents and other family members have joined together with strength and purpose to improve services for children with emotional, behavioral or mental disorders. Several states have mandated family participation in state and local mental health planning processes, and a new standard of family involvement in all aspects of service planning, implementation and evaluation is increasingly apparent. In addition to participation in planning at both the service delivery and systems levels, family members are also being hired in formal service delivery roles such as case manager and educational advocate (Ignelzi & Dague, 1995).

Because of the CASSP emphasis on interagency planning and service delivery, the public schools have been part of the systems change effort in many communities. Indeed, some of the school-affiliated programs featured in this publication are on the cutting edge in terms of family participation and family support. Other communities where the general reform effort in children's mental health is less apparent can build on and adapt these and other successful educational and service innovations, capitalizing on the growing national, state, and local family movement to develop new roles for families in pursuit of more integrated, family-friendly services.

A primary school related role for families of children with disabilities and the one promoted by the IDEA is that of advocacy. Families know best how their children perform in a wide variety of settings and situations. Families are a child's first advocate and the one source of support that is continuous throughout the child's educational career (as well as across the various agencies). This very necessity for continuity dictates the centrality of families in the entire educational process, in addition to advocacy for individual students, and particularly when special education services are contemplated or provided.

## Expanded Roles for Families: New Opportunities

Over the past 20 years considerable attention has been given to describing and categorizing the variety of ways that families are or can be involved in their children's education. Bauch (1994) reviews a variety of approaches to describing and categorizing the ways that families are or can be involved in their children's education. One way of thinking about family involvement is in terms of the intended target of influence, as exemplified by Gordon's (as cited in Bauch, 1994) categories of (1) parent impact mode, where energy and resources are focused on influencing the roles and behaviors of family members; (2) school impact mode, where attention is given to making the schools more responsive to parents and family members; and, (3) the community impact model, which posits a broad impact on individuals and community institutions. According to Bauch (1994) Gordon also identified six roles that parents can play when they interact with the schools. These are as: teacher of own child, decision-maker, classroom volunteer, paraprofessional, adult educator, and adult learner. A number of other authors also describe a variety of roles in which parents can or should be involved (see, e.g., Berger, 1991; Chavkin & Williams, 1993; Comer & Haynes, 1991; Dauber & Epstein, 1993). With the exception of Dauber and Epstein (1993), these authors only implicitly include criteria for describing family roles such as the location of activity (e.g., home or school), whether family members are engaged in direct educational roles such as tutor or classroom aide, or supportive roles (e.g., room parent, chaperone, fund raiser), the intensity of involvement, or the degree of influence that family members may have with regard to a variety of decisions.

We have chosen to organize our discussion of family roles in education according to the level at which family participation is focused. These are: (1) the individual student or family level; (2) the classroom level; (3) the building or school level; (4) the school district, educational service district, and state levels; and, (5) the national level.

## *Individual Student/Family Level*

Traditional forms of family involvement in education emphasize the role of parents in teaching or tutoring their own children, helping with or monitoring homework, and creating a home environment that is supportive to the educational process. When children have serious emotional, behavioral, or mental disorders or other disabilities, other important family roles emerge as paramount. In particular, parents and other family members should be centrally involved in the entire process of referral, assessment, planning, implementation, monitoring, and evaluation for special and general education services. Although the enactment of PL. 94-142 codified the importance of family involvement in the preparation and development of the Individual Education Plan (IEP), the promise of increased family involvement signaled by this law has yet to be fully realized (Turnbull & Turnbull, 1990). Beth Harry (1992a) summarizes the findings from a number of studies that emphasize the distinction between attendance at meetings and genuine participation. She also points out that "the participation of minority parents in special education programs stands out as even less involved and less informed than those of the mainstream" (p. 100).

As Turnbull and Turnbull (1990) and Harry (1992a) point out, the role of parents in the assessment and planning process is often minimal. Explanations for this phenomenon are very much dependent on one's perspective. School personnel may perceive parents as lacking interest or understanding of their child's disability, when in fact, families are overwhelmed or intimidated. Parents may feel that schools are excluding them from the planning process or withholding pertinent information when in fact there are administrative constraints on handling confidential information, or other barriers.

Fortunately, conceptual developments both within and outside of the education system have renewed the emphasis on family participation in the assessment and planning processes. In a special education study, Brinckerhoff and Vincent (1986) prepared parents for the IEP process by having them complete a developmental assessment of their child, record a family profile, and meet with a community/school liaison prior to the IEP meeting. This intervention had a positive effect on parents' contributions and programming decisions in the meetings. Henning-Stout (1994) proposes a shift from a focus on children's skills and deficits through standardized testing to a more ecological approach that takes into account the social context of the child's learning. From this perspective the child's various environments including home, classroom and social/peer setting are examined and adjusted to produce the best fit between the child's learning needs and the environment. Entitled "responsive assessment" (Henning-Stout, 1994), this approach to assessment considers parents and other family members as central informants and decision-makers in educational assessment and planning.

Including family members as central to the assessment process will require considerable change in most schools and in teacher education, as well. Young, Gable, and Hendrickson (1989) examined the extent to which special education teachers are trained to employ an ecological perspective including school, home, and community factors in their educational planning, and found that although ecological issues are addressed in teacher education, the bulk of both course and field time emphasized those factors that could be controlled within the classroom.

An emphasis on an ecological approach to assessment involving all relevant persons is also a cornerstone of assessment and planning for "wraparound" services in children's mental health (VanDenBerg, 1992). This approach emphasizes individualized services built around the specific strengths and needs of the child and family in eight domain areas including (1) a place to live; (2) family or surrogate family; (3) social (friends and contact with other people); (4) education/vocational; (5) medical; (6) psychological/emotional; (7) legal; (8) safety; and (9) other child-specific areas such as cultural and ethnic needs or community needs. Youth and family members participate in the wraparound planning process along with all other relevant service providers, including school personnel.

In a number of communities family members have been hired as members of interagency planning teams to support the involvement of family members in the assessment and planning process for their children. In Utah, at the Four Corners Mental Health Center, for example, a standing committee composed of service and education personnel includes a paid family member whose role is to provide information and support to families whose children's needs are considered in an interagency planning process (Margaret Thiele, personal communication). This process does not substitute for the IEP process, but the participation of family members and school personnel assures that educational planning is tied to the integrated service plan.

In this volume a similar approach is described by Lucille Eber, who asserts that "system of care leaders, including educators, need to recognize the importance of including parents as active partners . . . in this shift to more family-focused planning and service delivery" (p. 15). As Eber suggests, perhaps the most radical change for school personnel is the inclusion of services that go beyond the needs of the "special education child," and address the needs of the entire family. Clearly, such family-centered service cannot be funded solely with special education funds; in many cases a number of agencies come together to create a pool of flexible funds to support such interventions. In Oregon, for example, local school districts, child welfare, and mental health agencies, the State Medicaid agency, and a county level department of social services collaborated to form the Oregon Partners Project featuring pooled funding which could be used to support a broad range of services for children and families. This project was stimulated and partially supported by the Mental Health Services Program for Youth funded by the Robert Wood Johnson Foundation (Cole, 1993). Although the demonstration project has ended, many positive features of the program have been adopted within the current system.

Family roles at the child and family level also include a variety of information giving and receiving responsibilities, sometimes involving daily communication with teachers. Other responsibilities include activities such as structuring and monitoring homework, if necessary, and implementing and coordinating social and recreational aspects of the child's service plan.

### Classroom/Unit Level

Traditional roles for parents in the classroom include that of room parent, field trip chaperone, and volunteer aide. Family members may also serve as co-teachers, either on a regular or occasional basis. Inviting parents to appear as "guest artists" is one way to increase children's experience of diverse cultures and perspectives, as well as serving to strengthen ties with individual family members. For example, family members may be invited to share ethnic costumes, music and folklore, or talents and skills as diverse as magic, water-colors or veterinary medicine. The main objective is to positively involve family members in the educational process, and to acknowledge their strengths and contributions. Not all contributions to the classroom must be made in the classroom. Family members with access to computer equipment might assist with including photographs or other images in a newsletter, help the class set up a "home page" on the Internet, or correspond with members of the class by E-mail (Dwyer & Hecht, 1992).

Dwyer and Hecht (1992) assert that schools need to develop a better understanding of the needs and situation of families before developing a program to increase their participation. Issues to be addressed at the classroom level include expectations about "volunteering," school-related challenges, and family-related needs. An important issue about family members as volunteers is that it is often not reasonable to expect that family members should donate many hours of their time on a regular basis.

Generally, parents who assume "jobs" within the school should be paid for their work. School factors may also mitigate against increased family involvement, despite recognition that increasing family involvement requires flexible school environments that can accommodate family work schedules and other responsibilities (Comer & Haynes, 1991). Union rules that severely constrain the hours and schedules that teachers may work, or certification requirements that make it difficult to pay family members for their contributions may need to be revisited. Family-related issues may include work responsibilities, transportation and child care problems, or remuneration that is not sufficient or permanent enough to risk losing benefits (Comer & Haynes, 1991; Ignelzi & Dague, 1995). Family involvement in schools poses some potential threats to students as well. Some students may be embarrassed when a member of their family is a prominent visitor at school. School staff can help by assigning the adult to a role where contact with the student and her or his peers is minimal and by discreetly letting the student know how much the family member's support and work is appreciated. Of course, we could hope that once family involvement in schools is well institutionalized, children would be more concerned if someone from their family was not occasionally seen working in the school.

To make the most of family members' potential contributions to the classroom, parents and other family members need orientation, guidance, and in some instances, training, depending on the demands of the role. Bauch (1993) classified family roles in the school according to how much they demanded of teachers, recognizing the effort and planning required to assure that the needs of the school and the talents of parents are most effectively matched. All responsibility, however, need not fall on classroom teachers, and a number of authors describe specific roles such as "family school liaison" created to improve communication and promote school-family partnerships (Comer & Haynes, 1991; Chavkin & Garza-Lubeck, 1990; Kurtz & Barth, 1989).

Family members can also work collaboratively with school personnel to plan and implement family participation strategies (Friesen & Huff, 1990). For example, family members could provide an orientation for family volunteers to the structure and operating procedures of the school and classroom, or help to inventory and match family members' talents with classroom needs. Providing outreach to family members can also be undertaken by family members. In an Oregon program designed to provide families of kindergarten children with information about child develop, volunteer "parent home visitors" provided families with developmentally appropriate toys and an invitation to visit the school's book and toy lending library. These family volunteers were oriented and trained by a parent professional team. Family member volunteers or paid family staff can also make an important contribution to the challenge of individualizing outreach to families who have not previously been involved. Klimes-Dougan, Lopez, Nelson, and Adelman (1992) found that a simple strategy involving a specific invitation to low income parents resulted in higher attendance at a school event. Chavkin and Garza-Lubeck (1990) describe a number of effective multicultural practices to increase the active participation of families from diverse cultures and backgrounds.

Businesses can also promote family participation in their children's education. Mannan and Blackwell (1992) contend that business and industries interested in school reform place too much attention on school related variables, and not enough on work-related variables that might act as incentives for parents and other adults to get involved in the education of children. According to these authors, for example, AT&T allows employees to take leave on short notice to attend to school-related matters and some businesses have opened schools at work sites.

### Building/School Level

As important customers and stockholders of educational services, family members can play a number of vital roles in the overall design and implementation of the school's program. Family members can contribute to the curriculum development process by providing feedback about their children's responses to the curriculum and other aspects of the educational process. They can also participate in school governance bodies as a part of the planning, implementation and evaluation process for integrated service approaches. There has been much progress in the area of family-oriented evaluation over the last ten years, especially in the development of measures. There are now available a number of instruments designed to measure concepts such as the degree to which organizations are family-centered (Petr, 1995), a family-specific view of service coordination (DeChillo & Lebow, 1991), family empowerment (Koren, DeChillo, & Friesen, 1992), and the degree to which organizations provide culturally appropriate services (Mason, 1995).

Family members can play a unique and key role in staff development by providing school personnel with family perspectives of the educational process, suggesting outreach and communication strategies, and addressing issues related to family-school collaboration. Family members can also play other bridging roles such as mediating family-school, or children-school disputes.

Two major challenges are related to increased family involvement at the school, or building level. The first has to do with providing flexibility and choice with regard to the type and intensity of family involvement, realizing that these may need to vary over time. Comer and Haynes (1991) emphasize this point in a description of their well known school reform efforts. The family involvement program in their target schools is explicitly organized into three levels, and the opportunities and responsibilities associated with each level are communicated to all family members, along with the general message that their participation is important. Comer and Haynes (1991) report that as a result of their parent outreach and involvement program, attendance at major school activities increased from 15 to over 400 over a four year period.

The second major challenge is associated with the shift from school-controlled to shared decision-making with families. As Eber points out in this volume, considerable discomfort may be experienced by service providers, including school personnel, as family members assume more leadership and decision-making responsibility. Comer and Haynes (1991) describe the initial reluctance of school staff about family participation in governance and management, and recommend careful preparation for increased family involvement. They provide a number of practical tips that address issues such as preparation of staff for the change process, the importance of supporting and training parents, the development of clear role definitions, and the desirability of parent-teacher match.

### District/State Levels

At the school district, educational service district, or state levels, family members can provide effective leadership and advocacy. Organized family groups can be especially important in promoting policy change, as they can take formal positions on policy issues. Many have well-developed networks to communicate quickly on critical issues (such as resource allocations) with a large number of members. Parents may also initiate and implement needed program change. For example, the Oregon Graduate Alliance was formed by parents to promote better transition planning and programming for high school aged youth with developmental disabilities. They developed program initiatives to address gaps in school programs across the state.

Family participation in policy-related activities requires that family members have the opportunity to develop skills and have ready access to information necessary for full participation. Training materials such as those developed by Hunter (1994) provide foundation information to individuals and family groups about the policy-making and change processes. Educators and other service providers should work in partnership with family members, providing issue-specific information before and between meetings or other decision points.

Especially at the school district, or special service district level, it is also important for family members and school personnel to develop a common understanding about the extent of influence that family members are expected to have. Although families and school personnel may initially disagree about these boundaries, such discourse is much more desirable than failure to address this issue. Not infrequently, family members engage in policy or program related discussions only to be disappointed when their advice or perspectives appear to be disregarded. This problem is often related to the disparate expectations of the educational system, who see family input as advisory, and family participants got involved because they believed there was an opportunity to have an impact. Comer and Haynes (1991) explicitly address issues of influence and authority in their orientation and training for family members involved in their school reform efforts.

## National Level

Family participation in promoting reform at the national level takes place within existing federal agencies, and can be aimed at the legislative process. Family members, especially those who represent family organizations, may be invited to participate in identifying priorities for programs and research in a variety of federal education programs, including the Office of Special Education Programs, and the National Institute on Disability and Rehabilitation Research. Family members could also serve as part of the special education monitoring process at the national and state levels. Another important contribution of family members is to serve as members of peer review panels for education research and program grants. Turnbull and Friesen (1995) discuss the issue of family members on peer review panels and emphasize the importance of selection, training, and support for family members in the peer review process.

Singly, and as a part of coalitions, national family organizations participate in identifying issues, drafting and supporting legislation, and in organizing responses to proposed legislation and rule changes. At the national level, family organizations are challenged to keep abreast of policy issues and trends. It has been very important for organizations such as the Federation of Families for Children's Mental Health and the National Parent Network on Disability both to collaborate with professionals who understand the policy-making process, and to increase the capacity of family members to engage in a variety of activities related to the impact of education reform on students with disabilities.

## PRINCIPLES OF FAMILY PARTICIPATION

Many of the challenges and strategies identified thus far have been tied to specific levels of family participation. In this section we conclude with a set of general principles about family participation in education.

### Respect the Diversity of Families

Schools must strive for cultural competence and to demonstrate that they respect the diversity and varied experiences of all families regardless of how they are configured or the level of resources that they have. Language used in schools must be family friendly, jargon free, and respectful of the values, language, and culture of the children that they educate and their families. It is incumbent upon professional preparation programs to collaborate with all kinds of families in the educational enterprise.

### Have Clear Goals for Each Aspect of the Family Participation Program

The range of school related roles for families, including families with students who have disabilities, is limited only by the imagination and creativity of school personnel and family members. Nevertheless, having a clear and limited objective helps to recruit the right family collaborators and keeps the team focused once it is organized. Identifying partners is the first step in building the collaborative partnership. In order for the new family school partnership to work the philosophy and principles behind it must take root in the school system's heart. Institutional values and attitudes must be family centered and family friendly. A culture and belief system that says family members will be part of everything that this system does must be infused through every operation, department, and program of the system. Personnel must believe in a full and equal partnership with families and behave in ways that demonstrate their commitment to it.

### Develop Outreach Strategies That Are Individualized for Specific Parent/Family Collaborations

Educators need to reach out to the family and other groups that have a stake in the task they wish to undertake. For example, if expanding opportunities for inclusion of students with emotional, behavioral, or mental disorders in general education classes is the goal, teachers and family members of students in those classes, as well as family members and advocates for the students with disabilities who are to have this opportunity, need to agree with the goal and be involved in making decisions about how this will be accomplished.

Reaching out to meet and talk with families could mean going to their workplaces during lunchtime or to other locations where families congregate. Teachers can share their own views, give an overview of the tasks the school needs help with, ask family members how they think they can help, and find out what kinds of support they will need.

## Work with Family Members to Match Their Interests and Talents to Program Needs

Not all roles are right for all family members. Matching family members to the jobs that a school needs done is essential for success in the partnership. Unlike the interchangeable parts of a car coming off an assembly line in Detroit, one family member cannot readily be substituted for another. Effectively utilizing the unique skills and talents of family members in a school, classroom, or special education program requires screening, planning, and training similar to recruiting professional staff. Family members should build on their own strengths and the best interests of their children in selecting projects to work on and roles to play in schools.

## Be Realistic About Demands/Expectations of Family Volunteers

Other family and work obligations as well as logistics such as travel, meeting times, and child care arrangements affect the extent of commitment a family member can make to any task. The extent to which the school accommodates these as well as other individual requirements related to the extra effort associated with raising a child with a disability will influence the match between family members and the roles they play in schools. The best way for school staff to discover new school related roles for families is to talk directly with them. This is especially important given evidence (Hermary & Rempel, 1990) that family members and school personnel may have quite different ideas about what is likely to appeal to and motivate family members. A variety of networking strategies can be used to establish links with family run support, training, and advocacy groups or organizations in the community that focus their efforts on serving families with students who have disabilities. Educators can learn about the groups with which family members in their school are affiliated, arrange to meet with the family groups, and talk with them about what they like about the school and what they think should change.

## Provide Relevant Information and Training to Family Members

Families that are well informed about what is happening in school are better able to support their child's learning and feel more comfortable about coming to school when they have concerns. Family members will need information and training to perform their new roles well. The amount of training and the nature of the information will depend on the role. Someone who is going to handle the phones while the school secretary is on vacation needs to know how the phone system works but also needs to be told about how routine procedures (such as relaying messages to teachers during class time) are handled. This person also needs up to date information about the calendar of events and other school functions the public may call about. Someone who is going to serve on an advisory committee to the superintendent will need a different kind of preparation.

For the most part, even the most educated family members do not have good information about how school policy is established and about how state policy influences policy development and program design at the community level. This includes knowing about the organizational structures, knowing the names of key decision makers and how to contact them, and understanding the development of school budgets and how funding priorities are established. Family members who are planning to serve in a policy capacity also need to become familiar with all the resources that exist and what kinds of programs can be developed. Yet, families are likely to get their information about schools from the public media, what their children tell them and bring home, or the experiences of other family members and friends. Orientation sessions for family members should be tailored to informing them about key topics so they can participate in decision making with confidence and competence.

## Provide Support to Family Members for Their Participation

Working groups of all kinds, from individual IEP development to school board meetings, should be flexibly organized and scheduled so that family members can participate. Meetings where decisions are made should not be held without family members present. One way of institutionalizing a family centered philosophy is to include a family member as a permanent member of the interdisciplinary team that manages special education. In this way, there will always be someone with a family perspective on the team; someone who is well versed in the team's responsibilities and processes; someone who could constructively support participation of any family members representing the interests of a particular child; and someone who can sensitize the team to respect the strengths, culture, language, desires, and needs of the child's family. This individual could be paid directly by the school or the school could contract with a family organization to provide this service.

### Provide Support to School Personnel for Increased Family Participation

Any change in complex institutions such as a school system is difficult when it requires people to take on new roles and responsibilities and learn new skills. Training about new roles for families and ongoing technical support to help staff adjust to an expanded family presence in schools, therefore, are essential for all school staff. For example, staff in the teacher's lounge may feel constrained in talking with peers about what is going on in their classrooms when family members are present. School staff value this type of peer support because it helps both to defuse some of the pressure and develop creative solutions to problems. The school staff may need technical assistance and support to overcome their reluctance and see that family members can be part of their support system. Family members in this situation also need to learn how to "break the ice" and gain acceptance and respect of the school staff, and to maintain the confidentiality of these communications. There are many useful training packages that focus on building partnerships between families and professionals.

### Maintain an Inclusive Approach to Working with Family Organizations

One politically sensitive challenge concerns the selection of specific individual family members to serve on governance and policy making structures. It is essential that participation reflect the cultural, linguistic, and racial diversity of families in the community served by the school. At the same time, there may be several family organizations in a community each with its own special focus (e.g., chapter of C.H.A.D.D., the ARC, the Federation of Families for Children's Mental Health, AMI-CAN, or others). Teachers and schools may feel pressure to work exclusively with one or another of these. It is important that schools be able to work with all groups, make the table large enough to accommodate a variety of family viewpoints, and not get caught up in any friendly competition that may exist among the different organizations' agendas. No one organization can be expected to speak for all families.

Educational leaders should prepare a written description of the task that lists the skills or experience required of family members as well as the extent of commitment expected. Circulate this "job description" to established family organizations inviting them to nominate qualified individuals from their own leadership or individual members who have leadership potential. The invitation should be specific. There is a difference between asking family members to represent their organization's position and asking them to participate and speak with the voice of an individual with expertise on the matter at hand. Clarifying which hat the family member is wearing will prevent misunderstandings both within the working group as well as in the public arena.

### Build Capacity and Plan for Continuity in Family Participation

Family members, particularly when they are volunteering their time, may be called away for a variety of reasons. This possibility generates a need to develop redundancy in family leadership by having more than one family member on the team. Family organizations need to identify and train alternate members to provide backup when their "official" representative is unable to attend. Mechanisms such as conference calls and distributing duplicate packets of meeting materials between meetings can help family members exchange information.

### Build Family-School Partnerships That Are Reciprocal and Mutually Rewarding

Schools that value family involvement find ways to acknowledge their contributions. All volunteers in school deserve recognition regardless of the amount or type of work they do. Thank you notes, mention in the school newsletter, a pot luck supper, bumper stickers, and tee shirts are all ways school staff can let family members know how much they are appreciated. With the family member's permission, employers could receive a letter of recognition for the family member's community spirit.

## CONCLUSION

Family members can be enormously effective in promoting school reform, and can add to the quality and diversity of the educational experience at many levels. The integrated service approaches featured in this volume promise to respond to the needs of families and children with comprehensive and individualized services. The climate is right for change. There is national policy support for full family participation, and family members say that they want to be more involved. It is now up to educators to renew their commitment to family participation and to work with families and partners from other agencies to improve the quality of education, and ultimately, the quality of community life.

## REFERENCES

Bauch, J.P. (1994). Categories of parent involvement. *The School Community Journal*, 4(1), 53-60.

Bauch, P.A. (1993). Improving education for minority adolescents: Toward an ecological perspective on school choice and parent involvement. In *Families and schools in a pluralistic society* (pp. 121-146). Albany: State University of New York Press.

Berger, E.H. (1991). *Parents as partners in education*. New York: Merrill.

Brinckerhoff, J.L. & Vincent, L.J. (1986). Increasing parental decision-making at the individualized educational program meeting. *Journal of the Division for Early Childhood*, 11(1), 46-58.

Chavkin, N.F. & Garza-Lubeck, M. (1990). Multicultural approaches to parent involvement: Research and practice. *Social Work in Education*, 13(1), 22-33.

Chavkin, N.F., & Williams, D.L. (1993). Minority parents and the elementary school: Attitudes and practices. In *Families and schools in a pluralistic society* (pp. 73-84). Albany: State University of New York Press.

Chavkin, N.F., & Williams, D.L. (1985). Parent involvement in education. *School Social Work Journal*, 10(1), 35-46.

Chavkin, N.F., & Williams, D.L. (1989). Low-income parents' attitudes toward parent involvement in education. *Journal of Sociology and Social Welfare*, XVI (3), 17-28.

Cole, R.F., with Poe, S.L. (1993). *Partnerships for care: Systems of care for children with serious emotional disturbances and their families*. Washington, D.C.: Washington Business Group on Health, Mental Health Services Program for Youth.

Comer, J.P., & Haynes, N.M. (1991). Parent involvement in schools: An ecological approach. *The Elementary School Journal*, 91(3), 272-277.

Coughlin, P. (1989). The role of the social worker in facilitating parent involvement in special education. *School Social Work Journal*, 13(2), 34-40.

Dauber, S.L. & Epstein, J.L. (1993). Parents' attitudes and practices of involvement in inner-city elementary and middle schools. In *Families and schools in a pluralistic society* (pp. 53-71). Albany: State University of New York Press.

Davies, D. (1994, October 12). Partnerships for reform. *Education Week*, pp. 34-44.

DeChillo, N. & Lebow, W. (1991). *Help when it's needed: Community mental health crisis services for children and youth.* Portland, OR: Regional Research Institute for Human Services, Portland State University.

Dwyer, D.J. & Hecht, J.B. (1992). Minimal parental involvement. *The School Community Journal,* 2(2), 53-66.

Education for All Handicapped Children Act of 1975, PL 94-142. August 23, 1977). Title 20, U.S.C. 1400 et seq: U.S. Statutes at Large, 89, 773-796.

Education of the Handicapped Act Amendments of 1986, PL 99-457. (October 8, 1986). Title 20, U.S.C. 1400 et seq: U.S. Statutes at Large, 100, 1145-1177.

Friesen, B.J. & Huff, B. (1990). Parents and professionals as advocacy partners. *Preventing School Failure,* 34(3), 31-36.

Friesen, B.J. & Koroloff, N.M. (1990). Family-centered services: Implications for mental health administration and research. *The Journal of Mental Health Administration,* 17, 13-25.

Greenwood, G.E. & Hickman, C.W. (1991). Research and practice in parent involvement: Implications for teacher education. *The Elementary School Journal,* 91(3), 279-288.

Harry, B. (1992a). *Cultural diversity, families, and the special education system.* New York: Teachers College Press.

Harry, B. (1992b). Restructuring the participation of African American parents in special education. *Exceptional Children,* 59(2), 123-131.

Henning-Stout, M. (1994). *Responsive assessment.* San Francisco: Jossey-Bass.

Hermary, M.E. & Rempel, J. (1990). Parental and staff perceptions of individual programming teams: Collaboration in and beyond the conference. *Education and Training in Mental Retardation,* 25, 25-32.

Hunter, R.W. (1994). *Parents as policy-makers: A handbook for effective participation.* Portland, OR: Research & Training Center on Family Support and Children's Mental Health, Portland State University.

Ignelzi, S. & Dague, B. (1995). Parents as case managers. In B.J. Friesen & J. Poertner (Eds.), *From case management to service coordination: Building on family strengths* (pp. 327-336). Baltimore: Paul H. Brookes.

Individuals with Disabilities Education Act, PL 101-476. (October 30, 1990). Title 20, U.S.C. 1400 et seq: U.S. Statutes at Large, 104 (part 2), 1103-1151.

Katsiyannis, A., & Ward, T.J. (1992). Parent participation in special education: Compliance issues as reported by parent surveys and state compliance reports. *Remedial and Special Education,* 13(5), 50-55, 62.

Klimes-Dougan, B., Lopez, J.A., Nelson, P., & Adelman, H.S. (1992). Two studies of low income parents' involvement in schooling. *The Urban Review,* 24(3), 185-202.

Knitzer, J., Steinberg, Z., & Fleisch, B. (1990). *At the schoolhouse door: An examination of programs and policies for children with behavioral and emotional problems.* New York: Bank Street College of Education.

Koren, P.E., DeChillo, N., & Friesen, B.J. (1992). Measuring empowerment in families whose children have emotional disabilities: A brief questionnaire. *Rehabilitation Psychology,* 37(4), 305-321.

Kurtz, P.D. & Barth, R.P. (1989). Parent involvement: Cornerstone of school social work practice. *Social Work*, 34(5), 407-413.

Mannan, G., & Blackwell, J. (1992). Parent involvement: Barriers and opportunities. *The Urban Review*, 24(3), 219-226.

Mason, J.L. (1995). *The cultural competence self-assessment questionnaire: A handbook for users*. Portland, OR: Research & Training Center on Family Support and Children's Mental Health, Portland State University.

Palfrey, J.S., Walker, D.K., Butler, J.A. & Singer, J.D. (1989). Patterns of response in families of chronically disabled children: An assessment in five metropolitan school districts. *American Journal of Orthopsychiatry*, 59(1), 94-104.

Petr, C. (1995, Spring). Helping professionals and programs become more family centered. *Focal Point*, 9(1), 10-11.

Riley, R.W. (1994). Ingredient for success: Family involvement. *Teaching K-8*, 25, 12.

Schulz, J. (1987). The parents' role in special education. In Schulz, J. *Parents and Professionals in Special Education*. Boston: Allyn & Bacon.

Shea, T.M., & Bauer, A.M. (1991). *Parents and teachers of children with exceptionalities: A handbook for collaboration*. Boston: Allyn & Bacon.

Stroul, B. (1995). Case management in a system of care. In B.J. Friesen & J. Poertner (Eds.), *From case management to service coordination: Building on family strengths*. Baltimore: Paul H. Brookes.

Turnbull, A.P., & Friesen, B.J. (1995, April). *Forging collaborative partnerships with families in the study of disability*. Paper presented at the National Institute on Disability and Rehabilitation Research on Participatory Action Research. Washington, D.C.

Turnbull, A.P., & Turnbull, H.R. (1990). *Families, professionals and exceptionality: A special partnership*. Columbus: Merrill.

U.S. Department of Education. (1994). *Strong families, strong schools*. Washington, D.C.

VanDenBerg, J.E. (1992). Individualized services for children. *New Directions for Mental Health Services*, 54, 97-100.

Young, C.C., Gable, R.A. & Hendrickson, J.M. (1989). An ecological perspective to training teachers of the behaviorally disordered: Where are we now? *Behavioral Disorders*, 15(1), 16-20.

# Planning and Evaluating Integrated School-Based Services

## John Kalafat

### Spalding University

**SUMMARY.** This paper reviews some of the challenges to evaluation presented by integrated school-based services, and describes field-based evaluation approaches designed to yield valid and useful information about such programs. In place of the positivistic research paradigm, a multistage evaluation approach is called for that includes qualitative and quantitative and process and outcome evaluations. This approach is characterized by close collaboration between evaluators and program personnel that makes evaluation an integral part of program planning and operation. *[Article copies available from The Haworth Document Delivery Service: 1-800-342-9678.]*

One of the most promising efforts on behalf of children in recent decades is the collaboration between schools and other social and health agencies to provide more effective services for children. As the other contributors to this volume have surely documented, the establishment of integrated school-based services is a daunting undertaking due to the organizational complexities of the human service and school systems. The fact that integrated services must address, and to some extent reflect, these complexities presents an equally daunting challenge to the evaluator. This paper will review planning and evaluation strategies that may be best suited to integrated school-based services for children and youth.

---

Address correspondence to: John Kalafat, Department of Psychology, Spalding University, 851 4th Street, Louisville, KY 40202.

[Haworth co-indexing entry note]: "Planning and Evaluating Integrated School-Based Services." Kalafat, John. Co-published simultaneously in *Special Services in the Schools* (The Haworth Press, Inc.) Vol. 11, No. 1/2, 1996, pp. 209-224; and: *Emerging School-Based Approaches for Children with Emotional and Behavioral Problems: Research and Practice in Service Integration* (ed: Robert J. Illback, and C. Michael Nelson) The Haworth Press, Inc., 1996, pp. 209-224. Single or multiple copies of this article are available from The Haworth Document Delivery Service [1-800-342-9678, 9:00 a.m. - 5:00 p.m. (EST)].

Clearly, program planning and evaluation each represent substantive topics. Rather than attempt to address these areas separately, a central theme of this paper is that the development and implementation of integrated youth services consists of an ongoing, reciprocal cycle of planning, evaluation and implementation. In this process, program planners and evaluators must begin to "think like each other" and to build evaluability into programs from the start.

## CHALLENGES FOR EVALUATION

Many evaluators who have ventured into the real world of the interface of schools and community services speak of the major challenges that this field work presents. A partial listing of these challenges includes: first, many integrated service efforts, such as Kentucky's family resource programs, are rapidly expanding, full-coverage programs that encourage adaptability (variability) to local conditions (Illback & Kalafat, in press). Second, rather than providing narrow categorical services, a hallmark of integrated services is that they are family-centered vs. systems centered programs that seek to provide or broker dynamic, changing services in response to a variety of needs for a given child or family (Illback, 1994). Third, integrated school-based services are nested in organizations characterized by Crowson and Boyd (1993) as consisting of "submerged labyrinths of disconnected and often competing organizations, incentives, and allegiances" (pg. 141) and "Balkanized" (pg. 155) sets of stakeholders. Fourth, most integrated service efforts are not well-funded, circumscribed, demonstration programs. Rather, they are evolving, dynamic projects that "require an enormous amount of time to reach a stable [i.e., evaluable] level of operation" (Powell, 1994). Some of the implications of these conditions for evaluators can be illustrated by noting their relationship to threats to validity in traditional research designs.

### Threats to Validity

A sample of threats to *internal* validity include:

- *Sample Integrity* (affected by selection, attrition, comorbidity of needs/problems). Most recipients of integrated services are self-selected, based on motivation, awareness and a variety of felt needs rather than uniform defining characteristics. In fact, services are provided for children, parents, families, and the interface between families and schools and/or communities, all of which represent differing "units of analysis."

- *Comparison or Control Groups.* Full-coverage programs leave little or no room for comparison groups. They present ethical, political, and/or logistical problems with withholding services or randomly assigning families or individuals to particular services; and, factors that influence program participation are difficult to secure in a control or comparison group (Powell, 1994).
- *Treatment Integrity.* According to Weiss and Jacobs (1988):

> [clients] have considerable latitude in determining the amount and nature of their program involvement. Many programs individualize their services in accord with each family's strengths and needs; some include drop-in and other discretionary services, and most are structured to allow both program and [client] input . . . These characteristics make it difficult to define the "treatment" families receive and hence to use evaluation procedures that assume uniform treatment. (pg. xxii)

Moreover, treatments change "in subtle but important ways as staff learn, as clients move in out and as a conditions of delivery are altered" (Patton, 1990, pg. 52). Thus, it is impossible to standardize the treatment in a program responsive to diverse participation needs (Powell, 1988). Because "clients take from programs what they need" (Powell, 1994) programs may vary in dosage and thus, even where programs are implemented in some standard way as intended, we may conclude that interventions lack utility when they simply lacked potency (Felner, Phillips, DuBois & Lease, 1991).

Threats to *external* validity include, in addition to sample heterogeneity, setting or contextual factors. By definition, integrated services address childrens' concerns within the multiple contexts of family, school and community, each of which is comprised of subsystems, all of which influence program interventions and outcomes. Generalizability of evaluation results can be compromised by the differential effects of the settings themselves on program impacts. Bond and Halpern (1983) describe their cross-project evaluation as a multisite, multimethod demonstration in which methods were confounded with site and population characteristics. The built in flexibility and different perspectives of programs interacted with cross-project variability in client populations and communities to produce significant unplanned and uncontrolled variation. Such variation occurs even within a given local program. A national survey by Dunst, Trivette, Starnes, Hawley, and Gordon (1993) of family support programs for persons with developmental disabilities found that a variety of political, economic, and human factors, such as belief systems, influenced how practitioners rendered services to families. They found, as did Illback and Kalafat (in press) in their evaluation of school-based family resource centers, that program elements at one level (e.g., coordinators' helping styles) were often moderated by program elements at another level (e.g., principals' attitudes toward family involvement).

Schools in particular present a complex system that substantially complicates evaluation efforts. Crowson and Boyd (1993) note that evidence abounds that schools are small polities of teachers, students, administrators, service workers, and parents in either real or potential conflicts. In their evaluation of a single school-based program, Weinstein et al. (1991) described multilevel steps of change from initial joint planning, to positive teacher expectations, to high expectancy classroom practices and school policies, to motivated students, each of which can mediate program impact and lead to smaller and more variable program impact. Crowson and Boyd (1993) noted that "evaluation of integrated services for children shows a history of experimentation colliding with ubiquitous problems of institutional deficiency, professional training differences, resource constraints, communication gaps, authority and turf issues, and legal and leadership problems" (pp. 152-3).

Given these complexities, it is not surprising that evaluation of school-based services are also vulnerable to threats to *construct validity* due to the difficulties in devising measures that capture program impacts. The lack of availability of sufficiently valid and reliable measures that adequately capture program effects at such varying levels as parent, family, and community has plagued evaluations to date. Evaluators, program administrators, and program staff all share the concern that evaluations do not tap what really matters in integrated services (Schorr & Schorr, 1988; Ellwood, 1988; Larner, 1992). In addition, evaluators have succumbed to various stakeholders' pressures to assess too many program goals; and, to look for main effects when programs offering individualized services to heterogeneous groups of participants will at best show benefits spread unevenly across participants (Tivnan, 1988). Thus, evaluators struggle with the dilemma noted by Weiss (1988) to evaluate with inappropriate standard measures and risk no results, or evaluate with unproven measures and risk both credibility and results.

Weiss and other evaluators recommend taking the time to develop and pilot program-specific measures based on a clearer understanding–and ongoing clarification–of program methods and goals. However, Powell (1994) noted that instrument development is not a high priority among funding agencies. Also, the time necessary to pilot appropriate measures is part of another difficulty associated with the evaluation of integrated services: integrated services require a considerable amount of item to reach a stable level of operation. Cowen referred to this as things taking longer than they take (Felner et al., 1991). Thus, programs must reach certain levels of maturity, stability, specificity, and fidelity before summative or outcome evaluations are appropriate. This level of program maturity is referred to "evaluability" (Wholey, 1979), and a number of evaluators recommend that evaluability assessments precede full-scale evaluation efforts (Bond & Halpern, 1988; Felner et al., 1991; Illback, Zins, Maher, & Greenberg, 1990).

Finally, given the host of constraints involved in field studies of complex interventions, many evaluators warn against framing evaluations in oversimplified "does the program work" terms. Instead, more reasonable expectations of incremental gains in understanding program processes and impacts are recommended:

> It is self-defeating to aspire to deliver an evaluative conclusion as precise and as safely beyond dispute as an operational-language conclusion from the laboratory . . . When the evaluator aspires only to provide clarification that would not otherwise be available he has chosen a task he can manage and one that does have social benefits. (Cronbach & Associates, 1980, p. 318)

Even this partial list of "caveats from the trenches" may appear like the warnings that accompany televised stunts–"don't try this at home." However, experience in the field has also led to a growing consensus around a set of evaluation approaches that promise to yield more valid and useful information. Given the amount of time required, the lack of available funding for process and qualitative evaluations, and the academic incentives (and journal editor preferences) for microexperiments, one caveat remains: don't try this if you are going for tenure. With this in mind, following is a review of the strategies recommended for evaluation of school-based integrated services.

## EVALUATION STRATEGIES

### New Paradigm

In order to capture the processes and impacts of complex integrated service systems, there is a growing consensus for a shift from the positivistic research paradigm with its emphasis on pure variables devoid of contextual influences, manipulation and control of the process being studied, and neutral experimenter maintaining distance from passive subjects. Commenting on early attempts to create laboratory conditions, Jacobs (1988) noted a "serious mismatch between the richness of what could be studied and the paucity of acceptable techniques" (pg. 41). Beer and Walton (1987) suggested that intervention research was reaching a turning point where traditional methodology has proven limiting by its focus on single causes and on isolated episodes of change and by its failure to meet the needs of users. They noted that traditional science may be relatively precise about methodology and instruments, though often imprecise in depth and description of the intervention and situation–in other words, lacking ecological validity.

In an unusual special article with accompanying commentaries, Weinstein et al. (1991) were able to describe the many adjustments they had to make to design an ecologically valid evaluation of a school-based program. In what they described as a war between differing paradigms, they concluded that "psychological methodology and ecological questions are not comfortable bedfellows" (p. 401).

Writing from the Harvard Family Research Project, Shaw (1995) contended that the quantitative experimental design which can be applied to well-developed models and tightly controlled participation, is outmoded as a means to assess large-scale, dynamic, systemic efforts.

While evaluators have employed quasi-experimental designs (Cook & Campbell, 1979) for some time, there is also a growing acceptance of qualitative and case study evaluation. Qualitative evaluations consist of inductive analyses that begin with specific observations and build toward general patterns. Patton (1990) noted that the qualitative approach is especially appropriate for developing, innovative, or changing programs where the focus is on program improvement, and for exploring a variety of effects on participants, who, as noted earlier, vary in terms of their involvement in programs. As programs are implemented, they frequently unfold in different ways than were planned, as practitioners learn what works and what does not, and as priorities change. Such dynamic conditions call for a dynamic evaluation process that is capable of capturing and monitoring not only anticipated outcomes, but also unanticipated consequences, treatment changes, and context variables. Weinstein and colleagues' (1991) report exemplified this process, as they noted that their initial design was far too crude to fully capture the effects of the intervention, whereas the collaborative model and qualitative approach offered rich opportunities to increase their understanding of their evolving program. Qualitative approaches are not equivalent to unsystematic or "sloppy" evaluations. Sources such as Patton (1990) and Miles and Huberman (1984) provide detailed guidelines for careful qualitative evaluations.

Another departure from traditional designs that can add to our understanding of services is the use of single case designs. In his overview of research designs for school intervention research, Shapiro (1987) noted that in group designs, individual variability is treated as a source of error, and thus generalizations of group results to individuals is not possible (this is known as the 'ecological fallacy'). He notes that single case designs permit one to establish a functional relationship between implementation of the intervention and change. Also, single case designs more readily permit evaluation of interventions within the environment in which behavior is naturally occurring. Shapiro (1987) noted that the single case emphasis on studying intrasubject variability, combined with the features of precise specification of treatment conditions, repeated measurement, replication, and design flexibility, allows for more intensive investigation of variables which relate to outcomes. Yin (1989) provides an excellent guide to careful, systematic case study research. In particular, he notes that conclusions drawn from a case study lead to hypotheses that are confirmed or disconfirmed by subsequent case studies. Thus, conclusions can be bolstered by multiple case studies that are analogues to replications of experiments.

The use of qualitative and case study methods can be used in conjunction with, and often as precursors to quasi-experimental group designs that permit more generalizable conclusions. Werthhamer-Larson (1994) noted that they can assess the usefulness of more rigorous research that controls for more plausible interpretation by involving program staff in less threatening ways, exploring the characteristics of children, families and services related to positive outcomes, and showing whether there is any improvement to interpret. Ellwood (1988) noted that the strength of their "informal" evaluations rested in its flexibility and responsiveness to changing interests, circumstances, and opportunities; while formal evaluation is essential to establish credibility.

### Process Evaluation

Another common emphasis of the positivist research tradition is a search for summative conclusions. Such outcome results are often of limited utility to services development because of their "black box" approach to programs. Weiss (1988) indicated that the importance of systematically gathering information about program implementation and processes–of unpacking the black box–is an area of growing consensus in evaluation practice. Bond and Halpern (1988) reported that their "most radical strategic decision" (pg. 353) was to break the summative evaluation mold; to focus as much on hypothesis generation as on hypothesis confirmation, and, on understanding the nature of the problems addressed and the dynamics of intervention, rather than rigorous estimation of its usually modest average effects.

It seems that such process or formative evaluation serves at least two purposes. First, given the lack of control over levels of participation, differences in program components and implementation approaches, and a variety of other contextual variables that operate in community and school-based integrated service systems, our understanding of programs can be enhanced if these naturally occurring variations were identified, and their sources, bases and relationship to differential program impacts were explored (as opposed to lumping them into large "error variables" which will obscure program main effects). Second, such exploration can begin to identify the "active ingredients" of programs which would be critically important for enhancing the focus and intentionality of program staff, and for program replication. For example, in the Child Survival/Fair Start initiative, "it became clear that the heart and soul of services are caring relationships, not information, instructions, or procedures" (Larner, Halpern, & Harkavy, 1992, pg. 248). In regard to connecting process (active ingredients) variables to program impacts, studies have found a relationship between amount or duration of contact between providers and consumers and more pervasive and sustained effects (Heinicke, Beckwith, & Thompson, 1988; Powell & Grantham-McGregory, 1989). Again, the development of a trusting relationship between family and staff is quite likely mediated by, among other things, duration and frequency of contact.

It must be reiterated that process evaluations must address the complexities of the contexts or systems involved in integrated service delivery. Illback et al. (1990) noted that the education change literature makes it clear that systemic factors such as administrative support, school environment, and staff opportunities for involvement in the change process are all important to the success of any program. Indeed, Weinstein et al. (1991) reported that some teachers dropped out of their school-based intervention because of a lack of administrative support. Again, formative evaluation, which can include a substantial qualitative component, aims to clarify program features and dynamics. As such, it is not an alternative to summative evaluation, but instead, an important precursor that provides meaning to summative findings. In fact, a number of evaluators have outlined phases of evaluations that are tailored to the stages of program development, thus connecting evaluation to program planning. One of the more comprehensive models is Jacobs' (1988) five-tiered approach. Level one is a preimplementation stage in which evaluation consists of needs assessment and matching the proposed programs to the identified needs. Another role that evaluators can play at this stage is to keep program planners from reinventing the wheel by sharing models of successful programs from the literature. A number of resources provide models and guidelines for evaluated, integrated school-based services (Berman & McLaughlin, 1978; Crowson & Boyd, 1993; Dryfoos, 1994; Goetz, 1992; Huberman & Miles, 1984; Kagan & Weissbourd, 1994; Schorr & Schorr, 1988). Levels two through five are accountability, program clarification, progress toward objectiveness, and, finally, program impact. At each level, evaluative data contribute to the process and progress of program planning and development.

## Collaboration

This systematic collaborative process between program implementators and evaluators is the core of the interactive planning and evaluative process, and represents another significant departure from the positivistic model. As Weinstein et al. (1991) reported "Our negotiated study rocked the expectations of more formal relations between researchers and subjects . . ." (pg. 348). The term "negotiated study" is critical: evaluators must abandon their traditional distance from the program personnel and the programs themselves and enter into co-equal collaborative roles which result in modifications–actually enhancements–to both the program and the evaluation approach. As Weinstein et al. (1991) described the process, "We learned patience, we made trade-offs, but we also deepened our understanding" (pg. 347). There are several advantages or payoffs associated with this collaborative approach.

First, a collaborative endeavor reduces the resistance of program personnel and obtains the cooperation that is essential to successful program implementation and evaluation. Zins and Illback (in press) noted that many change initiatives flounder because the consultant did not have the skills to mobilize people around the change process, both initially and over the long run. Reporting on the Brookline Early Education Project, Tivnan (1988) reported that despite occasionally conflicting goals of service providers and evaluators, the benefits of close and long-term cooperative relationships were considerable. In particular, when practitioners are consulted and involved in evaluation it can dispel their impression of the limited utility of evaluation created by premature, global summative evaluations. They begin to see evaluation as a tool to demonstrate the utility of the program to consumers and other stakeholders, and ultimately to preserve the program (Illback et al., 1990). Recalling the layers and complexities of human service and school systems noted earlier, it is important to identify and touch base with as many stakeholders as possible. This will not only increase the validity of the intervention and evaluation, but may prevent resistance from cropping up later in the process.

A second advantage of collaboration is the increased validity of the intervention and evaluation due to evaluators' more complete understanding of the systems involved in the program's implementation. For example, discussions between program personnel and evaluators can help to develop measures that are tailored to local needs, populations, and contexts. This is the same process as that which contributes to the increased validity of the clinicians' conclusions based on solid rapport with the client.

Probably the central dynamic of a collaboration between evaluators and program personnel is to co-opt them into each other's paradigms. Gifford (1986) suggested that collaboration produces practice-sensitive researchers and research-sensitive practitioners. As practitioners are treated as partners rather than subjects or suppliers of data for esoteric research processes, and as they are drawn into thoughtful consideration of exactly what their program can accomplish and how it works, they become curious and interested in evaluation as an inherent component of their program planning, development and implementation process. As one of the teachers in Weinstein et al.'s (1991) project confessed, "I understand that you set up a program to help me discover things for myself but I guess I wanted to be fed information" (pg. 347). Weinstein et al. reported that, later, teachers became more comfortable exposing their own teaching practices to collaborative analysis and scrutiny; and, they began subscribing to journals, and calling the university for lists of courses and readings. As another example of this process, the involvement of evaluators in a family support program led staff to question the quality of the child care component, eventually resulting in the shift from a custodial to an educational focus (Johnson & Walker, 1991).

By asking questions and bringing information from other projects and from the literature, evaluators can accelerate the program development process by infusing relevant information and third party insights, and thus ultimately increase the evaluability of programs (Bond & Halpern, 1988). As Werthamer-Larsson put it, "Nesting intervention research within the service delivery systems stimulates investigations of school system processes that influence the delivery of services and of cost benefit and cost-effectiveness, thus forging strong links between research and system reform" (1994, pg. 122).

This cycle is called "action research" (Rapoport, 1985) and may have been best captured by the founder of the total quality management movement, W. Edwards Deming. Urging that planners and managers make decisions based on facts and data, rather than opinions, Deming created the Deming or Shewhart Cycle (Brassard, 1989).

This PDCA cycle represents the ongoing involvement of evaluation and data collection in the planning process as we *plan* the improvement or intervention, based on available data; *do* the interventions and collect data on them; *check* the results of the intervention and data collection; and, *act* to hold and institutionalize the gains, and continue the improvement process. In this process, program planning, implementation and evaluation are inseparable.

Once evaluation becomes part of programming, it can not only lose its threatening quality, but also become an exciting avenue to professional growth (Illback et al., 1990), as illustrated by a teacher's report of a presentation of evaluation findings at an American Education Research Association meeting: "As we read [our papers], we reflected on the growth that we had experienced as teachers, the effect we had had on our school, and the successes our students had shown . . ." (Cone, 1989).

This clearly represents an empowerment process that focuses on the role of knowledge creation and the expectation that program participants themselves will play major roles in defining research questions or problems, gathering data, determining the meaning of the data through collective analysis, and presenting the data to a larger audience for action (Powell, 1994). This is, of course, consistent with the empowerment philosophy inherent in many integrated children's' services initiatives (Dunst, Trivette, & Deal, 1988).

It must be noted that this collaborative process requires that the evaluators go into the "trenches" or the settings in which services are delivered. As Patton stated:

> When in doubt, observe and ask questions. When certain, observe at length and ask many more questions. (1990, pg. 7)

Not only will evaluators learn a lot through this activity, but they will enhance their rapport and credibility with practitioners who note their interest and see that they have observed how things "really work." Again, from the pure research paradigm, the question may be raised "is this unobtrusive?" Patton (1990) is unequivocal in his response when he states that the researchers' entry into a setting may not only create problems of validity and reactivity, but may make it a different setting altogether–forever. This, of course, is exactly the goal of a PDCA approach to program planning and implementation. From the positivist point of view, the intervention is "artificially" augmented by professional rewards experienced by practitioners such as Weinstein et al.'s teachers, and the involvement of evaluators is perceived as "noise factors" that cannot be replicated (Brophy, 1991). From the empowerment goal of making evaluation a part of practitioners' planning repertoire, this does not represent "noise."

If evaluators wish to assess program impact devoid of the influence of ongoing evaluation, which may not, in fact, occur in many settings, Rossi (1978) offers a model for doing so. He describes a three stage evaluation strategy: first, the program can be demonstrated to be effective under the most favorable delivery method (e.g., provision by a highly motivated team of practitioners and evaluators in a demonstration site). This helps to establish the internal validity of the intervention. Second, it can be demonstrated that the program can be delivered in a cost-effective manner (e.g., delivered by trained practitioners in a representative system). This helps to establish the external validity of the program. Third, a delivery system that can provide the program can be demonstrated to in fact do so at a level of quantity and quality necessary to impact the target population. It must be kept in mind, however, that these evaluations only provide *snapshots* of a dynamic process. Research leads to clarification for the moment, and, always, to further questions (Bardon, 1987). Cronbach (1975) described this as generalization decay, and noted that a conclusion is ultimately valid only as history. Thus, it is recommended that evaluation become a regular part of program planning and management.

Given that evaluation should be an integral component of service delivery, it is interesting to note the similarities between the recommended characteristics of field-based evaluation and those of integrated childrens' services delivery systems. For example, in his presidential address to the Section on Clinical Child Psychology, "Models for service delivery in children's mental health: Common characteristics," Roberts (1994) included a recognition of the ecology of the child, collaboration among agencies and among professionals, clearly defined missions and philosophies, replicable programs, and accountability and documentation of effectiveness. Such common characteristics between evaluation and service delivery systems can only enhance the melding of the two.

## *CONCLUSION*

The recommended approach to evaluating school-based integrated services begins with evaluators and practitioners joining to educate each other. The practitioners share their goals and objectives for the services, apprise the evaluators of the nuances of the systems, and help to identify the target populations and stakeholders throughout the system. Following Jacobs' (1988) model, the evaluators help the practitioners to document the need for the particular program within the community, and to demonstrate the fit between the needs and the program. Evaluators also share information about similar programs. Sample data might include social indicators (Struening, 1975), key informant, and survey responses.

Second, evaluators work with practitioners to set up automated management information systems that can develop accountability data (utilization, participant characteristics and satisfaction, costs, etc.) that can be used in the ongoing PDCA process.

Third, services (goals, intervention approaches, participant characteristics, participation patterns) become clarified through qualitative procedures such as observations, interviews, case studies, and MIS data. The goal at this stage is clear program specification. Illback et al. (1990) identified characteristics of well-defined programs including a clear logic or conceptual basis that connects needs, goals, and operations; identified target populations; clear goals and objectives or outcomes; resources (staffing, materials, and methods); and a plan of operation. Once a program is well-defined, appropriate measure of it can be developed.

Fourth, measurable indicators of program impact are collaboratively derived (clearly written objectives become outcome variables). Assessment of differential proximal outcomes among types of participants and levels of involvement is begun. An attempt is made to combine standard measures with established psychometric properties, with measures tailored to the specific program interventions and contexts. Some measures can be administered nested within structured interviews to ensure greater reliability and validity of responses. Data from each of these stages are continually used to modify and enhance program efficacy and efficiency. A good deal of adjustment in program operations and measurement occurs at this stage, as attempts to measure promote clarifications of processes and goals. Examples of proximal outcomes might include parenting skills, parent attitudes toward school, parent involvement with school, childrens' attitudes toward school, and self-esteem.

Finally, often between one and three years after initial implementation, evaluators and practitioners concur that program impact or distal outcome evaluation is appropriate. That is, the program is now considered evaluable. As Campbell (1983) put it: evaluate no program until it is proud. At this level, evaluation can consist of quasi-experimental designs with quantitative and qualitative participant-specific data collected over time, as well as cost-effectiveness information. Intervention-delay control groups, or comparison groups based on differing levels of participation can be employed. Distal outcome data might include enduring and/or lifestyle changes among participants.

Advocates for such action research applications must encourage academic researchers to become involved in field-based program development, and must find ways for funding sources to support long-term research commitments, as opposed to short-term, shifting program emphases. Ultimately, the promise of integrated school-based services may be fulfilled by the empowerment of evaluators and practitioners alike to blend evaluation, planning and intervention.

## REFERENCES

Bardon, J. I. (1987). The translation of research into practice in school psychology. *School Psychology Review, 16*, 317-328.

Beer, M., & Walton, A. E. (1987). Organization change and development. *Annual Review of Psychology, 38*, 339-367.

Berman, P., & McLaughlin, M. W. (1978) *Implementing and sustaining innovations.* Santa Monica, CA: Rand.

Bond, J. T., & Halpern, R. (1988). The cross-project evaluation of the Child Survival/Fair Start Initiative: A case study of action research. In H. B. Weiss, & F. H. Jacobs (Eds.), *Evaluating Family Programs* (pp.347-370). Hawthorn, NY: Aldine.

Brassard, M. (1989). *The memory jogger plus +.* Methuen, MA: Goal/QPC.

Brophy, J. (1991). I know I can do this, but where's my motivation? *American Journal of Community Psychology, 19*, 371-377.

Campbell, D. (May, 1983). *Threats to validity added when applied social research is packaged as "program evaluation" in service of administrative decision making.* Paper presented at the Conference on Family Support Systems: The State-of-the-Art. Yale University, New Haven, CT.

Cone, J. (1989, March). *The teacher and motivation researcher relationship: Bridging the gap.* Paper presented at the Annual Meeting of the American Educational Research Association, San Francisco, CA.

Cook, T. D., & Campbell, D. T. (1979). *Quasi-experimentation: Design and analysis for field settings.* Chicago: Rand McNally.

Cronbach, L. J. (1975). Beyond the two disciplines of scientific psychology. *American Psychologist, 30*, 116-127.

Cronbach, L. J., and Associates. (1980). *Toward reform of program evaluation.* San Francisco, CA: Jossey-Bass.

Crowson, R. L., & Boyd, W. L. (1993). Coordinated services for children: Designing arks for storms and seas unknown. *American Journal of Education, 101*, 140-174.

Dunst, C. J., Trivette, C. M., & Deal, A. G. (1988). *Enabling and empowering families: Principles and guidelines for practice.* Cambridge, MA: Brookline.

Dunst, C. J., Trivette, C. M., Starnes, A. L., Hamby, D. W., & Gordon, N. J. (1993). *Building and evaluating family support initiatives: A national study of programs for persons with developmental disabilities.* Baltimore: Brookes.

Dryfoos, J. G. (1994) *Full-service schools.* San Francisco: Jossey-Bass.

Ellwood, A. (1988). Prove to me that MELD makes a difference. In H. B. Weiss, & F. H. Jacobs (Eds.), *Evaluating family programs* (pp. 303-313). Hawthorne, NY: Aldine.

Felner, R. D., Phillips, R. S. C., DuBois, D., & Lease, A. M. (1991). Ecological interventions and the process of change for prevention: Wedding theory and research to implementation in real world settings. *American Journal of Community Psychology, 19,* 379-387.

Gifford, B. R. (1986). The evolution of the school-community partnership for educational renewal. *Education and urban society, 19,* 77-106.

Goetz, K. (Ed.). (1992). *Programs to strengthen families: A resource guide.* Chicago: Family Resource Coalition.

Heinicke, C. M., Beckwith, L., & Thompson, A. (1988). Early intervention in the family system: A framework and review. *Infant Mental Health Journal, 9,* 111-114.

Huberman, A. M., & Miles, M. B. (1984). *Innovation up close.* New York: Plenum.

Illback, R. J. (1994). Poverty and the crisis in children's services: The need for services integration. *Journal of Clinical Child Psychology, 23,* 413-424.

Illback, R. J., & Kalafat, J. (in press). Initial evaluation of a school-based integrated service program: Kentucky family resource and youth services centers. *Special Services in the Schools.*

Illback, R. J., Zins, J. E., Maher, C. A., & Greenberg, R. (1990). An overview of principles and procedures of program planning and evaluation. In T. B. Gutkin., & C. R. Reynolds (Eds.), *The handbook of school psychology.* (pp. 799-820). New York: Wiley.

Jacobs, F. H. (1988). The five-tiered approach to evaluation: Context and implementation. In H. B. Weiss, & F. H. Jacobs (Eds.), *Evaluating family programs* (pp. 303-313). Hawthorne, NY: Aldine.

Johnson, D. L., & Walker, T. B. (1991). *Final report of the Advance Parent Education and Family Support Program.* Report submitted to the Carnegie Corporation. San Antonio, TX: Advance.

Kagan, S. L., & Weissbourd, B. (1994). *Putting families first.* San Francisco: Jossey-Bass.

Larner, M. (1992). Realistic expectations: Review of evaluation findings. In M. Larner, R. Halpern, & O. Harkavy (Eds.), *Fair start for children* (pp. 136-158). New Haven, CT: Yale University Press.

Larner, M., Halpern, R., & Harkavy, O. (Eds.). (1992). *Fair start for children.* New Haven, CT: Yale University Press.

Miles, M. B., & Huberman, A. M. (1984). *Qualitative data analysis: A sourcebook of new methods.* Newbury Park, CA: Sage.

Patton, M. Q. (1990). *Qualitative evaluation and research methods.* Newbury Park, CA: Sage.

Powell, D. R. (1994). Evaluating family support programs: Are we making progress? In S. L. Kagan, & B. Weissbourd (Eds.), *Putting families first* (pp. 441-470). San Francisco, CA: Jossey-Bass.

Powell, D. R. (1988). Toward an understanding of the program variable in comprehensive family support programs. In H. B. Weiss, & F. H. Jacobs (Eds.), *Evaluating family programs* (pp. 267-285). Hawthorne, NY: Aldine.

Powell, D. R., & Grantham-McGregory, S. (1989). Home visiting of varying frequency and child development. *Pediatrics, 84,* 157-164.

Rapoport, R. (Ed.) (1985). *Research and action: Innovations for children, youth, and families.* London: Cambridge University Press.

Roberts, M. C. (1994). Models for service delivery in children's mental health: Common characteristics. *Journal of Clinical Child Psychology, 23,* 212-219.

Rossi, P. H. (1978). Issues in the evaluation of human services delivery. *Evaluation Quarterly, 2,* 573-599.

Schorr, L. B., & Schorr, D. (1988). *Within our reach: Breaking the cycle of disadvantage.* New York: Doubleday.

Shapiro, E. (1987). Intervention research methodology in school psychology. *School Psychology Review, 16,* 290-305.

Shaw, K. M. (1995). Challenges in evaluating systems reform. *The Evaluation Exchange, I,* 2-3.

Struening, E.L. (1975). Social area analysis as a method of evaluation. In E. L. Struening, & M. Guttentag, (Eds.). *Handbook of evaluation research* (pp. 519-536). Beverly Hills, CA: Sage.

Tivnan, T. (1988). Lessons from the evaluation of the Brookline Early Evaluation Project. In H. B. Weiss, & F. H. Jacobs (Eds.), *Evaluating family programs* (pp. 221-238). Hawthorne, NY: Aldine.

Weinstein, R. S., Soulé, C. R., Collins, F., Cone, J., Mehlhorn, M., & Simontacchi, K. (1991). Expectations and high school change: Teacher-researcher collaboration to prevent school failure. *American Journal of Community Psychology, 19,* 333-363.

Weiss, H. B. (1988). Family support and education programs: Working through ecological theories of human development. In H. B. Weiss, & F. H. Jacobs (Eds.), *Evaluating family programs* (pp. 221-238). Hawthorne, NY: Aldine.

Weiss, H. B., & Jacobs, F. (1988). *Evaluating family programs.* Hawthorne, NY: Aldine.

Werthamer-Larsson, L. (1994). Methodological issues in school-based services research. *Journal of Clinical Child Psychology, 23,* 121-132.

Wholey, J. (1979). *Evaluation: Promise and performance.* Washington, D.C.: The Urban Institute.

Yin, R. K. (1984). *Case study research: Design and methods.* Newbury Park, CA: Sage.

Zins, J. E., & Illback, R. J. (in press). Consulting to facilitate planned organizational change in schools. *Journal of Educational and Psychological Consultation.*

# Changing the School Culture
# Toward Integrated Services

Cindy Carlson

The University of Texas at Austin

**SUMMARY.** In this article, contemporary school culture is examined, as it relates to delivery of health and mental health services to children and families. Proposed changes are put forth that can help move from services as currently organized to integrated services as discussed herein. *[Article copies available from The Haworth Document Delivery Service: 1-800-342-9678.]*

Four forces within the United States–social and demographic changes, documentation of children's mental health problems, federal initiatives promoting comprehensive, coordinated, and consumer-oriented versus service-provider-oriented services, and the failure of public schools to adequately address children's mental health problems–have converged to

---

Address correspondence to: Cindy Carlson, Department of Educational Psychology, College of Education, SZB 504, The University of Texas at Austin, Austin, TX 78712.

Portions of this article are based on earlier work by the author individually and in collaboration with others. Earlier versions have appeared in the following: *The School Psychologist, 48*(2); *Professional Psychology* (in press); *School Psychology Quarterly* (in press); and the *Schools as Health Service Delivery Sites: Historical, Current, and Future Roles for Psychology: Report of the Schools a Health Service Delivery Sites Work Group,* Committee for the Advancement of Professional Practice, and American Psychological Association.

[Haworth co-indexing entry note]: "Changing the School Culture Toward Integrated Services." Carlson, Cindy. Co-published simultaneously in *Special Services in the Schools* (The Haworth Press, Inc.) Vol. 11, No. 1/2, 1996, pp. 225-249; and: *Emerging School-Based Approaches for Children with Emotional and Behavioral Problems: Research and Practice in Service Integration* (ed: Robert J. Illback, and C. Michael Nelson) The Haworth Press, Inc., 1996, pp. 225-249. Single or multiple copies of this article are available from The Haworth Document Delivery Service [1-800-342-9678, 9:00 a.m. - 5:00 p.m. (EST)].

create momentum for the establishment of school-based comprehensive, coordinated, and integrated services. The call for services integration is also related to calls for broad-based reform in education (e.g., *America 2000: An Educational Strategy,* 1990) and health, (e.g., *Healthy People 2000,* 1990). In fact, the interrelatedness of children's health and education are highlighted in services integration proposals to a degree that is unique in the recent history of either enterprise (e.g., *School-linked human services,* 1993).

Social and demographic changes may be the primary impetus for the current emphasis on overhauling the education and health systems of the nation. A sampling of indicators finds the following: 25% of children living in poverty with poverty being the primary impediment to achievement; 82% have working mothers; 50% live with single mothers, 55% of which are in poverty; 25% will not graduate from high school; 30% are at serious risk for school failure; 14% are children of teenage or unwed mothers (*Schools as Health Care Delivery Settings,* 1995; *Comprehensive and Coordinated Psychological Services for Children,* 1994). In addition, between 1981 and 1990, all categories of violent crime increased substantially for youths under age 18 (Goldstein, Harootunian, & Conoley, 1993). Changing demographics are also reflected in shifts in minority populations; and minority youth will represent the majority populations within four states (TX, CA, NY, and FL) by 2010 (Hodgkinson, 1992). These social and demographic changes are placing enormous strain, not only upon children and families, but also upon the nation's public schools.

A second factor encouraging reform of services delivery to children and families, is the improved documentation of children's health and mental health needs. It is widely accepted that 12-15% of children have a mental health problem in need of treatment, and 6% are severely emotionally disturbed (McElhaney, Russell, & Barton, 1993). Rates of psychopathology appear to be higher among disadvantaged groups (Tarnowski & Blechman, 1991). Moreover, children are at special risk for chronic mental health disorders because the risk factors associated with problems seldom occur in isolation, but rather reflect complex interactions of multiple factors (Saxe, Cross, & Silverman, 1988). As noted by one leading authority, "From the perspective of prevalence rates of emotional and mental disorders, seriousness of the disorders, age of onset and relationship to other problems, the situation has never been so bad" (Stroul & Friedman, 1986, p. 3).

The dismal picture of children's mental health spurred the development of a national agenda regarding children's mental health services as exemplified in the Child and Adolescent Service System Program (CASSP). Several of CASSP's guiding principles have had an impact on the movement to expand school-based services to children. CASSP guidelines state that children's services should be: (a) provided in the most normalized environment appropriate to the child; (b) community-based, preferably operating out of the school; and (c) governed by consumer needs, rather than by traditional agency configurations.

The final impetus to reformed service delivery systems can be observed in the documented failure of existing school-based services to meet the mental health needs of children. Very few schools have services for children with serious mental health needs that are a part of the regular education program (Duchnowski, 1994). As currently structured, when children have serious emotional or behavioral problems that are considered to affect their educational progress negatively, they are referred for remediation to the school system's division of special education, where services are provided under the Individuals with Disabilities Education Act (IDEA, 1990). IDEA has resulted in a system that is categorical in terms of how programs are funded, eligibility is determined, and service is delivered. Specifically, this act authorizes the provision of services necessary to educational achievement for children identified as mentally retarded (MR), learning disabled (LD), seriously emotionally disturbed (SED), physically impaired and other health impaired, including attention deficit disordered (ADD or ADHD). Researchers have uniformly reported poor outcomes for children identified as seriously emotionally disturbed and treated under IDEA (Duchnowski, 1994). Poor outcomes are documented each year in the "Annual Report to Congress on the Implementation of IDEA" (U.S. Department of Education, 1995). Additionally, Knitzer (1992) reveals that less than 1% of children are identified as behaviorally or emotionally disturbed despite significantly higher epidemiological estimates cited above. In short, as concluded by Duchnowski (1994), "If the outcomes for children who are serviced under this rubric [IDEA] are examined, one could readily reach the conclusion that the service system is in critical need of innovative service models" (p. 13).

In summary, there is agreement that the current system of mental health service delivery to children is inadequate, however, no single model of service delivery has evolved to replace existing services. Rather, guidelines or principles have been proposed to guide the development of more effective systems. Specifically, it has been recommended that services to children: (1) be available in close proximity and accessible without reference to physical, psychological, social, linguistic, sexual orientation, or other barriers; (2) be comprehensive and appropriate, in that they address the priorities identified by the family at a level of service sufficient to meet their needs; (3) be formulated and delivered such that the family perceives them to be an organized whole and can participate in them in an effective manner; (4) promote psychological competence and self-sufficiency versus dysfunction and pathology; (5) are oriented toward full participation, partnership, and empowerment of family members; (6) are sensitive to cultural, gender, racial, linguistic, class, disability, and sexual orientation issues; (7) are driven by a concern for the needs and desires of the consumers (i.e., children and families) and emphasize explicit outcomes stated in a positive manner (*Comprehensive and Coordinated Services for Children,* 1994).

A shift from the current reality of categorical services to proposed service integration will require substantial change in the existing school culture and organization. The purpose of this article is to examine contemporary school culture, as it relates to the delivery of health and mental health services to children and families, and to propose changes necessary to move from services as currently organized to integrated services as proposed. It is the view of the author and others (e.g., Sarason, 1990) that changing the school culture is best understood from the perspective of schools as complex social systems; therefore, this will be the starting point. Since complex organizations develop regularities in response to pressures from the environment exerted over time, the contemporary culture of schools and school-based services will next be viewed within its historical context. Third, the fit between the contemporary school culture and proposed integrated services will be evaluated. This article will close with a discussion of necessary changes, and necessary losses, implied by services integration in the schools.

## AN ORGANIZATIONAL SYSTEMS PERSPECTIVE OF SCHOOLS

Schools are complex social systems and any efforts to change services within schools must first and foremost understand the regularities of the system. The most widely accepted definition of a system is a series of elements organized in some consistent and enduring relationship with each other. Critical to systems theory are the notions of organization and consistency; the arrangement of elements in a system is not random, but patterned. The way elements are organized reflects not only the relationships between elements, but also of the organization as a whole.

Complex systems are organized hierarchically into smaller systems (subsystems) with boundaries to protect the differentiated functioning of the subsystems. Boundaries are defined by redundant patterns of behavior that characterize the relationships within that system or subsystem and which are sufficiently distinct as to give a subsystem its particular identity. Complex social systems arrange subsystems hierarchically. Subsystems that are superordinate hierarchically will have greater authority and power over lower subsystems and thus, constrain their behavior. Elements in subsystems that are lower hierarchically, however, are not powerless to exert influence. In fact recent studies in organizational behavior have emphasized both the impact of powerful individuals and groups on organizational contexts and situations in which the superordinate organizational context is ignored successfully by individuals and groups within the organization (Mowday, 1993).

School systems, like all living social systems, share common attributes. They are open, ongoing, goal-seeking, and self-regulated. The education system, as a public enterprise, is clearly open to the vicissitudes of public opinion and social change. School systems are ongoing in that they have a past, present and a future. The educational enterprise is also purposeful and goal-oriented. As an open and ongoing system, however, the goals of schooling may appear unclear and/or conflicting at any given time as they have emerged in response to diverse opinion and a changing social context. Clarity of goals, however, is critical as the organizational structure, the network of relationships, and the nature of the relationships within any system are relative to the purpose of the system. Self-regulation then reflects the system's essential monitoring of its progress toward its goals. If the system perceives itself to be performing in a manner consistent with its goals, then it will continue its present course without correction. If there is a discrepancy between performance and goals, the system will be motivated to change its course. For effective "self-direction" a system must continuously receive a full flow of three kinds of information: (1) information of the outside world; (2) information from the past; and (3) information about itself and its own parts (Buckley, 1967, cited in Broderick, 1993).

Thus, information exchange or communication is considered to be an essential characteristic of well-functioning systems. In addition, functional systems are characterized by clarity of roles and rules, clear and open boundaries, and a structure that optimizes the efficient accomplishment of the goals of the system. Moreover, self-regulating systems must have sufficient variety of responses in their repertoire to match the variety of inputs it encounters (Broderick, 1993). Lacking sufficient variety, the system has only three choices: (1) close down operations; (2) fall back on a standard default response; or (3) generate a new, previously untried response. This last behavior is termed in systems theory, morphogenesis, that is, literally the creation of a new form or structure.

According to Sarason (1990), complex traditional social organizations, such as the schools, are largely homeostatic, that is, they are unlikely to create new forms or structures. Rather, Sarason (1990) asserts it is a highly predictable fact that schools will accommodate to demands for change in ways that require little or no change in existing structure or form. Adaptation without change of structure or form in systems theory has been termed first order change. First order change constitutes additions and deletions to the existing system structure. This form of adaptation has characterized schools for the past 150 years (Sarason, 1990). Schools have added and deleted programs, added and deleted staff, added and deleted curriculum. However, the fundamental regularities and beliefs of the system remain intact.

Thus far we have been exploring the nature of the school as an organizational system, that is, examining information about the school itself and its parts. Following the recommendation of Buckley, that self-determination also requires an examination of one's history, we next turn to a review of the changing goals and related structure of schools, with particular attention to these changes as they have guided the development of contemporary school-based services.

## CHANGING VISIONS OF EDUCATION, SCHOOLING, AND SERVICE DELIVERY

As it is the past that has given shape to the current purpose and shape of public education, it is important to understand the origins of current school organization and relatedly school-based services. Schools, like all social structures, are organized or structured in a manner consistent with a vision of their purpose, which is embedded within the larger economic, social, and cultural milieu (Schlechty, 1990). Schlechty identifies three past visions of schools–school as a tribal center, school as factory, and school as hospital–all of which persist in some form today. Social services in schools emerged in reaction to the vision of schools as factories; therefore, we will next take a closer look at each of these visions for education.

The American public school system was invented at a time when the population was rural agrarian, white Anglo-Saxon, and the purpose of education was to promote republican/Protestant morality and civic literacy. Thus, the first vision of schools was as the tribal center with the purpose of schooling the induction on the young into the tribe. Curriculum focused on the ancient cultures of Greece and Rome, the classics of English literature (with their espousal of Anglo-Saxon values), and the early McGuffey readers which contained Protestant morality tales. Schools were small, often consisting of a single nongraded room and teacher, with close community links. Schools often served as the community center. Teaching was viewed as a sacred calling and social service, with the appropriate vows of chastity and devotion taken, somewhat akin to serving in the ministry. Teachers were hired and fired by the community. A teacher who did not live and teach consonant with community values would neither be hired or retained. Schooling was not compulsory and many children were educated at home. Therefore, children of limited mental ability were unlikely to be schooled, and children of differing abilities did not pose problems in ungraded or unmandated schools. Health care during this era was abysmal for all classes of people; however, when needs arose, they were met within the family and community. Provision of social services was not consistent with the goal of schools during this era.

Urbanization, industrialization, and the influx of non-English-speaking, non-Anglo-Saxon, non-Protestant people dramatically changed America to a heterogeneous culture of urban industrialists and factory workers living in cities. With this social and economic change, the essential purpose of schools shifted from the provision of a basic education and promotion of a common culture to serving economic purposes of sorting and selecting students in terms of their potential for carrying out work roles. The industrial society required a well-educated elite and masses trained for semiskilled jobs. One aspect of training was literacy to immigrants and a standardization of education for the masses. Thus, with industrialization emerged the vision of schools as factories and attendant was compulsory schooling.

In schools organized as factories, school leaders emulated industrial leaders. Efficiency became the prime value; differentiation, standardization, control, and rationality became the operating guides. Schools designed to sort and select begin with the assumption that standards must be established and maintained and that some, hopefully few, products (students) will not make the grade. In this vision students are viewed as products who enter as raw materials to be molded, tested against a common standard, and inspected carefully before being passed on to the next workbench for further processing. Products that do not meet the quality control test are eliminated from the system. In short, they drop out of school. Students from poor families simply are not good raw material for the educational enterprise. Thus, a new concept was introduced to American education with restructuring schools as factories–school failure. School failure was operationalized into the structure of schools with the graded classroom, the graded reader, school grades, the tracking system, selective athletics, etc.

In the vision of schools as factories bigger is better; the more products produced for the least cost, the better the system. The vision of schools as factories is also consonant with hierarchical organizational structures, bureaucratization, centralization of administrative functions, and increasing differentiation and specialization of function. In the school as factory, the role of principal shifted from chief priest to factory manager. The goal became running a tight ship and keeping the assembly line running with a minimum of down time. The well-ordered school, with lines of obedient children and classes scheduled every 53 minutes, comes to mind.

In the school as factory, two distinctive views of teachers emerged. In one view, teachers were highly skilled technocrats, similar to accountants or engineers; when this view prevailed the emphasis in schools was on curriculum design, methods of instruction, and adoption of the latest innovations. In the second view, teachers were seen as skilled laborers (versus real professionals), or seen as less intelligent than other professionals, such as doctors or lawyers; when this view prevailed in schools, the emphasis was on control structures that limit teacher decision-making and instructional freedom. The unionization of teachers might be viewed as both a reaction to and perpetuation of this view of teachers as skilled laborers.

The harsh realities of urbanization, and immigration 150 years ago spurred a third vision of schools–schools as hospitals. With urbanization and immigration emerged unparalleled levels of social concern regarding health and sanitation, poverty, violence, and criminal activity, especially on the part of children. Schools came to be viewed as the setting from which both children and their families could most easily be reached. The purpose of schools as hospitals was to redress the pain and suffering imposed on children by the urban industrial society. In short, the function of the school as a hospital was to redress the imbalance created when raw materials of different quality enter the system, and thereby, equalize the disadvantages of children in society such that there is equal opportunity for success within the American economy.

In the social reform era of the early 1900s, the view of schools as hospitals was the impetus for a variety of health and social services to be provided to children in schools by physicians, dentists, enthusiastic volunteers, and social reformers, from outside the school. Schools incorporated health curricula, and schools experimented with open air education in an effort to deal with the prevalent respiratory ailments of students. Medical inspectors, or medical visitors (known later as school physicians), were a routine part of the urban schools. They emphasized vision and hearing screening, good health habits, cleanliness and exercise. Their services were expanded to include testing for tuberculosis, psychological inspection, dental inspection, providing nutritional data, and sometimes provided services for the school staff. School physicians gave way to school nurses whose duties also included home visits and the investigation of chronic attendance problems (Dryfoos, 1994; Fagan, 1992). Volunteers, external agencies, and social activists frequently collaborated and/or co-funded services with the schools. Services included free/inexpensive meals, transportation, special classes for sickly or handicapped children, playgrounds, recreation, summer vacation schools, visiting teachers, as well as vocational counseling and job placement. Schools were often used in evenings to teach adult classes in English and sewing, as well as to provide counseling in job training, welfare services, and civic instruction (Tyack, 1992).

As educational reformers called for more health and social services, schools were pressured to take over many of these externally provided services and to hire their own cadre of service providers. Thus, the professions of school social work, school psychology, and school guidance all emerged, almost simultaneously, in the early 1900s in the urban northeastern United States to assist in solving problems which were affecting the child's school progress. Speech and language pathology was one of the more recent additions to school social services, with widespread assignment occurring in the 1940s.

From 1920 to 1960 many of these non-academic social services were assimilated by the schools and organized bureaucratically under the rubric of pupil services. However, in so doing, these services underwent a transformation (Tyack, 1992). The new internal school program and new practitioners lost the former qualities of zeal, child advocacy, focus and coordination with the community. Often the targeted populations were modified so that many of the internal school services were also provided to the middle and upper classes rather than being limited to the impoverished. Indeed, in some cases, services were shifted away from the poor populations. In times of budget cuts, for example, more affluent communities were able to maintain internal school health and social services, while schools in less prosperous communities were forced to eliminate them (Tyack). Thus, when external pressures were strong, schools collaborated with outside providers, agencies and volunteers in order to assure the availability of services they were unable to provide internally.

The civil rights movement of the 1960s, with its emphasis on equal treatment of the handicapped, and accompanying legislation, necessitated the organization and provision of special education services in all schools. This spurred the development of coordinated pupil services in schools lacking organized components. Thus, the final addition to school pupil services was special education, and special education became a formal vehicle for the delivery of psychological and health services within the schools (Fagan, 1992).

Schlechty (1990) argues that, despite the fact that up to fifty percent of any school budget is devoted to noninstructional costs, neither the schools nor the public has wholeheartedly accepted the role of schools as hospitals. If they had, Schlechty points out, teachers would view themselves as service delivery professionals (as do psychologists, counselors, social workers, and speech pathologists) whose primary obligation is to meet the needs of their individual clients, or students, regardless of the cost. The teacher would serve as the primary care physician in the vision of schools as hospitals. As such s/he would have primary responsibility for the progress of the child, most likely over multiple years, as well as responsibility for coordination with other specializations of special services to the child. In the vision of schools as hospitals, the curriculum becomes the prescription, and the ideal prescription is highly individualized. In the school as hospital then heavy emphasis would also be placed on diagnostic testing, use of scientific instruments, and empirically-validated interventions/prescriptions.

In summary, three goals for schools and schooling have emerged in the history of the United States: (1) socialization; (2) preparation of a workforce; and (3) provision of equal opportunity. These goals have conformed to three visions of schools–schools as tribal centers, schools as factories, and schools as hospitals. The professional roles and organization of services associated with the provision of social services in schools emerged within the vision of schools as hospitals; however, these services developed and matured within the vision of schools as factories. We will next examine the challenges that this organizational structure poses for the delivery of integrated services to children.

## CONTEMPORARY CULTURE AND ORGANIZATION OF SCHOOL-BASED SERVICES

### Formal Organization

Although it is acknowledged that the formal organization of social services varies from school to school and from district to district, examination of a sample organizational chart (see Figure 1) indicates that bureaucratization, hierarchy, and specialization are characteristic of school-based services. Consistent across all organizational structures is the separation of social services from the instructional components of the education system. In general, specific units are created around the catego-

FIGURE 1. Organizational Model for Pupil Services (Large-Sized School District)

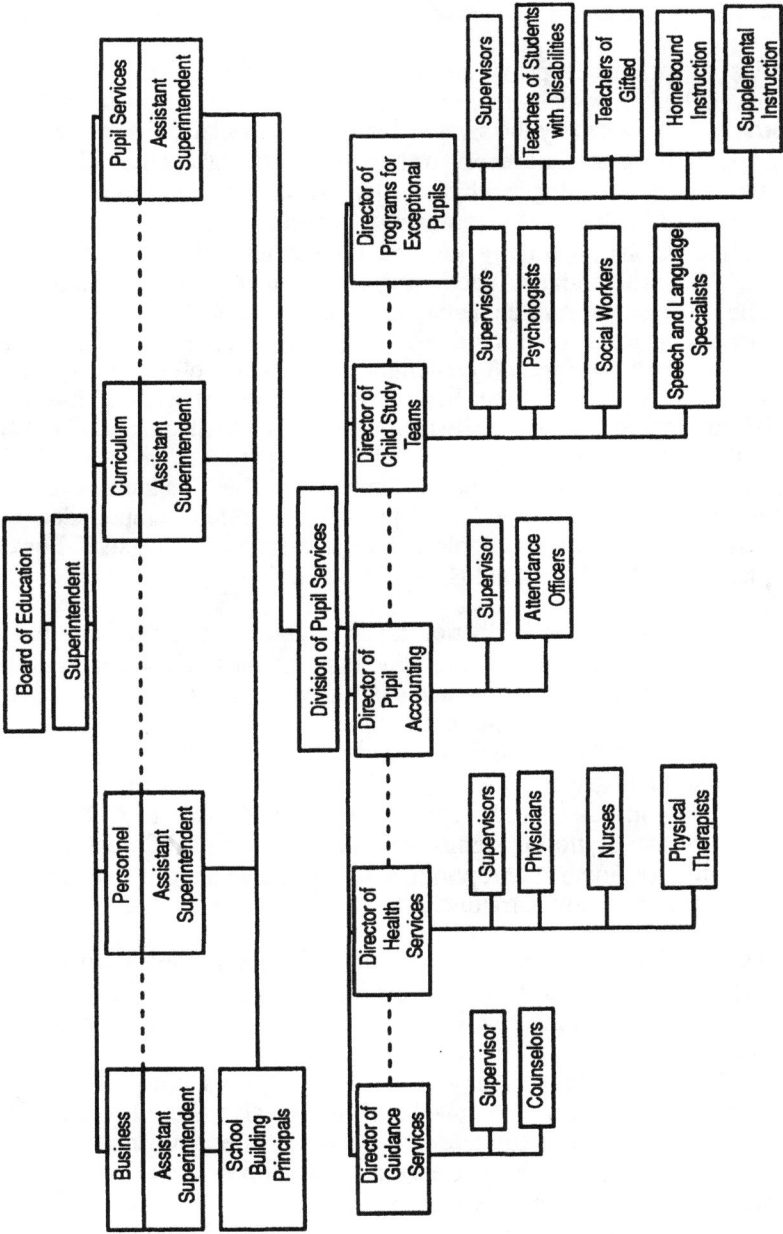

ries of personnel providing the services (e.g., units for counselors, psychologists, social workers, health workers). In large-sized school districts, as provided by the sample chart, these specialized services of social support personnel are even further separated organizationally from one another into groupings with distinctive administrative lines of authority.

Formal hierarchical organizational structures assume the value of specialization and optimally provide boundaries between subcomponents such that differentiated functioning can occur without undue interference. The professional role demarcations within schools have been further cemented in professional standards and in state and federal legislation which control the licensing and credentialing of each professional specialty as well as regulate the school-based practice of that specialty. Thus, school-based services are historically characterized by "balkanization" consistent with the factory vision of schools in which products are sent to different autonomous specialty areas for completion. This "balkanization" of social services and professional specialties is often compounded by the assignment of several schools to the same social service staff. For example, as noted by Farrar and Hampel (1987):

> In one California district, a career counselor is available two days each week, which is less time than the nurse has (four days) or the district counselor (two and a half days, for attendance, parent conferences, and troubleshooting), but more than the social concerns (sex, drug, alcohol) counselor's short daily visits or the appearances of the psychologist, who is responsible for two other schools. Specialization, in other words, applies to time and place as well as to task. Further scattering stems from the existence of different lines of authority. Some staff report to superiors in the building, whereas others work for administrators in the central offices. (p. 100-101)

As such, it is not uncommon for staff to be confronting similar concerns and/or working with the same troubled children, yet working in isolation from one another, thereby limiting efficacy and wasting resources (Adelman, 1994).

The "balkanization" of school social services not only reflects the traditional factory vision of education, but also the ad hoc manner in which services and programs are usually created and incorporated into schools (Adelman, 1994). Being a system open to public opinion, the creation of social services programs in schools has usually been in response to legal mandates, currently pressing social or demographic problems, and extramural funding for specific programs and populations. The creation of existing pupil services clearly reflects a response to pressing social problems and/or legal mandates versus a self-directed evaluation of the needs of the system. In recent years, with increased public attention to social problems and demographic changes, schools have seen a proliferation of programs, each with its own set of offices, personnel, and eligibility criteria. Schools, in fact, have been termed a veritable "shopping mall" of social services, with an array of specialists and programs available to help (Dryfoos, 1994; Farrar & Hampel, 1987). How can it be that with so many service providers and programs, the needs of children are still not being met?

Nader (1990) has argued that balance and coordination are principal issues. Coordination can be challenging as the services are so disparate, programs are developed and operationalized in an ad hoc manner, and coordination efforts are not strongly promoted by school administrators. In addition, Nader (1990) notes that coordination is negatively affected by the unequal equity and power of many services. In medium and large school districts, the services with strong historical traditions (i.e., social work, school psychology, health) have often retained autonomous identity and authority. On the other hand, in small districts, where comprehensive and coordinated services were historically nonexistent, the development of pupil services, encouraged by federal mandates for special education, have been accompanied by struggles for leadership status among disciplines. These observations are supported by the ethnographic study of Farrah and Hampel (1987) who found that unless mandated by law, interdepartmental coordination of social service activities occurred only if propelled by strong individual personalities.

## Informal System of Service Delivery

The contrast between the formal and informal organizational structure of school-based social services was highlighted in a recent ethnographic study (Farrar & Hampel, 1987). These researchers found that whereas the formal organizational structure of school-based social services was characterized by balkanization, i.e., specialization of time, place, and task, the actual delivery of services was governed by informality except where clarified or required by legal mandates.

Informality characterized the social service system in multiple ways. Whereas there was little confusion about how to handle problems that were regulated either by laws or district policy, (i.e., physical impairments, medical problems, child abuse, possession of illegal weapons, suicide), for problems of drug and alcohol abuse, or other psychologically or emotionally-related problems, there was considerable informality in matching students with services, with clear-cut policies and regulations the exception, not the rule. There was also a lack of systematic record keeping (despite complaints about excessive paperwork), such that the frequency of student problems, number or kinds of referrals, and referral outcomes were not compiled. Furthermore, despite a somewhat rigid formal organization, the roles and responsibilities of social service providers within the informal organization were negotiable. For example, there was considerable flexibility in how far an individual social service provider might choose to extend his or her workload, whether or not to involve parents, or how much time to allot to particular tasks. Moreover, it was common for social service personnel to disagree on a course of action, or if in agreement, to both insist that it was the responsibility of the other party to carry out, and thus reduce the efficacy of operations.

Informality was also observed to govern the ways that social service staff linked with external community service providers (Farrer & Hampel, 1987). Referrals to external agencies and service providers were inconsistent across personnel, schools, and school districts, and the reasons for referral were quite varied. In some cases referrals were avoided because school-based social service staff feared losing their raison d'etre; in other cases referrals were not recommended for fear of parental reprisal or fear that the schools would be held financially accountable for the cost of external services. Despite these barriers, the sheer numbers of children in need demanded many referrals to community agencies. Referrals, however, were generally made based on a personal relationship between the school and the community agency staff, versus a systematic relationship, and there was rarely much follow-up by the school on referrals once made.

The results were replicated by Adelman (1994) in his study of school-based services in a large urban school system. Adelman concluded: "[programs] . . . were not coordinated with each other; they were are not linked with community services (an especially critical problem for students from low income families); and there was little systematic interface between education support programs and instructional programs in the schools" (Adelman, 1994, p. 7). Surprisingly, Adelman (1994) observed a high level of awareness displayed by district personnel regarding structural and operational deficiencies, as well as awareness of policy initiatives emanating from the state that stressed service integration and school-community agency linkages. Awareness, however, did not appear to translate into action due to a variety of school service support personnel concerns. Service personnel concerns centered on issues of: (a) role responsibility, (b) accountability, (c) procedural guidelines, (d) threat regarding loss of jobs, and (e) having a voice, i.e., power regarding policy and planning.

## Goals/Orientation of the System

Because organizational structures, both formal and informal, emerge in service of the goals of the system, the contemporary organization of school-based services must be viewed within a context of school system goals. As noted previously, Schlechty (1990) has argued that schools have three goals which remain salient today: socialization; preparation of a work force; and opportunities for equalization. Health-related services developed outside of the school system in response to the goal of equalization of opportunity; however, over the course of the past century, these services have become embedded within the school system with its primary goal of sorting and selecting students. The priority of the goal of sorting and selecting is consistent with the delivery of services by categorical programs, the use of stringent eligibility criteria, and helping professional roles to sort and select despite training in service delivery. School counselors, for example, despite training in the delivery of counseling services, are primarily involved in the sorting and selecting of students for tracking; school psychologists, despite training in consultation and prevention, are primarily involved in the sorting and selecting of students via individual psychological assessments for services eligibility under IDEA. In short, contemporary school-based services are structured primarily to sort and select students.

Another criticism which has been leveled against existing school-based service delivery structures is the focus on individuals (Sarason, 1990). Sarason argues that by organization, ideology, and preparation, school personnel accept the responsibility for dealing with the problems of *individuals*. The focus on individuals, is not only inefficient, but it discourages the adoption of a preventive stance towards the educational and mental health problems of children, families, and school personnel.

Finally the orientation of existing services are based on a model of deficiency and pathology. Such a model establishes helping professionals as experts in the remediation of children's difficulties such that they can learn while disempowering those systems most closely involved with the child–the parents and teacher. This model has been increasingly challenged in our contemporary milieu (e.g., Dunst & Trivette, 1987), as not only disempowering individuals to solve their own problems in the future but also as sustaining a dependency on caretaking which can no longer be sustained by the more circumscribed economy.

In summary, it is clear that the impetus behind the movement supporting coordinated and integrated services derives from appropriate concern regarding the failure of the current specialized, fragmentary, balkanized, and categorical approach to social service delivery to meet the needs of children, families and schools. As noted by Chaskin and Richman (1992), the following weaknesses in the system are evident: (a) rather than dealing with the needs of the whole child or family, we engage in an atomistic approach to discrete problems; (b) rather than addressing the root causes of children's problems, we attack their symptoms and leave the systems that serve children intact; (c) lack of coordination among service providers leads to waste, frustration, and the perpetuation of a client-provider system in which those seeking help are moved powerlessly through a labyrinth of bureaucratic prerequisites and protocols.

## CHANGING THE SCHOOL CULTURE TOWARDS INTEGRATED SERVICES

It is clear that social services as currently organized and operating in schools do not provide a good fit with the goals of coordination and integration of services. A comparison of the characteristics of the traditionally organized school-based social services and those presumed to be needed for coordinated, comprehensive services appear on Table 1. Changes in formal structure, informal practices, system goals and orientation to services delivery all appear to be necessary to move from the traditional configuration of services to coordinated, integrated, and comprehensive services to children.

### Changes in Formal Organization

Integrated services requires a formal organizational structure and culture that foster collaboration and teamwork versus autonomous, uncoordinated functioning. Adelman (1994) has recommended the development of an *enabling component* within existing education support services. "Enabling" is defined in Webster's dictionary as providing with the means or opportunity; making possible, practical, or easy; giving power, capacity, or sanction to. "The enabling component is a school-based/linked comprehensive, integrated programmatic approach to preventing and ameliorating those barriers to learning that are not accounted for by efforts to restructure the instructional and management components" (Adelman, 1994, p. 11). The creation of an enabling component requires a major restructuring of school support services, integration of school support services with other programs, and enhanced linkages with community resources. One aspect of the enabling component described by Adelman is the use of program focused school-based "teams." School-based teams

TABLE 1. Comparison of Characteristics of Traditional versus Coordinated Services Cultures

| Traditional Services | Coordinated Services |
|---|---|
| *Formal Organization* | |
| hierarchical | collaborative teams |
| rigid | flexible |
| autonomous | coordinated |
| specialized | specialized |
| services categorical | services based on need |
| services separated from instruction | school-based services integrated with instruction |
| *Informal Organization* | |
| poor record keeping | accountability/measurement of outcomes |
| unclear policies | clear but flexible policies for all student needs |
| individual role latitude | clear roles but collaboratively determined |
| responsible for a part | responsible for the whole |
| *Orientation to Service Delivery* | |
| provider ease | customer satisfaction |
| expert role | learner, collaborator role |
| deficit focus | strength focus |
| tertiary treatment | primary prevention |
| individual focus | systems focus |
| categorical solutions applied to all | solution-generating, problem-solving |
| *System Goals* | |
| sort and select | success for all |
| cost containment | cost containment |

may vary in scope and theme, e.g., crisis teams, resource coordinating teams, child study teams. Critical to the success of teams are the following: (1) participation of every staff member in some team; (2) job descriptions and reward structures that require teamwork; (3) appropriate expertise among team members; (4) leadership; (5) use of computer technology to enhance team communication; and (6) a clear goal of cost effectiveness and efficiency (Adelman, 1994).

An alternative proposal for the use of teams to alter how school-based services are conceptualized and delivered has been articulated by Rosenfield (1992). Rosenfield suggests the implementation of interdisciplinary *instructional consultation teams* (IC-Team). The IC-Team model is based on three critical assumptions that challenge traditional beliefs within schools: (a) all students can learn; (b) a critical area for change is the student-teacher relationship in the classroom; and (c) optimal schools have a highly collegial, problem-solving orientation with numerous opportunities for teachers to interact and provide feedback, support, and ideas to one another. Two specific outcomes have been associated with IC-Teams: (a) a shift in the systematic referral process from a focus on student deficits to restructuring the environment of the student to enable learning; and (b) a restructured management system based on a collaborative, problem-solving culture with a school support team at its core.

In summary, one consistently proposed formal organizational change for school-based services is a shift from multi-level, top-down, hierarchical, formal organizational structures to the completion of work through on-site collaborative teams, which may be reconfigured as tasks change or are completed. Such a restructuring does not omit the need for specialization; however, it dramatically changes the way in which specialists are utilized. Rather than being grouped together in autonomous units, where they are responsible for completion of their piece of a product, (e.g., intelligence testing), specialists are placed on teams where their expertise is essential, and the team is responsible for completion of the entire goal, e.g., the child's success in school.

## *Informal "Culture" Change*

Changing structure is considered to be the most powerful producer of behavioral change within an organization because it addresses the underlying organizational opportunities and constraints on behavior (Mowday, 1993; Senge, 1990); however, a critical aspect of organizational structure is the informal culture or behavior patterns which operate despite overt policies. Given the demonstrated inadequacies of the existing informal services delivery culture, a shift to comprehensive, coordinated, and integrated services would appear to be enhanced by the following: (a) the development of comprehensive and clear policies for linking resources both within the system and external to the system; (b) a shift from autonomous role definition to coordinated, but flexible, role definitions; (c) the infusion of a culture of results in which documentation of outcomes is welcome as a mechanism of self-regulation and problem-solving; (d) increased personal responsibility for outcomes related to the whole of the child in his/her milieu.

It seems clear that at least one aspect of informal culture change is the role of a strong leader in promoting such changes. As previously noted, coordination between social service programs only occurred within school-based services when strongly promoted by the administrator for pupil services (Farrar & Hampel, 1987). Organizational behavior studies confirm that leaders have influence, especially when an organization is small and young, by making decisions that affect the structure of the organization and by shaping the thoughts, feelings, and actions of people inside and outside the organization (Mowday, 1993). Recent studies further confirm that not only powerful leaders, but also powerful groups, can take actions that influence the organization structures, processes, and performance (Mowday, 1993). Underlying the influence of both individual leaders and groups, however, is an aggregation or consensus of individual thoughts, feelings, and behaviors.

*Beliefs/Orientation*

The informal culture or organization of school-based services is intrinsically linked with the beliefs or orientation of service providers regarding their role and responsibilities. Accompanying any successful structural change must be a change in the beliefs members hold regarding their role and capacity for change (Rosenfield, 1992; Senge, 1990). Coordinated, integrated and comprehensive services demand a reshaping of service delivery beliefs as follows: (a) from provider ease to customer satisfaction; (b) from an individual focus to a systems focus; (c) from a focus on careful diagnosis, such that the "right" treatment can be applied, to a focus on problem-solving and solution-generation such that the most appropriate and culturally sensitive solution can be tried; (d) from a tertiary treatment orientation to a prevention orientation; and (e) from a view of self as expert helper to a view of self as learner, collaborator, and enabler.

Senge (1993) argues that the development of shared vision among members of an organization, such as school-based social services, is essential to the organization because it provides the focus and energy for learning which is necessary for change. When people truly share a vision, they are connected, bound together by a common aspiration. Moreover, shared visions create the excitement that lifts an organization out of the constraints of bureaucracy and compels courage to change. Shared vision also fosters risk-taking and experimentation. As noted by Schlechty (1990), the emerging knowledge-work society demands that organizations worry more about doing the right thing than doing things right, e.g., by the book. Finally, a shared vision changes people's relationships with the organization, such that it is no longer "their school," but rather "our school." A shared vision is also the first step in allowing people who have previously mistrusted each other to begin to work together. As noted by Sarason (1990), "People rarely embrace a restriction or alteration in the scope of their accustomed powers" (p. 29), and power struggles among school-based service providers appears historically endemic (Nader, 1990). Shared vision and purpose then would appear essential to the promotion of coordinated and integrated services among service providers who have a history of power struggles and autonomous functioning.

### Changes in System Goals

Integrated, coordinated services are consistent with the goal of redressing the inequities of society such that children learn. What is clear from previous discussion is that in the traditional formal and informal organizational structure of schools, the needs of children and families have not been paramount such that an equalization of opportunity can occur. Rather the accomplishment of this goal has been compromised in school-based social services where the system goal of sorting and selecting has been paramount. Two options would appear feasible: if comprehensive and coordinated services are to remain embedded within the education system, the goals of the instructional and social service system must become more congruent; if this is not feasible, then the establishment of comprehensive and coordinated services may fare better in community-based, school-linked models where system goals can remain distinct.

A greater congruence between educational and social service goals appears possible given the changing economic base of the nation from manufacturing products to the production of knowledge. Since a primary goal of education is the preparation of a work force, the changing demands of the economy exert strong pressures on schools to change their structures accordingly. According to Schlechty (1990), in the schools of the future knowledge-learner society teachers will no longer be sources of information, but rather guides to information sources. Students will become more active in the manipulation of their knowledge, and become collaborators in their education. Conditions of work will require one to learn to function well in groups or teams versus the current emphasis on individual, competition. In short, the goals of schooling must change from sorting and selecting students for factory work to ensuring that each student is successfully able to manipulate knowledge. The primary goal of schooling then must become student success (Schlechty, 1990).

School success for all reflects a dramatically different goal than the sort and select goal of the previous school as factory vision. Applied to the delivery of services it suggests that social support services similarly must adopt a goal of success (versus a focus on deficiency as evident in such concepts as resistance, lack of motivation, lack of parent involvement). Moreover, a focus on success shifts the burden of responsibility from the client as a savvy consumer to responsibility on the provider for identifying the appropriate resources and motivational strategies such that success is insured. The shift to a success-oriented goal similarly argues for careful documentation of outcomes, with a focus on the achievement of results, such that corrective actions can be taken versus a documentation of compliance with legal mandates or bureaucratic procedures regardless of results.

In sum, the provision of comprehensive, coordinated school-based services to children and families will require a qualitative change in the formal structure, informal operating procedures, belief systems of individual providers, and goals of the system. Although by no means exhaustive or comprehensive in scope, proposed changes include restructuring into site-based teams, improving policies and accountability procedures, and developing a shared vision that is consistent with the goal of success for all students regardless of the raw materials with which they enter the school system.

## GETTING FROM HERE TO THERE

"Changing a system is not for the conceptually and interpersonally fainthearted" (Sarason, 1990, p. 46). As noted earlier, schools are largely homeostatic systems which will attempt change through additions and deletions to the system. According to Sarason (1990), if educational reform (and we might assume school-based social service reform) proceeds as it has in the past with change by addition or deletion–that is–doing more of the same–it will be doomed to failure. Rather systems theory argues that in periods of significant external or internal developmental pressure, systems must restructure. Restructuring in systems commonly requires: (a) challenging the adequacy of existing reality/vision; (b) providing an alternative reality/vision; and (c) trying alternative role relations and transactional patterns that fit the new vision (Senge, 1993; Schlechty, 1990).

Clearly, such substantive change in the structure and beliefs of a system do not occur rapidly. Rather change, both individual and organizational, proceeds through distinct stages (Senge, 1993). In Stage One new cognitive capacities are developed. People/organizations see new things and can speak a new language. They may have difficulty translating these new cognitions into actions, or they may initiate new behavior sequences, but the basic rules and values of the system remain the same. In Stage Two, people/organizations begin to experiment with new action rules based on new assumptions and shared visions. These new patterns of behavior remain unstable and may regress under stress. In Stage Three persons and organizations can string together rules and roles for relating that consistently reflect their new cognitions and language. Stage Three reflects the development and institutionalization of a new structure.

The process of change in systems has also been described as comprising the distinct stages of Insertion, Destabilization, Resolution, and Deletion (Terkelson, 1980). In the Insertion Stage the need for change becomes manifest and is recognized by members of the system. In the Destabilization Stage perturbations occur as the system attempts to incorporate new behavioral sequences while meshing with some preexisting elements. Behavior is likely to be more variable and conflictual during this stage as there is anxiety and uncertainty about the future. Trial sequences consisting of merged elements of new and of preexisting structure are tried. One of these sequences is eventually adopted as the most effective solutions, and a compromise structure gradually takes shape. This stage is termed Resolution. At the same time as this change process is emerging, a parallel process of Deletion occurs, through which now obsolete behavior sequences and structures are removed. There are differing emotional reactions to the stages of Insertion and Deletion. Whereas Insertion evokes frustration, anxiety, and uncertainty, Deletion gives rise to the experience of loss in its various forms of hurt, sadness, irritability, and anger (Terkelsen, 1980). It is therefore important to keep in mind that the process of change, however exciting in its opportunities, is normatively accompanied by multiple negative emotions, which may undermine the change process.

## CONCLUSION

Schools and their attendant goals have transformed across history in conjunction with major economic and social change. Dramatic economic and social changes in the contemporary milieu suggest that a restructuring of school-based services from balkanized, inefficient, and piecemeal efforts toward comprehensive, integrated, and coordinated services to children and families may be possible. Such a restructuring of school-based services to children and families are most likely to succeed with strong leadership, shared vision, congruence of instructional and social service goals, and restructuring into learning teams that eliminate wasteful, disempowering bureaucracies.

Although the economic and social change forces in contemporary society are compelling, the forces for homeostasis in the traditional, complex social system of the schools are strong. If schools fail to restructure to meet new economic challenges, and rather attempt change through additions and deletions to the system, the possibility of significant reform in school-based services to children and families will be sorely constrained. Concern for the plight of children's services should they be embedded within the rigid bureaucracy of the schools has lead some to argue for the advantages of community-based models (Chaskin and Richman, 1992). Given the homeostasis of the traditional school system, establishment of comprehensive, coordinated services for children may be more feasible outside the school system.

Regardless of location, the establishment of comprehensive, coordinated children's services will require a reconceptualization of role and patterns of behavior among service providers. Changes in self-perceptions of role, changes in behavior patterns, and changes in power, are unlikely to be accomplished easily as significant structural change is uniformly accompanied by mixed emotions. The role of strong leadership, the capacity to build a shared vision, and adequate training for required behavioral changes, are essential, particularly in the early stages of transformation. One cannot help but be empowered, however, by the opportunity to create a service delivery system in which the goal is success for all children and needs of children are paramount.

## REFERENCES

Adelman, H. S. (1994). *Restructuring education support services: Toward the concept of an enabling component.* Unpublished manuscript, University of California at Los Angeles.

American Psychological Association. (1994, August). *Comprehensive and Coordinated Psychological Services for Children: A Call for Service integration.* Washington, DC: Author.

Bricklin, P., Carlson, C., DeMers, S., Paavola, J., Talley, R., & Tharinger, D. (1995). *Schools as health service delivery sites: Historical, current, and future roles for psychology,* (July, 1995). Report of the Schools as Health Care Delivery Sites Work Group, Committee for the Advancement of Professional Practice. Washington, DC: American Psychological Association.

Broderick, C.B. (1993). *Understanding family process: Basics of family systems theory.* Newbury Park, CA: Sage.

Chaskin, R. J., & Richman, H. A. (1992). Concerns about school-linked services: Institution-based versus community-based models. *The Future of Children, 2,* 107-117.

Dryfoos, J. G. (1994). *Full-service schools.* San Francisco, CA: Jossey-Bass.

Duchnowski, A. J. (1994). Innovative service models: Education. *Journal of Clinical Child Psychology, 23,* 13-18.

Dunst, C. J., & Trivette, C. (1987). Enabling and empowering families: Conceptual and intervention issues. *School Psychology Review, 16*(4), 443-456.

Fagan, T. (1993). *The School's Role in Primary Health Care.* Unpublished manuscript.

Farrar, E., & Hampel, R. L. (1987). Social services in high schools. *Phi Delta Kappan.*

Goldstein, A., Harootunian, B., & Conoley, J. (1994). *Student aggression: Prevention, management and replacement training.* New York: Guilford Press.

Hodgkinson, H. L. (1992). *A demographic look at tomorrow.* Center for Demographic Policy. Institute for Educational Leadership. Washington, DC.

*Individuals with Disabilities Education Act of 1990,* 20 U.S.C. 140 (1990).

Knitzer, J. (1992). *Unclaimed children.* Washington, DC: Children's Defense Fund.

McElhaney, S. J., Russell, M., & Barton, H. A. (1993). *Children's mental health and their ability to learn.* National Health/Education Consortium. Washington, DC.

Mowday, R. T. (1993). Organizational behavior: Linking individuals and groups to organizational contexts. *Annual Review of Psychology, 44,* 195-229.

Rosenfield, S. (1992). Developing school-based consultation teams: A design for organizational change. *School Psychology Quarterly, 7*(1), 27-46.

Sarason, S. B. (1990). *The predictable failure of educational reform.* San Francisco: Jossey-Bass.

Saxe, L., Cross, T., & Silverman, N. (1988). Children's mental health: The gap between what we know and what we do. *American Psychologist, 43*(10), 800-807.

Schlechty, P. C. (1990). *Schools for the 21st century.* San Francisco: Jossey-Bass.

Senge, P. M. (1990). *The fifth discipline: The art and practice of the learning organization.* New York: Doubleday.

Stroul, B., & Friedman, R. (1986). *A system of care for severely emotionally disturbed children and youth.* Tampa, Fl: University of South Florida, Florida Mental Health Institute.

Tarnowski, K.J., & Blechman, E. A. (1991). Disadvantaged children and families. *Journal of Clinical Child Psychology, 20*(4), 338-339.

Terkelsen, K. G. (1980). Toward a theory of the family life cycle. In E. A. Carter & M. McGoldrick (Eds.), *The family life cycle* (pp. 21-52). New York: Gardner Press.

Tyack, D. B. (1992). Health and social services in public schools: Historical perspectives. *The Future of Children, 2,* 19-31.

United States Department of Education. (1990). *Goals 2000: Educate America Act.* Washington, DC: Author.

United States Department of Education. (1995). *Sixteenth annual report to Congress on the implementation of the Individuals with Disabilities Education Act.* Washington, DC: Author.

United States Department of Health and Human Services. (1990). *Healthy people 2000: National health promotion and disease prevention objectives* (DHHS Publication No. PHS 91-50212). Washington, DC: U.S. Government Printing Office.

United States General Accounting Office. (1993). *School-linked human services: A comprehensive strategy for aiding students at risk of school failure.* (GAO/HRD-94-21). Washington, DC: U.S. Government Printing Office.

For Product Safety Concerns and Information please contact our EU
representative GPSR@taylorandfrancis.com
Taylor & Francis Verlag GmbH, Kaufingerstraße 24, 80331 München, Germany